First Edition

Don Wood

You Must be out of Your Mind! Practical Solutions from the Inspired Performance Institute, First Edition

For more information about the author and the Inspired Performance Program™ (TIPP), visit the Inspired Performance **Institute at:**

3218 E Colonial Drive
   Orlando, FL 32803
   407-600-2438

www.inspiredperformanceinstitute.com

ACKNOWLEDGEMENTS

Writing this part of the book reminds me of those moments when you're about to thank people for their help at an event, and the whole time you're thinking, "I hope I don't forget someone important!" (In fact, does anyone bother reading this part of any book? Most likely, it's the people who check to see if you acknowledged them by name.) Nevertheless, at the risk of forgetting someone important, here goes:

Starting in chronological order provides some safety since it will make it easier to remember who influenced me first. There is no doubt that God knew me before I was ever born, so let's give Him the **first acknowledgment.**

There is no doubt in my mind that I would not be the person I am today without the influence of my parents. They adopted me when I was four days old—I'm lucky that I won the parent lottery! They are amazing people. You probably noticed I used "they are" as opposed to "they were." I say it that way because, in my mind, they have never left me. I smile when I think of them. Their support is still with me and within me. For example, I originally created this book as part of my course require-ments for my doctorate. This was something my mother always told me: "You're going to be a doctor, I can see it clearly." Her wisdom is astonishing! How did she know, even when I had no interest in being a doctor? She knew better. I know she is very proud of me, and that makes me smile.

My father was brilliant. (He married my mother, didn't he?) He was book smart. You could ask him any word in the dictionary, and he could tell you what it meant. I remember him telling me as a boy that between his brother and him they could tell you the definition of any word in the dictionary. He'd say, "Go ahead; ask me any word," and when I would ask him for the definition of a word he would say, "my brother knows that one." Did I mention where I got my sense **of humor?**

My atmospheric conditions growing up were quite remarkable. I loved sports and, as a result, I must acknowledge the many inspirational coaches who influenced me as a young man. Sports are a great teacher. Hard work and discipline are the keys to success in both sports and life, and those lessons were instilled in me early and often. As an example, a coach once told me that if I wanted to be great at something I would need to lose a lot. At the time, it didn't make sense. How could losing make me better? Now I truly understand what that **advice meant.**

How did my friends growing up influence me? I shared a passion for sports with my neighborhood friends throughout my childhood and teenage years. However, it wasn't until I met my best friend at eighteen that I can say I knew about real friendship. It's important to note that I married my best friend: I won my second lottery! Her name is Bridget, and there's no way I would be writing this book if she didn't enter my life. Besides being my best friend, she is also an amazing research assistant. She spent many hours proofreading the very early drafts of this book. Sometimes she can overwhelm me with new information to read, yet it all fits perfectly into our model. She is resourceful, inspirational and brilliant. Her quest and drive for knowledge in order to help our struggling children is what led us to develop the Inspired Performance Program (TIPP). You're going to hear more about her throughout the book, and you'll see how much she changed me, my life, and this book. I love **her unconditionally.**

I also need to acknowledge the lifeblood produced from my friendship with my best friend, my children who gave me a purpose in life: Brandon, the eldest, my best friend, business partner and friendly––but fierce–– golf competitor; Ashley, my middle daughter, a Crohn's survivor and a young woman with a mental toughness that rivals my father's; and Tyson, the youngest, who suffered three head injuries and has inspired me to look for answers that also created the Inspired Performance Institute. Watching them being born, enjoying sports, and having fun in our epic Christmas celebrations are some of the greatest highlights of my life, and I am proud that those memories are the beautiful gifts they bestowed on me. I hope to lead them by example and leave them a legacy for their children. I love them unconditionally.

Professionally, I would like to acknowledge several people. I am honored and privileged to work with renowned neuropsychologist, clinical statistical researcher and child psychologist Dr. Alex Gimon. He has been a continuous wealth of knowledge and inspiration and has opened new avenues for healing for my youngest son Tyson, because he was the first doctor to recognize that he suffered a traumatic brain injury (TBI). Bridget and I can't thank him enough for his dedication to Tyson––and, most importantly, for being a loving Christian man.

Trauma therapist Dr. Jon Connelly opened my eyes and ears to a new way of healing people from trauma. His training allowed me to see the path to performance was to eliminate the traumatic or disturbing events affecting the mind on a daily basis. From him, I learned the most efficient way to reach peak performance—and adapt those models to **our clients.**

I must also recognize the contribution of the staff and executive management at Florida Christian University. Their support has been instrumental in the development of the Inspired Performance Institute. As of the date of this writing, the Inspired Performance Program is now a part of the FCU curriculum and is currently tied in with their landmark SOAR program. They were also responsible for my first international speaking engagement in Curitiba, Brazil. I also thank the Portigliatti family for their combined spiritual guidance and focused business expertise. Also, a special thank you to Dr. Josie Oliveira, Dr. Polanco, and Pastor Braga for their encouragement and support on my spiritual and **educational journey.**

The Inspired Performance Institute is connected to the University of Central Florida's Business Incubator, a community partnership program is designed to offer resources to new and growing companies in order to become successful businesses. With seven offices throughout Central Florida, our main office is located in the Orlando Incubator office. Besides receiving constant access to university-provided resources and partnership opportunities with other local startups and businesses, we are also exposed to the university's student base so we can help them gain valuable internship experience and future employment opportunities as they graduate.

As a result, the Inspired Performance Institute has already benefited from this student base. For example, we hired José E. Romero, a Technical Communication major from the University of Central Florida. Throughout this collaboration, José has provided his advice and expertise in shaping the direction for this book by researching, writing, editing, and proofreading content. In addition, Bridget and I met our best friends, Jim and Shelley Bowie, through the UCF Business Incubator program. They have watched and supported us on this adventure since we set up our first office with UCF in 2009, and to this day we treasure such an important relationship.

Dr. Leslie Hamilton was a great find. We were both speaking at a local women's empowerment seminar and immediately connected with similar worldly perspectives. She has also added her literary expertise with the foreword and assisted in proofreading the early drafts of this book.

Last and not least, I thank the many clients I have worked with over the years who gave me an insight into new approaches that are now part of the Inspired Performance Program. Thank you to all.

media.org/wiki/File:Eeg_gamma.svg. Used under the

Table of Contents

CHAPTER ONE

Why do You Need to be Out of Your Mind? 1

CHAPTER SIX

You Must be Out of Your Anxious Mind 169

CHAPTER SEVEN

Table of Figures

Tables

LIST OF ABBREVIATIONS

ACE	Adverse Childhood Experiences
ADHD	Attention Deficit Hyperactivity Disorder
ads	Advertisement(s)
ADVANTAGE	Assessment of Differences between Vioxx and Naproxen To Ascertain Gastrointestinal Tolerability and Effectiveness
AMA	American Medical Association
APA	American Psychological Association
ASHS	American Society of Health-System Pharmacists
BAP	*Beneficial, Applicable, Possible criteria*
BPD	*Borderline Personality Disorder*
CBT	Cognitive Behavioral Therapy
CDC	Center for Disease Control
CHC	Coalition for Healthcare Communication

COX	Cyclooxygenase
DID	Dissociative Identity Disorder
DTC	Direct-to-Consumer Advertising
DEA	US Drug Enforcement Administration
DSM	Diagnostic and Statistical Manual of Mental Disorders DSM5
DXM	Dextromethorphan
EDMR	Eye Movement Desensitization and Processing
EEG	Electroencephalograph
Fps	Frames per Second
GABA	Gamma-Aminobutyric Acid
GAD	Generalized Anxiety Disorder
Hi-res	High Resolution
HPA	Hypothalamic-Pituitary-Adrenal Axis
Hz	Hertz
Lo-res	Low Resolution
LSD	Lysergic Acid Diethylamide

Mg	Milligrams
NCO(s)	Noncommunicable Disease(s)
NIDA	National Institute on Drug Abuse
OCD	Obsessive-Compulsive Disorder
OTC	Over-the-Counter Drugs
PTSD	Post-Traumatic Stress Disorder
R&D	Research and Development
REM	Rapid Eye Movement
RRT	Rapid Resolution Therapy
TBI	Traumatic Brain Injury
tIPP	Inspired Performance Program
UCLA	University of California, Los Angeles
WMD	Weapons of Mass Destruction

INTRODUCTION

BY DR. ALEX GIMON, PH.D.

In my private practice as a licensed psychologist spanning more than 33 years and the prior nine years working as an educator at the university level, I have utilized the many different treatment techniques taught to me and which have been developed over the subsequent years, to diagnose and treat thousands of students and patients. I have been on an unending journey to find that "perfect answer" to the ever-present question of how to fix the psychological problems of the burgeoning number of clients I see each year, when the time and cost factors necessary to effectively evaluate and treat my patients have become more and more limited each year by social, economic and political factors out of my control.

When I first met Don Wood and learned of his work, I was skeptical at the thought it could so quickly and effectively help those suffering from PTSD, and other personal traumas which normally take years to address. I am now very pleased to present to you a procedure which properly administered in a professional setting, is unique in its effectiveness in providing therapy and healing for the escalating number of psychologically ill in the world, in an immediate and very time and cost-effective way. This Inspired Technique has been tested on hundreds of people who have volunteered for the program or have asked to participate. Not all were looking for help, but nonetheless, greatly benefited from the extraordinary relief and peace gained from **this procedure.**

The author started this work by taking a look at normal behavior versus learning through the school of hard knocks. He documents a history of the development of psychology as a separate medical field, and informs the reader about counseling techniques and medications clearly and concisely. To relate the need for an effective technique that does not involve medications or long-term therapy for effectiveness, he also gives a very personal, brave, and beautiful presentation of how individuals may be hurt in life, by presenting his own family's developmental history in *Chapter 2, A World of Hurt.*

In order to understand the crucial need for a therapeutic intervention to address the escalating problems suffered by people worldwide, the author elaborates in *Chapter 3, How Your Mind Works* and various parts of the brain, in terms easily understood by the layperson. In *Chapter 4, Atmospheric Conditions, or, Your Mind Could Not Have Done It Every Other Way,* the author begins the presentation of his compelling technique. In *Chapter 5, Getting Your Mind to Alpha State* he describes how the brain's electric waves work for us and the four states of brain waves. His technique begins at one level, which takes you into the important **Alpha State.**

In Chapter 6, the author goes on to present the Mind of Anxiety, and explains how his technique takes you *Out of Your Anxious Mind*. Chapter 7 describes how Trauma and Chronic Illness contributes to Being Out of Your Mind, and how to fix these conditions utilizing his technique. Finally, in Chapter 8, the author concludes with *Clearing Your Way to Success*.

This book is a new way for today's counselors to help a growing number of traumatized patients effectively, especially with the restrictions placed upon them by managed health care and health insurance companies. It is also an excellent self-help book that educates those suffering from trauma or illness to better understand their problems, the status of current evaluation of treatment modalities, and how to best address their problems effectively. I am very happy to lend my support to such an innovative program, which may change the way we deal with trauma in **our field.**

FOREWORD by Dr. Leslie Hamilton, Ph.D., LMFT

Over the past seventeen years of clinical work as a licensed marriage and family therapist, I have counseled men, women and children, helping them process their experiences differently, unveiling and co-creating preferred narratives, in order to improve their quality of life. I have studied social constructionism, cognitive-behavioral therapy, and narrative therapy, among other therapeutic modalities, and made significant progress with many clients, helping clients become more aware of "the stories they tell themselves," allowing them to take greater responsibility in identifying "unhelpful"

stories––maladaptive neurological programming––and
replace them with more "helpful" stories––developing new neural pathways through neuroplasticity. This
process has been deliberate, relying upon conscious
awareness in the context of talk therapy, but was sometimes undone in moments of dysregulation in a client's
nervous system. The origins and triggers of the dysregulation were sometimes known, often not, but the
consequences were evident. To a point, my feelings of
frustration and ineffectiveness sparked my curiosity for
the field of neuroscience and fostered innovative ways
to help my clients find peace.

I first met Don Wood at a Women's Empowerment
conference in Orlando, Florida, where we were both
presenting on our respective ideas for creating desired
change. A dear friend used to say, "The world was
divided up into two groups: people who get it...and
people who don't." I'm not quite sure what "it" is, but I
knew that when I heard Don speak, he got it. His words
resonated with me: While the parallels in our work were
obvious, his presentation linked bodies of research and
knowledge that greatly expanded my understanding of
the cognitive processes that were sabotaging my clients'
efforts and provided a structured program for quickly
and effectively addressing the disruptions. I felt his work
was the missing link I had been searching for, and I even
referenced to that fact in my presentation that same
day. I knew in my core that he was onto something and
I wanted to learn more about it.

When Don and I sat down to talk for the first time,
I was struck by the clarity and simplicity with which
he described his work. I was truly inspired by the

testimonials of the many professionals, athletes, veterans, women, and children he had quickly helped. But, while I was impressed with his work, it was Don's heart that inspired me the most. Keenly aware of how trauma is passed down from generation to generation––or as I like to say, that "hurt people hurt people," ––Don knew that in order to stop the cycle, we need to clear the glitches in the wounded psyche that lead people to perpetuate abuse despite all logic and rational thought. Don expressed a desire to see people optimizing their human potential, performing at their best and truly enjoying their lives.

The human mind is a fascinating mystery which remains vastly unknown, akin to the origins of the universe and the great abyss of the earth's deepest oceans. We have grasped elements such as the electrical impulses, chemical messengers, and intricate networks of connectivity that synergistically orchestrate our sensory experience and how we show up in the world. Yet, so much remains unknown. Our mind is the interface between the subjective "I" and "everything else." It determines not only *how* we perceive the world, but also *what* we perceive in the world. Research in the fields of neuroscience and psychology have identified how each one of our minds filters sensory data differently due to differing life experiences and biological make-ups, resulting in each one of us experiencing a unique and different reality. Don's work draws from multiple disciplines and techniques to create a unique and innovative program that clears the disruptive glitches or "error messages" hindering our perceptions and experiences of the world, and our performance within it. He has created a proverbial reset button that helps recalibrate mental processes to be more efficient and productive. And the results have been nothing short of amazing, along with the hope this program instills in its clients.

I believe Don's program, when properly delivered by a skilled practitioner, will revolutionize the mental health field and improve the quality of life for so many. It already has. The effectiveness of the NEURO techniques on panic attacks and anxiety has been astounding, and there is empirical data to support these results that is currently being processed to provide the validation needed to earn the credibility the technique warrants. It is an honor to work with Don to bring this program to the world. And I look forward to seeing the tears of relief in the eyes of those it heals.

It is with great pleasure and anticipation that I introduce to you, Don Wood, his neuro-technique, and the Inspired Performance Program. Enjoy!

Dr. Leslie Anna DeVol Hamilton, Ph.D., LMFT

CHAPTER ONE

WHY DO YOU NEED TO BE OUT OF YOUR MIND?

"Doctors do not like to talk about cure. Too many illnesses are remitting and relapsing—that is, they seem to go away only to return again at a future time. Psychiatric conditions, in particu-lar, tend to be chronic. [...] They are, in short, an exaggeration of normal."

—Frederick Neumann,
   Ph.D., 2013, par.1

What do you, dear reader, define as normal? What, do you believe, distinguishes "normal people" from others? Something that's too strange, bland, confusing or––above all––*out of your mind* takes over and invades you. Maybe you've suffered from very harmful, very embarrassing, or very blasphemous thoughts that are anything but normal. Or perhaps you are struggling to open a business due to all the times you've failed at very normal activities, and even the faintest hint of success

I

makes you feel anything but normal. Or, despite all the talk of sticks and stones and broken bones, names like "fat," "ugly," or "dumb" still haunt your dreams–and it's even worse when your loved ones become those who hurt you. Let me reassure you: whatever you do and whatever you feel, *there is nothing wrong with your mind.* **Your pain is just a symbol of the hard knocks you've traveled throughout your life.**

But is a school of hard knocks necessary to provide character in the face of adversity? Or is only "hard knocks" just a coping mechanism people use after experiencing disturbing or traumatic events? Some people wear it like a badge of honor. Others rage against the world, their family, and themselves, their minds tainted by the past they never chose to live through. If that helps, why should we stop them? But what about those moments in your life that you don't speak of because they aren't "normal?"

You see, everyone has been through traumatic or disturbing events at various times throughout his or her lives that seems out of the blue or shockingly unordinary. Sexual assault, abuse, death and grief, terrorism, or the unwieldy forces of nature––you name it, and it's already happened somewhere on the planet today. Or the trauma could be commonplace events that caused you so much distress: a biting dog, a finger cut, a pink slip, or an F in that College Statistics class you love to hate. Even today, commonplace events from the past can still be disturbing to process, and disastrous to recover from. Then why do some people appear to be more high-functioning and over-achieving than others, even though they've been through similar difficult experiences? Even if such a question becomes an all-consuming reality to either the victim or the client, I would rather focus on understanding how the *solution* is more important than the *why*. The solution involves bringing your mind into balance, being present and at peace. I'm sure you've read books that tell you the secret to success and happiness is to be "present" and "in the moment." Great advice! However, did they ever bother to explain *how* to accomplish this?

In short: you must be *out of your mind*! Your mind has developed certain error messages from life events and experiences, creating a series of glitches in the way your mind works. That's what the purpose of this book is. I will teach you how to correct these glitches and operate your mind with peak efficiency. When your mind is clear and present, everything naturally lows, and you'll recognize how your life will be much easier when you can place all your energy and attention on the right now!

A Short History of Psychology

Now, why isn't everyone using such a revolutionary process? To understand that answer, let's take a brief look at the history of psychology and its impact on the study of human behavior:

• Psychology can be traced all the way back to 387 B.C., when the Greek philosopher Plato stated that the brain is the mechanism that produces mental processes. His term, *psyche*, is translated as the "soul" which consists of three distinct parts: the *logical*, or separating reality from fiction through reason; the *spirited*, which is "competitive and seeks honor and victory;" and *appetitive*, which itself is derived into *necessary*, *superfluous*, and *lawless* necessities that seek fleshly fulfillment (Fenstermaker, 2013; Hartfield, 2011)

- In 335 B.C., Aristotle stated that the heart was the center of human reasoning and developed the first known psychological text in history, titled *Para Psyche*, or "About the Mind." In the book, he explored how the mind, indistinct from the soul, is the main reason for the body's existence. In addition, Aristotle also examined the role of balancing thoughts and influences in the body, which formed the basis of Freud's psychoanalytic theory (Shuttleworth, 2013).

- It was 1774 when the role of psychology as a science was carved through the work of German physician Franz Mesmer, who theorized that the mind could cure some mental illnesses. Originally called "mesmerism," his process is now known as *hypnosis* and, despite his successes with psychosomatic blindness, convulsions, and even hemorrhoids, Mesmer was completely denounced by both the Viennese and Parisian medical communities as a fraud due to his unorthodox practices involving animal magnetism and dramatic group sessions that rubbed the Enlightened community of the time the wrong way. Nevertheless, to him we owe the word "mesmerized"––to be spellbound and held to the complete attention **of something.**

- In 1859, Charles Darwin published his theory of "Survival of the Fittest," which, despite its controversial stance on evolution, offered the basis for evolutionary psychology to develop. Moreover, Darwin's Theory contributed to developing comparative psychology through the study of animals to draw conclusions about human behavior. It helped recognize individual differences through concepts like intelligence (drawn from natural selection), and addressed the role of biology and genetics in psychology (Tanner, 2008).

- The first American Ph.D. in psychology was issued in 1878 to G. Stanley Hall, who developed "genetic psychology" under the influences of evolutionary theory. Dr. Hall wrote *Senescence* (1922)––a treatise on the "crisis of aging"––and made psychology a respected profession in the United States by founding the American Psychological Association (APA). He also fostered important developments in the "child study movement" and considered childhood as "merely an extension of embryological development" (Grezlik, 2005).

- One year later, the first formal laboratory of psychology was founded in Leipzig, Germany by Wilhelm Wundt, where he studied human emotions, behaviors, and cognitions. Known as the "Father of Experimental Psychology" and the "Founder of Modern Psychology," Wundt transformed psychology from its theoretical and philosophical basis to an experimental one, detailing psychology as the "investigation of conscious processes in the models of correction peculiar to them." (Alvarado, 2011). (In America, the first laboratory of psychology was established in 1883 at Johns **Hopkins University.)**

- Most people have heard of Dr. Sigmund Freud, the landmark psychoanalyst who started his therapy practice in Vienna, Austria in 1886, and whose work started the theory behind personality development. Freud's work developed the role of the psyche between the id (instincts), the ego (reality), the superego (morality), and the conflict between them. Other concepts of psychoanalytic theory developed by Freud include psychosocial stages of development and dream analysis. (Sigmund Freud's The Interpretation of Dreams: The initial response (1899-1908) .

- In 1896 at the University of Pennsylvania, Lighter Witmer developed the first psychological clinic, which is now recognized as the birth of clinical psychology. At this point, psychology transformed into a practical venture that could help patients under a carefully conducted methodology (Baron, 2006).

- In a famous 1901 study on classical conditioning, Russian psychologist Ivan Pavlov conditioned dogs to salivate every time food arrived and a bell rang. The dogs would salivate as soon as they saw the food. After a period of time, Pavlov could get the dogs to salivate even if there was no food present. Because of this experiment, the theory of classical conditioning, or learning by association, was born (McLeod, 2014).

There have been many other significant developments after this time by such people as Alfred Adler, Carl Jung, John E. Watson, Jean Piaget, Erik Erikson, B.F. Skinner, Abraham Maslow, Alfred Bandura, and Aaron Beck. The list of men and women who have dedicated their lives to the work of psychology is invaluable. You could argue that other names should be included on this non-exhaustive list, and you are right. However, an exhaustive treaty being precluded, I include only the above, which serve as the foundational basis for the Inspired Performance Institute's programs **and education.**

A Better Solution: Wagging the Dog?

It's noteworthy that I stopped with Bandura and Beck, even though many others have made significant steps in many aspects of psychology beyond the sixties and seventies. During these turbulent times, I believe there was a significant and potentially dangerous shift to the use of pharmaceuticals. For over fifty years, we have seen a dramatic dependence on the use of pharmaceuticals to solve all of life's issues. The pharmaceutical machine is so powerful that these companies are dictating American healthcare policy––in other terms, the tail is wagging the dog. This is not to dismiss the number of breakthroughs in our quality of life through the development of drugs. But for some, drugs serve as the *only* answer, and this eschews anything else. However, they are not the only answer: in ten years, neuroscience has made significant steps in understanding how the brain works and these advancements––these are what I truly see as the *real* answer to rapidly and safely removing any internal blockages to happiness.

Hurdles to a Better Solution

Pharmaceuticals have become the most common solution in any medical intervention today. The pharmaceuticals' potential for harm is a concern. According to a 2013 study at the Mayo Clinic, four out of five adults in the United States use prescription medications, and almost 33% of these adults will use five or more medications on a daily basis. Researchers for the American Medical Association learned that drug use among adults age 20 and older rose to 59% in 2012 (Dennis, 2015). How is this beneficial? How did this get so out of control? What can we as consumers do in order to rein in this overarching control to our quality **of life?**

Part of the problem started about twenty years ago when steps were taken to speed up the Food and Drug Administration's (FDA) approval process for drugs. A fee is charged to any pharmaceutical company seeking a review and approval of their drug for distribution, allowing the FDA to expand their staff and in turn approve more drugs on a faster basis. However, the funds aren't adequately distributed for post-marketing surveillance and safety, creating an underfunded and overwhelmed system where side effects and safety issues are not discovered until well after the drugs are mass-marketed in large quantities throughout the medical system––and well within the consumer's reach (CL Ventola, 2011).

This multi-billion-dollar industry needs to convince people they are sick. Big Pharma companies spend billions of dollars to get the message out––"you need help, and we have *just* the *right* medicine for you!" Billions of advertising dollars are spent each year. A Kantar Media report suggested pharmaceuticals spent over $5 billion dollars in 2016 on direct-to-consumer (DTC) advertising. This investment has paid off, as in 2016 Americans spent a record $457 billion only on prescription medications (Llamas, 2016). Furthermore, the lobbying power of Big Pharma is legendary to the point that the United States and New Zealand are the only countries that legally allow DTCs to operate. Due to such ubiquitous position in the consumer market, this may lead you to believe that our large prescription drug consumption is cost-effective, when the opposite is true: Americans pay more for drugs and devices than any other country in **the world.**

A Nielsen Media report shows that DTCs appear on television at a rate of eight ads per hour of programming, and the costs of these ads vastly exceed the money spent on research and development (R&D). Critics believe these ads adversely affect the doctor/patient relationship; for instance, patients are coming in asking for these prescriptions they learned about through television because they feel informed about how to best handle their personal issue. However, the billions spent on these direct to consumer ads are only a fraction of the money spent by Big Pharma to promote their products. Companies spend billions more on working with doctors to write prescriptions for the newest and most expensive brand-name prescription drugs or devices for uses that have not been approved by the FDA. This practice is called off-**label marketing.**

Does Big Pharma Face Any Consequences?

Big Pharma does not get away with these practices without some consequences. Big Pharma must pay billions of dollars in criminal and civil settlements due to marketing fraud. DTC ad supporters argue that they educate and empower the public to make better health care choices. At the same time, doctors and critics will argue that Big Pharma only wants to sell expensive products with unknown side effects. To this end, the American Medical Association (AMA) and American Society of Health-System Pharmacists (ASHS) have been calling for a ban on these ads Stephen R. Permut, MD, 2016).

Despite the controversy, these advertisements create benefits that far outweigh the consequences for Big Pharma. A 2011 Congressional Budget Office Report revealed that drugs commercialized through direct-to-consumer ads had nine times more prescriptions than those without direct-to-consumer ads (Campbell, 2011). Also, another Kantar Media report showed two out of three adults would take action after being exposed to a drug or medical device advertisement, and 40% will make an appointment with their doctor. Still, American consumers feel confident about the dangers associated with the use of these drugs or devices; according to a survey conducted by Harvard and STAT, 76% of American consumers believe that drug companies adequately explain the side effects and risks of their medications (Llamas, 2016).

THE AMERICAN CONSUMER'S (ERRONEOUS) PERCEPTIONS OF DRUG SAFETY

To make matters worse, consumers believe the FDA only approves new drugs if they are better than what is currently being prescribed. However, there are no federal requirements or regulations requiring the FDA to approve new drugs because they are better––in fact, FDA approval does not necessarily mean the product is endorsed or recommended for public consumption. That said, a Pew (2013) survey concluded 43% of Americans believing only *completely safe* drugs can be advertised, whereas an article from the Journal of the National Cancer Institute suggests DTC drug sales increased 43% against 13% for all other drugs. Still, consumer watchdog organization Consumer Reports argued drug ads should be banned since they encourage patients and doctors to turn to medication when nondrug options might work just as well or with even better results. So, what are the medical community's thoughts on this matter?

The medical community's thoughts appear to be that doctors and pharmacists favor banning these direct to consumer ads altogether, reasoning that such ads encourage patients to demand newer and more expensive drugs when more cost-effective choices are available. As an example, an article in the *Journal of Clinical Oncology* concluded that 94% of nurse practitioners said patients had asked for an advertised drug, and 74% had patients who requested inappropriate drugs for their conditions. Unfortunately, doctors still wrote prescriptions for more than half of these requests (Abel, Lee, & Weeks, 2007).

In 2015, the AMA's policymaking body voted to support an advertising ban for prescription drugs and devices. As stated by Board Chair Dr. Patrice A. Harris, "Today's vote in support of an advertising ban reflects concerns among physicians about the negative impact of commercially driven promotions, and the role that marketing costs play in fueling escalating drug prices" (AMA, 2015). As part of his concerns with DTC advertising, he equates the "inflated demand" for drugs with the disregard for the appropriate circumstances against other non-invasive treatments (AMA, 2015).

Months after the vote, the American Society of Health-System Pharmacists voted for the same ban. According to CEO Paul W. Abramowitz, "For decades, pharmacists practicing in hospitals and clinics have been the leaders in recommending and initiating evidence-based medication therapies in partnership with physicians and other prescribers—and in helping patients achieve optimal and cost-effective medication therapy outcomes" (2016). With these hardline stances from both medical organizations, there's finally a growing awareness of the degrees in which misinformation and irresponsibility have encouraged ill-informed patients to seek out pricey drugs without measuring its side effects or consequences.

In a 2013 survey, 81% of doctors agreed DTCs promote the overuse of medications. As an example, drug companies jumped on "Low-T" campaigns for testosterone with drugs like AndroGel, Axiron, and Aveed. These drugs were approved by the FDA to treat men diagnosed with clinical hypogonadism, a condition that causes low testosterone. By championing these drugs as the new fountain of youth, promising increased vitality and sexual prowess, drug companies enticed millions of men to visit their doctors demanding these drugs *without* a clinical diagnosis. Dr. Sidney Wolfe of the advocacy group Public Citizen notes that drugs such as AndroGel are widely used––out of 7.5 million yearly prescriptions, AndroGel patches and vial drugs number 5 million, while 2.5 are for the injectable form––but a vast majority of men are not benefiting from the drug.

Over-prescription was so ubiquitous and widespread that in 2015 the FDA released a warning stating there was no evidence the drugs were safe or effective for low libido and fatigue––key symptoms of low testosterone featured in these ads (FDA, 2015). Despite the warning, the testosterone therapy craze continued. As Wolfe argues, millions of men are exposed to a drug with benefits that do not outweigh the risk of potentially fatal heart attacks and strokes. Likewise, several studies linked these drugs to increased odds of cardiac problems, creating over 7,000 lawsuits from men who claim the drugs caused numerous health issues. As Diana Zuckerman, President of the National Center for Health Research believed, "Obviously, the companies are paying a lot of money for these ads for a reason. They know it affects how many people take these drugs and how many prescriptions are written" (Llamas, 2016).

Other studies point out the connection between the number of prescriptions and these direct to consumer ads. As an example, doctors have prescribed medication for attention deficit hyperactivity disorder (ADHD) about 25 times more in the United States than in the United Kingdom, a country that *does not* allow

direct-to-consumer ads *and* where ADHD as a diagnosis is rare and controversial, as in the rest of Europe
(Kelley, 2013). There are many controversial questions
regarding the validity of an ADHD diagnosis, including
treating it with powerful antipsychotics. A video report
stated that drug companies make $13 billion each year
in prescriptions to treat ADHD (Wired, 2015).

In 2007, Dominick L. Frosch, Ph.D., a professor at
the UCLA David Geffen School of Medicine analyzed
the relationship between overmedication and DTC ads
by examining 38 unique television drug ads targeted at
treating common ailments, including high blood pressure, cholesterol and depression. Frosch concluded that
the ads employed emotional appeals to encourage view-
ers that medication is the only way to live a managed,
carefree, and happy life (Thomas Elli, 2007). Because,
as Zuckerman explained, *persuasion* is the main goal of
pharmaceutical companies, the consumer's awareness of
the product is oftentimes clouded by the drug's novelty:
"It is educating you to tell you that this product exists
and that it's great" (Llamas, 2016, **block 10**).

Intermission

You must be thinking, wow, so far all that I've read
feels like a history lesson. You must be wondering,
where are the solutions? Don't worry; the answers are
coming. There is a good reason for all this information.
You see, in order to understand the solution, you must
first identify the problem. It's important to note that I
do give credit to Big Pharma for some amazing drugs
that have saved lives. However, my concern is how many

drugs are being prescribed and for how long people are taking these drugs. What I'm pointing out is that there are other solutions, and some drugs do have a role in the healing process. The issue is the amount and length of time they are **being prescribed.**

So allow me to give you some good news during this pause into this heavy reading: A gentleman I worked with had been in a car accident where he rolled his pickup truck three times. (I'll refer to him as Tom) Tom's main issue was he had his seven-year-old son in the pickup truck with him. A chiropractor referred him to me because she was more concerned about his mental than his physical state: Tom would break down crying during his treatments and would describe suffering from panic attacks even while driving to her office for treatments. Her staff was afraid for him as he was leaving the office. Tom was on anxiety medication and without taking that he may not have been even able to get to her for treatments. The chiropractor called me and asked if I could see him as soon as possible.

When I first met Tom, I realized very quickly that he was not doing well. His hands were shaking so badly he couldn't even sign his name or fill out any of the forms I asked him to complete. Tom looked physically fit, and he was. A former sheriff's deputy, he now worked in construction, which is a very demanding physical job. However, he was unable to return to work after his accident and now was worried about how he was going to pay the bills. Tom was also concerned that he would lose his visitations with his son due to his trauma—Tom loved his son very much, and this accident was a cruel reminder of how precious life is and how close he came to losing him. The accident itself wasn't the issue for Tom—his emotional disturbances came from the fear of losing his son. (You are going to learn more about how Tom's mind was working as you read this book, so I don't want to give away too much at this point.) However, there is a reason why I put Tom's story in at this part of the book. The purpose is to let you know there are alternatives to using medications. Tom needed the medications only for a short period of time until he went through our Inspired Performance Program. Tom is off his medications, driving without the anxiety and panic attacks and most importantly, back to work. The anxiety medication served its purpose; it got him through a period of time. Now it's possible that without going through the Inspired Performance Program (TIPP), Tom would have continued to stay on the medications for who knows how long.

Now, let us examine the role of Big Pharma.

WHO ADVOCATES FOR BIG PHARMA?

There are also many advocates for direct-to-consumer ads who argue that they are educational and promote awareness of treatment options. For instance, John Kamp, the Executive Director of the Coalition for Healthcare Communication, believed "patient empowerment" is the goal of DTC advertising by helping patients start conversations and collaborate with healthcare providers: "Active, empowered patients who are expected to be very active in their healthcare lead the culture in our times [...] it is important for consumers to be a part of the decision-making, to learn about options that are available to them and discuss them with their doctor" (Llamas, 2016, block 8). It's important to point out that the New York-based Coalition for Healthcare Communication (CHC) is a lobbying organization that advocates for the "free flow of truthful health-care information" and actively promotes the role of DTC advertising as freedom of speech (Coalition for Healthcare Communication, 2017).

Kamp's vision of patient-centered communication is accurate, to a point: a 2014 study published by the Iran Red Crescent Medical Journal argued that "patient participation in healthcare decision is a sign of valuing humanity and [the] individuality of a patient" and is considered both "a legal right" and "an international gold standard" upheld by healthcare providers (Vahdat, Hamzehgardeshi, Hessam, & Hamzehgardeshi, 2014, p. 6). That being said, nowhere in the study do the researchers refer to advertisements or marketing plugs as effective methods for communication between patients and healthcare providers. Rather, patient participation in healthcare is more of a two-way street, where both the patient and the healthcare provider are both engaged and committed in improving their knowledge, methods, and cognitive and emotional connections in healthcare.

It's also common for pharmaceutical companies to use celebrities in their marketing campaigns, such as athletes, actors, or newscasters. This relatability allows companies to market a drug to a certain niche or create awareness of a disease or condition that celebrities are personally involved in social media and television. So, why use celebrities in the ads? Because it works—and creates huge dividends! To wit, a 2005 news article revealed that celebrity endorsement fees ranged from $200 thousand to $500 thousand [$250 thousand to $626 thousand in 2016, adjusted for inflation] (Associated Press, 2015). Even then, there are times when the use of a celebrity can help; in 2000 Katie Couric promoted colonoscopies by having hers done on national television. Three years later, a study published in the Archives of Internal Medicine noted there was a 20% increase in colonoscopies, more so in American women and people under age 50 (Healy, 2003; Cram et al., 2003).

However, even though celebrity ads may be viewed in a positive light, there have been times when they promote a dangerous drug—and the ramifications have been disastrous. To explain, former Olympic athletes Bruce (now Caitlyn) Jenner and Dorothy Hamill promoted the painkiller Vioxx, marketed by Merck to reduce the strain of rheumatoid arthritis (RA), carpal tunnel syndrome, and cancer prevention. In 2003, both celebrities appeared on the CNN talk show *Larry King Live* alongside Dr. John Klippel, then the head of the American Arthritis Foundation, touting the drug's lack of side effects—even when the company's 1999 pre-trial study revealed heart issues and labels being placed by the FDA in 2001 (King, 2003). Vioxx accounted for $2.5 billion in sales for Merck, and 84 million worldwide took the drug.

A year later, Merck recalled the drug because people had heart attacks after using it. The Merck recall became one of the largest healthcare settlements in history, where the company was forced to pay over $4 billion dollars in order to resolve over 35,000 lawsuits. Stocks plunged 27%, and Merck lost over $28 billion dollars in market value (Collins, 2006; Topol, 2004).

Even Kim Kardashian has been caught in the crossfire of drug marketing in social media. In 2015, she "praised a drug, Diclegis, to treat morning sickness in her Instagram account, expressing her excitement that it had been studied and there was no increased risk for her pregnancy" (LaMattina, 2015). Even though the FDA sent a warning letter to Quebec pharmaceutical Duchesney for "false and misleading advertising," social media conversations spiked five times, her Instagram post garnered, 450,000 likes, and Duchesney's "brand awareness" was markedly increased (Friedman, 2015; Heine, 2011).

MARKETING TO DOCTORS

But what about marketing to doctors? Why do pharmaceuticals spend so much more on marketing directly to doctors? Because it works! Most people would assume that these companies would promote directly to doctors. However, it's surprising to see how effective this practice is on influencing the medications prescribed to you. The methods used on doctors to promote their products include free meals, speaking and consultation fees, and sponsoring lectures and symposiums. A 2016 study reported that doctors who accept free meals from pharmaceutical companies are more likely to prescribe a pharmaceutical company's promoted drugs. By evaluating publicly available data from 279,669 physicians on Medicare prescriptions for statins, blood pressure medications and antidepressants, researchers reported that one free meal would equate to higher rates of prescribing heavily promoted drugs like Crestor, Benicar and Pristiq (DeJong et al., 2016). While researchers were careful to state the study exhibited no causality, there seems to be an association between the free meals and the number of drugs prescribed.

Other studies show different relationships between payments and prescribing drugs or devices, such as a 2016 ProPublica analysis revealing "doctors who received industry payments were two to three times as likely to prescribe brand-name drugs at exceptionally high rates as others in their specialty" (Ornstein et al., 2016). Another Pew study (2013) reported that pharmaceutical companies spent more than $27 billion on drug marketing, with 88% of spending on marketing to physicians and the rest on consumer advertising (mainly through television commercials). This approach is designed to "influenc[e] doctors' prescribing practices" (par. 1). Moreover, a 2000 study of sustained physician interactions with pharmaceutical representatives revealed that "attending sponsored [continuing medical education] events and accepting funding for travel or lodging for educational symposia" increased physicians' rates of prescribing such medication (Wazana, 2000, p. 373

SEEDING TRIALS

There's another and even more disturbing practice that drug companies have undertaken, recently known as "seeding trials," or just another controversial way to market their drugs to doctors with considerable criticism from experts. Hochauser (2009) defined seeding trials as "clinical studies primarily intended to promote use of the study drug by physicians and/or to convert physicians into advocates for the drug" (p. 1). In 1994, David A. Kessler argued that seeding trials serve as "thinly veiled attempts to entice doctors to prescribe a new drug being marketed by the company" under the guise of a scientific basis (Kessler et al., 1994). Likewise, Elliott (2011) commented that promoting "pseudo-studies" that have no "scientific merit" is exploitative for both patients and consumers in general, especially those vulnerable or in dire need of the drug (par. 4).

The general practice of these clinical trials is to employ a doctor frequently prescribing a competing drug against the one being studied and pay them a high fee to participate. Because of this, it is not until litigation against the drug company initiates, that the true purpose of the seeding trials will be revealed. It does not help that drug companies are not required to disclose the purpose of these trials to any review boards, physicians or patients. Also, there is not much information available to the public about these practices. In essence, many clinical trials have become "marketing in the guise of science" (Rennie, 2008).

This brings us back to the issue described earlier about Merck and the marketing of Vioxx, exemplifying how litigation developed the issues from the seeding trial during legal proceedings against Merck for its pain reliever Vioxx. The seeding trial was named ADVANTAGE (Assessment of Differences between Vioxx and Naproxen to Ascertain Gastrointestinal Tolerability and Effectiveness), and its purpose was to assess the drug's gastrointestinal safety. The results of the trial appeared in numerous peer-reviewed medical journals; however, there was a problem: neither doctors nor researchers actually *designed* the trial.

Internal documents from the company reveal that Merck's marketing team designed the trial, and as such included reaching "a key physician group to accelerate the uptake of Vioxx as the second entrant in a highly competitive new class and gather data important to this customer group" even if, ironically enough, Merck's marketing team received important prizes such as the Best Physician Program Award for their contributions to improving physician service quality (Hill et al., 2008, p. 255). Eventually, Merck removed Vioxx from the market after an alarming number of patients taking Vioxx suffered heart attacks and discovered the hard way that seeding trials only serve to deceive patients, doctors, researchers **and advocates..**

Ross, one of the coauthors of the Vioxx report, explained three consequences of seeding trials. First, they undermine scientific integrity. Second, patients are not properly informed and cannot consent to the clinical trial. Finally, the medical literature suffers from bias and ethics concerns (Soucheray, 2012). In another alarming statistic, half of all clinical trials undertaken—legitimately or not—have not published results to the public: "When clinical trial information is kept hidden, it means governments and regulations are at risk of making the wrong decisions [and endangering public health]" (Lane, 2016).

OFF-LABEL MARKETING

In addition to seeding trials, there is the additional problem of drug companies using *off-label promotion,* or the practice of marketing a drug to doctors for a use not approved by the FDA. While healthcare providers are not forbidden to prescribe a drug for an off-label use (and one out of five medications prescribed by them are off-label), it is illegal for a drug company to promote a drug off-label, because the FDA has not reviewed any data regarding the safety or effects for its prescribed––or intended––use. Unfortunately, this practice happens more than we know; as reported in pediatric and psychiatric practices, there are times when more *off-label* than *on-label* use is occurring, especially for severe mental health or physical problems. As Dr. Michael Carome, Director of Public Citizen's Health Research Group, said, "Off-label promotion can be prosecuted as a criminal offense because of the potential for serious adverse health consequences to patients from such promotional activities" (Almashat, Wolfe, & Carome, 2016; Llamas, 2016; Public Citizen, 2010, par. 4). On the other side, supporters of this practice include people like John Kamp: "The drug sponsor, the company that manufactures the drug, is usually in the best position to talk about off-label because they know more about the safe and effective use of their drug than any other institution" (Llamas, 2016). So, if we follow his argument, are there examples of how off-label drugs can be beneficial?

Certain off-label marketing usage is permitted to manufacturers under certain circumstances, and certain guidelines exist that establish the difference between *communication* and *promotion*. To illustrate an appropriate off-label promotion, companies may "respond to unsolicited requests from health care professionals about unapproved [yet recommended] uses for the drug," may distribute "peer-reviewed journals and reference books" detailing off-label uses, and may support CMEs discussing off-label uses of such medication (Richardson, Kesselheim, Spatz, Lott, & Gnadinger, 2016). However, in addition, the companies must submit all promotional materials to the FDA before disseminating to the public in a process known as *advisory review* (Ventola, 2009).

There are cases where patients may receive access to life-saving treatments. To illustrate, many experimental cancer treatments help patients who have suffered with conventional treatments to no avail. Nonetheless, you must wonder if the *true* intentions of drug companies are noble in *every* situation. Because FDA-approved drugs have some very limited––and profitable––legal uses, drug companies like to use off-label practices in order to pad profits. Officially, drug companies state they are against the illegal practice of off-label use. Unofficially, they provide incentives for reps to sell these off-label uses to doctors, health care providers and hospitals.

There are cases when drug representatives are fired if they disclose the ethics of this practice, even if state and federal whistleblower protections forbid companies to do so. An example is former Acclarent sales representative Melayna Lokosky, who was fired for exposing Johnson & Johnson's deceptive marketing practices (Llamas, 2016). In 2015, Lokosky filed a whistleblower complaint in the Los Angeles Superior Court, accusing Acclarent of off-label promotion of its Relieva Stratus MicroFlow Spacer for an unproven drug-delivery use, stating that insurance companies paid for medically unnecessary, misbranded Acclarent devices that were marketed to physicians for unproven off-label use. Moreover, a Massachusetts federal court indicted two Acclarent executives for fraud when they marketed Acclarent's Relieva Stratus MicroFlow Spacer off-label for steroid delivery when the FDA only approved it for opening sinuses (Llamas, 2016; The United States Attorney's Office, District of Massachusetts, 2016).

The antipsychotic drug Risperdal, also marketed by Johnson & Johnson, is at the center of one of the most publicized cases of off-label marketing in recent years. In 1993, the FDA only approved Risperdal to treat schizophrenia in adults. However, Johnson & Johnson began marketing Risperdal to high-risk groups such as children and the elderly in order to treat ADHD, anxiety, sleep difficulties, depression, and hostility—despite the fact that in early clinical trials, researchers found substantial side effects, including hormonal disorders, diabetes, and stroke (Brill, 2016). Disregarding the evidence, Johnson & Johnson's Janssen unit exploited both groups by openly flouting drug marketing laws (Brill, 2016). The FDA denied approval to Johnson & Johnson for the use of Risperdal for the elderly in 1999 due to unexplained deaths from heart-related issues and strokes in elderly patients taking the drug. Specifically, Johnson & Johnson "failed to fully explore and explain what appeared to be an excess number of deaths" (Brill, 2016).

A disturbing side effect of Risperdal involved *gynecomastia* a condition, where young boys and men develop breasts. This was a side effect Johnson & Johnson knew about, but continued to make 20% of its revenue by selling Risperdal to children *and* without FDA approval. Furthermore, the company colluded with respected academics who boasted about Risperdal to pediatricians. In 2015, Alabama resident Austin Pledger, who suffered from gynecomastia due to the effects of Risperdal, won one of the many lawsuits filed in state and federal courts. Mr. Pledger took Risperdal at age 8 in order to treat severe autism and ADHD. He was awarded with $2.5 million dollars after testifying how he developed size 46DD breasts as a teenager after taking the drug (Brill, 2016).

Drug companies pay billions of dollars in fines to the Department of Justice for breaking the law. To date, the largest settlement involving a pharmaceutical company came from the popular antidepressant paroxetine (Paxil) by GlaxoSmithKline, who promoted the drug to children younger than 18 despite not having FDA approval. Eventually, the company paid over $3 billion in criminal and civil charges, since companies undertaking this practice face prosecution for exposing patients to serious health hazards without their knowledge or consent (Public Citizen, 2010). As a result, federal and state governments and pharmaceutical manufacturers reached a total of 373 settlements totaling $35.7 billion in 15 years, with the largest type of financial penalties resolved from "off-label promotion of pharmaceuticals" (Almashat, Wolfe, & Carome, 2016). So why would the drug companies keep promoting off-label uses even when fined billions of dollars? Because it's extremely lucrative: about a fifth of all their revenue comes from off-label prescriptions as reported by Cozen O'Connor's

Life Sciences Practice Group (Lefkowitz, 2017). So, can you see why it makes business sense to sacrifice a few hundred million in fines to bring in billions **in revenue?**

A lack of oversight and an excessive number of loopholes complicate the circumstances in seeking justice for victims. As reported by Bobelian (2013), the practice of off-label prescriptions "is simply too lucrative to pass up," and major pharmaceuticals can easily recover their lost profit to legal suits by other means, including––you guessed it––off-label marketing. Look at Risperdal: In 2002, off-label prescription use accounted for 75% of Johnson & Johnson revenue and, according to court documents, Risperdal was Johnson & Johnson's second-best-selling drug. By using off-label marketing promotions, Risperdal sales in 1994 amounted to $172 million ($314 in 2017, adjusted for inflation), and by 2005 sales increased tenfold to $1.7 billion ($2.1 billion, adjusted for inflation). By the time the Justice Department reached a settlement with Johnson & Johnson in 2013, the company had almost 20 years of profit from off-label use (Brill, 2016).

So, What's the FDA Doing to Protect Us?

How could the government let this happen over and over again? As Zuckerman explained regarding FDA practices, "The FDA has written policies that sound good, but the reality is very different from the written policies" (Llamas, 2016). If you asked most people, they would tell you the FDA is an important entity protecting the public. Yet, even if we recognize the need for governmental oversight, more than half the public believes thinks the FDA is doing either a fair or poor job of regulating the drug companies. And here's another surprise: Did you know that the FDA has not deemed many advertised drugs as "safe?"

So, what's the FDA doing about policing and controlling the drug companies? Apparently very little, because the FDA's guidelines for drug companies are voluntary, since: "In most cases, federal law does not allow the FDA to require that drug companies submit ads for approval before the ads are used" (Food and Drug Administration, 2009). Only the agency would intervene and ask for a company to pull out an ad if it violates a law. Michael Carome believed the agency has done poorly in this regard, and must be "vigilant" and dedicated in its enforcement against companies openly flaunting the agency's laws (Llamas, 2016). Barbara Brenner, executive director of Breast Cancer Action, stated that the agency's "lack of resources to identity violations" forces consumers to be the responsible party to bear the burden of DTC monitoring (s). The agency's role in regulating social medical is an equally important to address. As the Kim Kardashian/Diclegis controversy shows, how can the FDA ensure the accuracy of a social media promotion and still monitor the validity of "person-to-person pharmaceutical recommendations?" (Greene & Kesselheim, 2015).

Unfortunately, the chances of eliminating direct-to-consumer drug advertising are slim to none; even if politicians and physicians lobby to limit the effects of DTCs, drug companies spent $5.2 billion on lobbying in 2015, and only 25% of such lobbying money, or about $1.3

billion, was spent lobbying towards five drugs: Humira, Lyrica, Ellquis, Cialis, and Xeljan (Robbins, 2016). Our Constitution protects the right to advertise, and powerful lobbyists spend millions of dollars to defend those rights so long as the information presented in the commercial is not "false or misleading" —which, as discussed earlier, it oftentimes is (Furberg, Furberg, & Sasich, 2010). Any attempts at getting legislation passed to stop these ads would most likely fail. To this end, Kamp, the Executive Director of the CHC, offered a solution: that the FDA and other regulators ensure companies tell the truth while watching for "false and misleading" information (Silverman, 2016).

Do No Harm?

Now, this book was not written as an indictment of the drug companies, doctors, nor the FDA. The information provided in this chapter illustrates why any new non-drug solutions would meet fierce opposition and receive scathing criticism from a multi-billion-dollar industry with their proverbial finger on the pulse of any new trends that would oppose any threat to drug solutions revenue. That makes sense, since such companies are obliged to protect the shareholders within the company. However, the answer is *not* with the drug industry. As explained before, that does not mean pharmaceuticals are completely self-serving—there are times when medications are necessary, and there have been wonder drugs that have saved countless lives. However, why are so many people taking so many prescription drugs daily, especially when his or her conditions do not improve?

To clarify, I am amazed whenever I ask someone on anxiety medication if it improves their symptoms. Admitting the medication is ineffective, people continue taking the drug out of fear or uncertainty about what would happen if they stopped taking the medication. That makes no sense to me! Taking medication for a symptom only works as a palliative, not a catch-all for the disease; when the medication courses through the body, the anxiety lays dormant. I believe they feel better because they are *conditioned* to feel better with medicine. Likewise, it is not uncommon for drug addicts to say he or she immediately feel better when they know they just "scored" and the dealer is handing over the drugs. The drug user has not even touched the drug, and they already feel better. How can you **explain that?**

DRUGS ARE POISONS

Essentially, "all drugs are poisons," and every medication interferes with normal cellular processes in some way. To counteract this, physicians prescribe only drugs that (positively) react to the body's processes (Orac, 2016). Moderation is key since the effects of medication are dependent on both quantity *and* quality of the drug. One amount can speed you up, and a different amount can slow you down. Too much and the drug can kill you. This begrudging confession is one that every doctor, pharmacist, marketer, and consumer needs to take to heart. Of course, there are times when a drug is necessary. But remember––drugs are still drugs, and any distortion to the body's homeostasis can be destructive. Some people see drugs as the *only* solution for his or her ills; if not careful enough, the drugs can become *the* problem."

Using this drug-as-poison perspective, let's take a look at one common drug, aspirin. Because aspirin "permanently inactivates an enzyme" and "poisons the [platelet]," it works as a "blood thinner" by blocking its power and capacity to create cyclooxygenase (COX) enzymes, which are involved in the production of inflammation (Orac, 2016) No wonder the aspirin does wonders as a pain reliever, fever reducer, inflammation easer, and heart attack reducer!

Let's take another look at a drug called Warfarin. Even though this drug is used as a blood thinner, the drug began its days before human consumption as rat poison marketed under brand names Rat-A-Way and Lurat. Rat-A-Way was very effective because it was both odorless and tasteless, which made it easier to feed to rats. While many chemicals related to rat poison are also used as drug treatments, this does not mean that Big Pharma looks for creative ways to poison us; it suggests that, depending on the dosage, drugs can be either therapeutic or deadly. In lower doses, Warfarin inhibits coagulation because the drug interferes with a set of proteins that allows the blood to coagulate. At concentrated dosages, Warfarin will cause extensive internal bleeding, the same way the drug operates in killing rats. Before its release date, the drug was considered too strong to prescribe to humans. When Warfarin was introduced in 1954, it assisted in reducing the risk of strokes by two-thirds. But there was a catch: patients would now be dependent on this "light" version of rat poison for the rest of his or her natural lives. Warfarin is still prescribed today and is presently one of the most widely used anticoagulants in the **United States.**

In the 1980s, everybody was saying "Just Say No to Drugs." In our current society, we are currently facing polarizing and divisive sociopolitical pressures to decriminalize drugs like marijuana. At the same time, primary health care providers are prescribing handfuls of psychotropic drugs to address undiagnosed physical and behavioral complaints. If a patient complains of pain, anxiety, sleep disorders or depression, that unlocks the medicine chest, garnering unwanted dangers such as prescription drug abuse and addiction. To that end, we need to be *very* careful of what we consume. No longer is the addict a beggar languishing on a street corner. Now, people from all walks of life are affected––doctors, lawyers, mothers, fathers, brothers, and sisters–– with unseemly prescriptions from their well-meaning, but often misguided family doctor. In a world filled with con-veniences and instant gratification, these prescription drugs destroy lives, shatter relationships, and eradicate the livelihoods of productive members of society. For all intents and purposes, we appear to accept, rational-ize, and minimize the legalized danger of drugs in **our culture.**

No drugs, whether legal or illegal, can take the power from you to change your life by simply getting out of your mind. This is your new reality: there's a life-chang-ing adventure ahead of you. There will be moments of breakthrough discovery and powerful actions that will have you clear your mind without drugs, diets, or wasting time and money under a knife. In this book, you will find the various tools you need in order to be out of your mind should you choose to continue reading this book––all without harmful drugs. I will give you a hint: it involves changing lifelong, ingrained behavior patterns within you. It's not a quick-fix, but it's possible. It involves facing your innermost fears and failures in life *without* the use of dangerous drugs. It involves clearing your mind of past emotions. Most importantly, it involves learning how to truly love yourself while getting yourself out of the confines of your mind.

CHAPTER TWO:

A WORLD OF HURT

I do not know about you, but my parents' generation believed that adversity makes you tougher. Even today, Americans still prize the "self-made man," the person that beats the odds through hard work and success. Even today, many believe that going through tough times strengthens your character and matures you to better face adversity––and thrive. There's no doubt that life's experiences provide important lessons one can learn throughout life. For American psychologist Abraham Maslow, brushes with potentially stressful and traumatic events serve as important steps to growth (Joseph & Butler, 2010). Even if suffering may be self-imposed, accepting the trauma as temporary and having an optimistic outlook towards the future allows you to experience greater events of inner peace (Hampton, 2014a).

But how would this adage apply to someone *currently experiencing* trauma? How can this be, you might ask? How can you use these words to confront someone who has experienced the worst kinds of pain in the flesh? Of course, you've seen people who suffered horrible tragedies and unspeakable crimes, yet despite

34

the odds, they've succeeded. Is it right to expect every-body to do so? Their success does not mean the trauma of the past no longer has a powerful hold on them.

Perhaps, for some of those survivors, they are in for a world of hurt.

MY LIFE AND HERS

My father was a man with a calm and tranquil demeanor. He was very smart. He never lost his cool. He never became upset. He came from a long line of English lawyers and barristers, but was sickly, and the cold, wet English weather was slowly harming his body. As a teenager, he suffered from bronchitis and asthma, so his family sent him to Canada in order to relieve his symptoms. When he traveled to Canada, he fell in love with my mother—and her beautiful country, never wanting to return to England and become a lawyer. Dis-traught by his son's defiance, my grandfather disowned him—and from that point on, he had to survive on his own in the harsh, yet opportune Canadian environment. This environment transformed him into a stronger man.

He had a bad neck. He had bronchitis. He had numerous stomach issues—yet he never missed a day of work. He never complained, and he never explained his illnesses away. One of the best compliments my mother ever gave me (or so I thought) was in high school when I woke up ill and vomiting. When my mother saw me, she was surprised that I was still ready to go to school! Surprised, she remarked, "Oh, I heard you throwing up. I didn't think you were going to school." I responded, both succinctly and resigned, with a hint of ignorance and innocence, that I had things to do in school.

She responded with a certain scoff and gracious dismissal, "You're just like your dad," which in my naïve, teenaged mind, I considered the perfect complement: no matter what happened, I would still go to school and fulfill my obligations, just like my father would do.

I knew my father loved me deeply without question—but he was never an affectionate person by nature. Maybe it was his British stiff upper lip. Maybe it was the rugged nature that slowly turned him aloof, yet never distant with his loved ones. My mother was the complete opposite: she always hugged me and showered me with love and affection, offering me her kindness with deep serenity. We weren't wealthy, but I never remember wanting for anything, and only if I really wanted something would I be asked to work for it. From that, I learned good discipline and fiscal prudence while growing up in the middle-class Toronto suburbs. At the same time, I had to melt my aloofness away so I could to show affection to others. In hindsight, I was both blessed and spoiled with a warm and loving family, naively believing that everybody I knew lived in a beautiful and peaceful home where people would love and respect each other, even if the world would spin out of control.

Compare my idyllic, middle-class Canadian life with that of my wife, Bridget. On every level, she was a loving mother, a kind and dedicated housewife. If you ever met her, you'd *never* be able to tell she still suffered and relived the horrible abuse she experienced as a child at the hands of her father. You see, Bridget developed survival instincts very early in life as she discovered that living in an abusive home environment shouldn't be known outside of the home. She learned that dysfunction must be kept away from the public's judgmental and prying eyes. What would they think about her if they knew that her father was a raving lunatic or a charming sociopath? Why would she be the one responsible to shatter the illusion? As noted by Vangelisti (1994), the child feels keeping secrets would protect the family from falling apart and blunt any questions of a family member's identity. When everyone outside of the family saw him as the charming businessman, the loving and caring father, who would argue that his family was everything to him? This hypocrisy was broken inside the home where his family became the lightning rod for his anger. Since then, my wife has lived, and survived, in a world of hurt.

My wife was born in Ireland, but she moved to Canada when she was only one year old, as her parents looked at Canada with eyes of opportunity. With them, Bridget's father also exported a vicious temper, one we still believe was caused by untold amounts of trauma during his own life. Anything could trigger his temper, and the alarm was eerily unpredictable. For any child growing up, that is a frightening way to live: things would fly across the room; the children would scatter; he would be screaming and yelling, throwing tantrums —and then, thirty seconds later, the kids would come out of their hiding places, and everything would be back to normal, as if nothing ever happened. He'd taunt his victims, saying things like, "Are you still hanging on to that? It's over." In his mind, he could never understand

why his family would still feel anger, frustration, or resentment for the abuse *he* inflicted—if he could ever call
it abuse. In his mind, what's the point of resentment if
no harm was ever done?

Her father was charming and generous to a fault.
Desperately wanting to be liked, he would purchase
people's affection with things. His façade, however,
constantly broke down, and inside the home he would
project his frustrations onto his vulnerable family. In my
mind, I observed the major tell-tale signs of a textbook
sociopath: his lack of empathy for others, his self-serving nature, his controlling behavior by force, and anger
as his favorite tools for manipulation. Anger also became a good way to get people to back down, as I once
saw a big guy get scared of him. When people get angry,
others never know how to deal with it. Her dad learned
that lesson over the years: If he can growl and scream
louder than everybody else, they would back down.

If pity wouldn't cause you to bend your will for
him, then his temper would wring the choice out of your
hands. If something was in his way or he perceived any
exploitable weakness, he would seize the opportunity
to its full advantage. In fact, he was so emboldened by
weakness that he was deathly afraid of any challenge
to his strength. Still, he never used his anger on me because he knew his mind games wouldn't work on me—I
was a hockey player, so he was conscious that I would
knock him out in a heartbeat! That said, on a certain
occasion, I would see his nasty side and, even if his anger was never directed at me, it never stopped being an
unsettling experience. Even his positive attributes were
a double-edged sword, as his supposed "generosity"

was only a ploy to buy love and disguise his spendthrift ways to appear wealthier than he actually was. In other words, he attempted to portray an image of success that naturally channeled into his family.

He wanted to be remembered as a macho man who felt he was smarter than he really was, longing to make his presence heard, good or bad. I remember one cold winter night when Bridget, then my girlfriend, and I were sitting on the couch when, suddenly, her father's car got stuck in the snowy driveway. I saw a raving lunatic stomp in the house, screaming, yelling, and forcing the kids out of the house in order to dig his car out of the driveway. He shouted obscenities and somewhat empty threats should they not do exactly as they were told. Everybody inside the house—except me—darted into the driveway. I was stunned at the scene!

For Bridget, the fear of living with a mercurial father forced her to predict when the temper would arise. He would say something, and somebody would get hit. Her older brothers bore the brunt of his physical abuse while my wife looked up helplessly before them. They fought back, argued, and openly rebelled against their father, but my sensitive wife would be forced to live her life under the radar for fear of confronting *any* type of anger. She treated her past like a closely guarded secret, afraid that revealing it would expose the world to the far-from-idyllic reality that Bridget's family lived.

I knew my wife grew up in a traumatic household, but I always asked myself: why did she continue to live in fear? She was safe with me. She had a beautiful house with very beautiful children. Yet, as much as I tried making her world a bit safer, my wife kept reliving her past with the same intensity of a helpless child. If I would express any disagreement with her, she would suddenly ask, "Oh, why are you upset?," and I would be surprised at her random accusation. She would answer in a regretful and rueful tone, "The way you said it sounded like you were upset."

I was naïve. Even when we had our disagreements, she would listen so carefully to what I said and project her father's actions on to me. Bridget's mind went back to the memory of her father starting to get frustrated. Her perception was so attuned to recording any abrupt changes in my voice and my demeanor that her mind automatically geared towards self-protection. In turn, she learned to read people's intentions because that helped her survive. For me, however, there was no logical reason why she reacted the way she did, and she would also be unaware of why she was being hurt by someone she loved, *again*.

Did I really say that? Well, yes, I did: a little girl would naturally love her father, even if it means depending on their abuser and victimizer when hurt (Alford, Martin, & Martin, 1985). So, you can imagine the confusion children experience when their protector lashes out at them; their survival instincts are engaging, and a young mind is a sponge that analyzes and interprets every environmental cue to the best of its ability. An impressionable young mind without much life experience would interpret distorted meanings and internalize the dysfunction at an early age, and beliefs formed at an early stage will transform into the behaviors these traumatized children will display throughout the rest of their lives, unless serious corrections are made.

For Bridget, faith served as a lamp to her feet because she grew up believing there was a better way, full of hope and opportunity beyond her father's abuse. Yet even as a Christian, she never felt herself capable of forgiving her father. Everybody wanted her to forgive and forget, to let go and let God handle it if she wanted to enter the Kingdom of Heaven—but the past was still there, invading her conscience. Until these images were cleared, she would live with the distortions in her mind, toiling between her expectations and her reality. Without her faith, she would have ended up in a worse place.

Her brother ended up as an angry, bitter alcoholic who—just like his father—needed to pick a fight at every turn in order to feel validated. Her younger brothers, believe it or not, loved their father even though they still dealt with a bevy of anger issues directed at others rather than their father. They knew their father was an angry guy, but they saw something in him that they liked. They were younger, so it helped that time and a newfound affluence slightly calmed him down, even though here was still manipulation and favoritism, pitting one sibling against the other in order to build his own chiefdom amidst the competition to carry out his favor.

The ongoing nightmares were a much more perplexing experience. In her nightmares, Bridget would see a shadow lurking at the door. She could not distinguish that sinister presence. Yet Bridget believed that person had killed everybody in the house, and she had to pretend to be dead if she wished to survive. I would listen to her sobs and labored breath while she fought the nightmare, almost trying to keep quiet as if she continued to reject her dreams. Instead of screams and shouts and punches akin to a horror movie, there were pants startling enough to throw her sleeping body into total panic. Startled myself, I would have to gently wake her up and comfort her. This would happen once a month on average, sometimes more frequently, and sometimes less. As Borelli (2015) suggested in her article about the symbols of nightmares, murder reflects *forced change.* In other words, Bridget's subconscious mind was *forcing her* to deal with the trauma she may have pushed back during waking hours while she was asleep.

As I researched the causes for her distress, I've finally learned that her father could not have done it every other way. It did not mean she had to let him off the hook for all the damage he had deliberately caused throughout the years—that would have been an affront to the concept of justice. Instead, she understood something painful must have happened in his life that created such explosive anger and vindictiveness. She finally had the power to clear, sweep, and bank her own mind. She could finally feel safe. As I developed the techniques, everything in Bridget's emotional life calmed down. It changed her life! There were no more nightmares. She can comfortably make assertive decisions on her own, responding differently to the various changes in life. She no longer looks at her life with fear, and those are the same experiences of hundreds of people who have completed the Inspired Performance Program. If I witnessed how this program transformed the life of someone near and dear to my heart every day, then I know my clients living in a world of hurt will experience the same relief Bridget had by getting out of their minds and into the present.

What is Trauma?

Even if trauma is a commonly used word describing a highly stressful event, we need a superior way to describe trauma if we wish to better understand what it means. The Merriam-Webster Dictionary defines *trauma* as "an emotional upset" or "a disordered psychic or behavioral state resulting from severe mental or emotional stress or physical injury" (Merriam-Webster, 2007). On the other hand, the Oxford Dictionary defines trauma as "a deeply distressing and disturbing experience" (Oxford Living Dictionaries, 2007). While those definitions illustrate a *popular* way to understand trauma, in reality, living through it causes both physical and **emotional distress.**

Trauma is best described as an event that produces extreme stress and overwhelms the individual's ability to cope, often arising from one-time dramatic incidents like car accidents, terrorism, surgeries, or natural disasters; or chronic and repetitive experiences, such as child abuse and neglect, combat, and domestic violence. Because each person responds differently to events, defining trauma is a very subjective endeavor as each survivor, and institution, interprets the event through their own set of **atmospheric conditions.**

When an individual experiences a traumatic event, the event will create numerous negative psychological effects because the trauma overwhelms the individual's ability to cope, leaving them suffering through a litany of fears, including death, annihilation, mutilation, or psychosis. These trigger the limbic system, our survival brain, to intervene. The individual feels emotionally, cognitively, and physically overwhelmed. The most common events creating this overwhelming situation include abuse of power, betrayal of trust, helplessness, pain, entrapment, confusion, **and loss.**

The more helpless and endangered you feel, the more psychologically traumatized you will be in the long term. The impact of the trauma is much more insidious when the physical and emotional injuries are caused by someone whom the victim is dependent upon and through no fault of his or her own, rendering recovery far more complicated. In fact, the majority of people seeking treatment for trauma are survivors of violent physical or psychological wounds inflicted by a person. If the event was carried out through an ongoing romantic or parent-child relationship, the issues are increased and eventually magnified as treatment becomes even more complex.

To demonstrate how this works, let me by share with you several stories of former clients who asked for my help and got amazing results through the Inspired Performance Institute. That being said, I must make a very important disclaimer: I refuse to call them "case studies" because my former clients are people, not merely scientific participants or guinea pigs in a clinical trial. Like you and me, my former client's have thoughts, dreams, and aspirations. These men and women wish to grow. These men and women wish to succeed. However, something inside them, something very deep inside them, was holding them back, and it became my duty to break down those walls and help them become empowered and emboldened to walk them into the future. The names used are not real because I wish to protect my former client's identities—but their stories are real, and their successes, too.

THE STORY OF SARAH, THE UGLY DUCKING

In 2015, a business colleague, who very well understood the principles of performance, asked me to come to Indiana and work with some of his management staff. The Program was described to the employees as an innovative tool to clear events and experiences that were creating conflict for their minds, in order to improve their performance levels. While I met with several managers during the day, Sarah's story stuck out to me because, as soon as she walked in and sat down, she started sobbing uncontrollably.

I asked her softly, "So, I see something has happened. What's going on? Where is this coming from?"

She responded, "I've had a very difficult life. I have children, I've been married three times, but I know I'm ugly." She just came out with it, treating as if it were a sudden bombshell: "I'm ugly, I know I'm ugly, I can't look at the mirror, I can't!"

Mind you: even though Sarah was a successful telemarketing professional, her personal life was crumbling. Despite being a very attractive woman in her mid-sixties, Sarah was a telemarketing professional who *knew* she was ugly and nobody else could convince her otherwise—in fact, she chose telemarketing as a career because she did not need to be seen by everybody. She avoided being in any family pictures and, should she be forced to, she always stood in the near end of the frame. That way, Sarah could cut herself out when the photographer took the picture. No one in her office, not even her boss, would suspect Sarah had a very low self-esteem! No one would even know she developed that skill of hiding thanks in no small part to her mother's troubling insistence of secrecy. Going through this, I realized this was coming from some past experiences: certain events during her life that traumatized her, and it became my job to discover the root of her distress. There had been years of reinforcement underlying that belief. The key was to find the events causing the disturbance and update those reinforced beliefs.

One of the first questions I ask my clients relates to what emotions are they *currently experiencing,* because that would lead the direction of the treatment. One of the best parts of the process is that I do not need to analyze *what* happened. In fact, I do not really *need* to know every detail about the distressing events. When I asked that question to Sarah, she slowly revealed her past. When she was a child, her mother suffered numerous psychological problems. Sarah's mother would brush her and her sister's hair; but as she did, she would take the brush and hit them on the head, hurling at them insults such as "stupid" and "ugly." Her father never knew of the abuse because, in his presence, she was a doting housewife and loving mother; but behind his back, she would viciously neglect her daughters, depriving them of food and hitting them constantly. Sarah and her sister suffered because her mentally ill mother projected something repulsive into abuse against her daughters, which forced them to suffer "severe stresses and limitations" and as a result, both were at greater risk of developing mental illness themselves (Mattejat & Remschmidt, 2008; Alford, Martin, & Martin, 1985).

Even though the sisters grew up suffering the same trauma, their paths widely diverged: compared to Sarah, who became a well-functioning adult with a loving family and a successful career, her sister became a drug addict and a prostitute who died due to a drug overdose during her thirties. Despite her thin veneer of fortitude and success, Sarah was attracted to people who treated her badly, locking herself into marriages that would never last. Her three husbands told her she was stupid, which gave her comfort from her past emotional abuse. If both sisters experienced the same trauma at the hands of their mother, why did they travel different paths?

Sarah's coping skills were clearly more desirable than her sister's because she developed a more appropriate way to adapt to her *atmospheric conditions*. I will describe this term later, but in the meantime suffice it to say Sarah had other events and experiences that provided her the improved ability to successfully adapt to her environment. Other influences came into Sarah's life, especially ones to which she adapted successfully. Our survival depends on our ability to adapt to our environment, and the same holds true for the rest of the animal world: adapt, evolve or become extinct.

As she described the abuse at the hands of her mother, Sarah kept sobbing uncontrollably. At this point, being in touch with her feelings allowed her to safely experience these emotions so I could safely clear them from her mind. In Sarah's case, her past brought her an immense feeling of sadness and ugliness. At the same time, I did not show sympathy—not because I did not care about her emotions, but I choose not to validate or encourage her emotions through any outward expressions of sympathy or pity. In other words, I did not want my client to feel okay for experiencing emotions that shouldn't take hold of her anymore. Instead, I let her understand her experiences and that there is nothing wrong with her mind.

Sarah cried because her subconscious mind continued to relive the real-time experiences as she described them. You see, your subconscious mind is where trauma is stored, and your subconscious mind operates in the moment, fully present all the time. This is simply a glitch in the way the human mind operates. I let Sarah know we were going to clear this glitch from her mind that day, and the trauma would no longer have any power over her. Smiling through her tears, she said, "how?"

Not only was the event a stuck experience from the past, her conscious mind created its own distorted meaning and embraced it: "What does it mean about *me*?," she asked in her conscious mind. In Sarah's case, the immediate answer was lodged in her mind; the abuse meant she is ugly because that is what she learned from her mother it and was repeatedly reinforced. The emotion arose from the event, and the meaning from the conscious mind's overanalysis attempting to find *any* patterns.

Once I learned how to identify that subconscious trick, I encouraged her to choose two or three kinds of events for clearing. I also asked her about a time she remembered being centered and present, which would help her so they could contrast the distressing emotions experienced against those during serene times through visualization—a symbol, if you will. Instead of me telling my client what to do, I aim to collaborate with my clients so they can look at opportunities and feel deserving of being okay. Because of this, she can focus her thoughts based on three important criteria: her thoughts should be *beneficial*, or something that would lead them to become the best they could be; her thoughts should be *appealing*, or something they would like to do and/or achieve; and finally, her thoughts should be *possible*, or something that is realistic or feasible to complete. I call this the *BAP criteria*, and that helps my clients clear up important thought processes (**Figure 1**). By asking the right questions, clients like Sarah learn to appreciate the most beneficial, appealing, and possible results for their future.

Upgrading the mind is a process, and our goal is to keep the client present while recalling that old data, understanding that the client is in the office, sitting there, talking to me, and experiencing these confusing, traumatic images at the same time. The mind can't be in both places at the same time. We have the client see the trauma from the outside through detachment and (adaptive) dissociation. Once it understands that those images are no longer real, the mind will process them, automatically beginning a process of mental clearing. Our techniques are both different and adaptable for every client, ranging from active data recall to scrambling and data confusion. As a collaborator, I guide my clients to automatically update their mind images. In the end, the mind calms down on its own. As I applied these detachment techniques with Sarah, she learned how to recall past events without experiencing *any* emotion, to which she responded, "No. It's gone." In the end, clients understand to separate emotion from previous events, realizing that it does not make sense to feel emotional about something that happened in the past.

Three hours later, Sarah was finally able to discuss her childhood without being overwhelmed. She looked relaxed and could not stop smiling and laughing, giving me a big hug before she left the room. I heard her walk past her manager's office and say, radiant, and enlightened, "I'm not ugly," to which I heard a humorously confused reply of "OK?"

Before I called the next person for a session, Sarah showed me her family pictures and said, "Oh, here are the pictures of some of my children and my daughters' weddings." Her daughters were beautiful. Her grandchildren were beautiful. And Sarah? In every picture she was at the very end, half of her face barely on the frame. Now, you'd never see the grandmother at the end of the picture; they are generally the matriarch of the family, so you'd expect a woman like Sarah front and center of the picture, but right there, she was only but a small sliver outside of the frame.

So I said to her in a soft voice, "I look at this, and I see how beautiful your children and your grandchildren are. Now you can see how it made no sense that you could not have been ugly and produce that. You're beautiful. And your children are beautiful." She could see the beauty in her children. Now, she finally learned to see that beauty in herself, laughing and smiling on her way to success.

Three months later, I received a sudden voice-mail from Sarah that said: "I just wanted to let you know that I've been to several Christmas parties, wearing my new dresses and feeling beautiful. Thank you for everything; you're my angel."

Figure 1: Graphical description of BAP (Beneficial, Appealing, Possible) criteria and guiding questions.

How Abuse Compounds Addiction

Some effects of abuse are easier to recognize. As an example, physical bruises and broken bones, burns from cigarettes, swollen faces, and drastic changes in behavior are major signs of alarm in children. Doctors, school teachers, or caretakers may be in the best position to first recognize these signs of abuse. Unfortunately, abusers use various methods of intimidation to force the child to cover up the abuse. For this reason, Kadlec (2015) described many causes of secrecy in abuse, including children with a pleasing personality who loves and wishes to protect the abuser from danger; coaching from an abuser and/or an accomplice, especially if one of the accomplices is reliant on another person for financial support; and blame and fear placed on the child.

It's also difficult to recognize the signs of neglect in the passive child who is rarely communicative at home, or who may be locked up and left hungry, fending for themselves. Even bodily changes in a neglected child's body or changes in behavior develop slower and can often be misidentified for ill health or a shy personality. In fact, Boyce and Harris (2011) addressed basic issues regarding the impact of child abuse, including a lack of clarity surrounding its definition; the impact of social context on abuse; the mechanisms in which abuse exerts its effect; and the steps needed to prevent abuse in a clinical setting.

As a result, child abuse leaves a host of physiological, spiritual, emotional, and social consequences that are carried with the victims for the rest of their lives. As you see in Sarah's story, child abuse significantly increases the risk of people turning to drugs and alcohol to cope. A 2013 study conducted by researchers at UCLA determined that "individuals reporting low levels of love and affection and high levels of abuse in childhood had the highest multisystem [biological] risk in childhood" (LaBier, 2013; University of California––Los Angeles Health Service, 2013; Carroll, Gruenewald, Taylor, Matthews, & Seeman, 2013).

Complicating matters is the brain's nature, which is programmed by early life experiences. If the environment is calm and nurturing, this will orient a child to thrive in the most excellent conditions. In contrast, a tense or stressful environment will predispose the child to experience, fear, and somewhat crave, scarcity, anxiety, panic, and chaos. This is materialized through a 2004 Child Welfare Information Gateway report stating how the "root causes" of child abuse and neglect involve the child's natural temperament, family, and society (Allard & Hunter, 2010).

A large body of literature demonstrates that suffering through stressful childhood experiences combined with internal and external types of stress, such as school, homework, and even financial pressures, increases the odds that an individual will suffer from addiction, diseases, psychiatric problems, and higher death rates. Regardless of adverse experiences, what matters most is the cumulative effect of stress a child suffers through. Teicher (2002) expounded the potential outcomes and expressions of abuse: "Internally it can appear as depression, anxiety, suicidal thoughts, or post traumatic stress; it can also be expressed outwardly as aggression, impulsiveness, delinquency or substance abuse."

A common theme in addiction treatment is the incidence of children being humiliated early in life, even if it were unintentional. For instance, a teacher may attempt to motivate a student by "singling out" without realizing what else in the student's home life may affect school performance. Ironically, several addiction treatments emphasize a fast-paced, confrontational method to "break" addicts, even if research shows it is ineffective and leads to even greater psychological harm. In other words, the "tear 'em down to build 'em up" philosophy of addiction is still present today (White & Miller, 2007). It is not uncommon for people traumatized as children to feel victimized by confrontational treatment, causing disturbances of their post-traumatic stress disorder (PTSD) and addiction.

Even in non-confrontational addiction treatments, admitting "powerlessness" as the first step to recovery is problematic on its own, as "it is of our [human] nature to feel we have control over the people in our lives, as well as any situation or thing that crosses our path" (LaPierre, 2015; Powers, 2015). Additionally, forcing addicts to accept their "powerlessness" is only contrived at best and threatening at worst, because many are unable to control their abusive circumstances as a child and reliving such lack of control only furthers the addiction. As a result, the current structure and model of addiction treatment tend to be punitive, shaming, rigid and prone to victim-blaming, which resembles the chaotic atmosphere of their environment (Wood, 2016).

In addition, more than three million *reported* cases of child abuse and neglect are made each year in America due to "pervading dysfunctional and destructive belief[s]" that physical violence is acceptable to child rearing (Perkins, 2017).

Beyond culturally ingrained values of privacy and individualism, one attitude regarding the perpetuation of child abuse in America comes from the controversy of corporal punishment in schools. In the 2013-2014 school year, more than 160,000 children were

disciplined through school-sanctioned corporal punishment, which is legal in 4,460 school districts and 19
states, and disproportionately affects black boys and
children with disabilities (**Table 2**). It does not help that
80% of adults surveyed in 2011 have admitted to spank-
ing and physically punishing children, even though
this distances the trust between parents and children
and only serves to reinforce parental authority through
fear (Society for Research in Child Development, 2016;
Gumbrecht, 2011).

   In addition, a study suggests that "[White American children] who were spanked more were more likely
later to be involved in partner-to-partner domestic violence, face academic and health risks, and fall behind
in a whole host of social indicators," including poverty,
employment, and lack of societal integration (Hanes,
2014). Furthermore, studies have suggested that physically punished children struggle more in "fighting
inflammation" and fending off bacteria (Koul, 2012).
Moreover, Koul (2012) detailed the author's personal
experience with physical punishment and its short- and
long-term consequences:

> The research suggests that, regardless of culture,
> being hit by a guardian affects children's health.
> I'm far more concerned about the intangible
> consequences, the ones that can't be measured:
> the queasy feeling of resentment that lingers
> long after your parents struck you, the change
> you go through after someone hits you for just
> not being good enough [...]

Neuroscientists believe that factors like the nature of the trauma, the extension of bodily integrity, the timing of the abuse, the frequency of the abuse, the relationship between the child and the perpetrator, and a strong support system—should there be any—after trauma will define the damage to the child's neurological system, at a high societal cost. In July 2013, the Child Welfare Information Gateway displayed a report detailing the potential negative outcomes of abuse on physical, psychological, behavioral, and societal grounds (Child Welfare Information Gateway, 2013; **Table 1)**

Table 1: Brief list of risk and protective factors for child abuse..

	Risk Factors	Protective Factors
Child	Difficult or slow to warm up environment Age Premature birth Physical/cognitive/emotional disability	Good health Above-average intelligence Positive self-esteem Help-autonomy balance
Parents & family	Lack of trust Poor impulse control Domestic violence Substance abuse	Household rules and structure High parental education Supportive family environment Parental stability
Society &w Environment	Low socioeconomic status Unemployment Community violence Lack of access to quality medical care	Access to healthcare and social services Adequate housing Participation in a religious faith Consistent parental employment

Note: Adapted from "Risk and protective factors for child abuse and neglect," by Child Welfare Information Gateway, 2004.

TRAUMA AND THE LIMBIC SYSTEM

An important relationship exists between abuse and the limbic system, the "primitive midbrain region that regulates memory and emotion" (Perkins, 2017). The limbic system is composed of two parts: the *amygdala*, which filters and interprets information that helps define how the body and the brain will react to a threat; and the *hippocampus*, which determines the importance of the processed information in order to store it to long-term memory (**Figure 2**). Abuse damages the body's alert systems to the point where the brain defines every major event through the lens of danger; as neuroscientist Bruce Perry discussed the consequences of a startling abuse response, "A maladaptive amygdala makes an abused child recoil in fear at the drop of a hat" (Kendall, 2002; Perkins, 2017).

When a child is exposed to continuous and over-whelming stress early in life, such as abuse, the stress alters the production and release of his or her stress-regulating hormones involved in the addiction process, like epinephrine, dopamine, serotonin and gamma-Aminobutyric acid (GABA). Survivors of abuse typically have lower than normal levels of important neurotransmitters, which are altered and, if not carefully changed, may lead to irreversible damage in the abuse-ravaged body. Another effect of stress is the release of sugar into the bloodstream, which causes issues such as Candida overgrowth and insulin resistance. Even more alarming, a 2010 Nurses' Health Study II research found a relationship between moderate to severe "physical abuse" and a 26% to 54% higher risk of adult-onset diabetes; unwanted sexual touching, 16%; forced sexual activity,

34% if it occurred only once and 69% if more frequently
(Perkins, 2017; Cassels, 2010)

ADVERSE CHILDHOOD EXPERIENCES

When I explored the subject of abuse and its relationship to trauma, I was surprised to learn that research
on the links between childhood stress and adult illness
only began in 1996 with the Adverse Childhood Experiences Study (ACE), conducted by Kaiser Permanente
and the Center for Disease Control (CDC). The results
revealed are both stunning, and alarming for American public health: over 60% of Americans studied in
the most recent survey reported suffering one or more
types of ACEs, even though "trauma" was loosely defined
through various experiences such as living with addicted
parents or someone suffering from a mental illness,
divorce or parental separation, abuse, and even death.
As a result, child abuse can be considered as a "'cause
of causes' for disease" as various coping mechanisms,
including excessive smoking and drinking, obesity, or
sexual promiscuity are results of such abuse (Maunder
& Hunter, 2017). In a summary (Felitti, 2015):

• Children who experienced more than one ACE were
two times as likely to be diagnosed with depression as
adults.

• Women who experienced three or more types of
childhood adversity had a 60% higher risk of developing an autoimmune disease as an adult.

• CDC statistics divulged that the annual cost of
healthcare resulting from patients with a history of

abuse and trauma is $124 billion dollars annually.

• People experiencing six ACEs are 460 times more likely to become an IV drug user, and 3100% to 5000% more likely to attempt suicide.

• Two-thirds of the American population have at least one ACE, and one-fifth of those had four or more ACEs.

Vincent Felitti (2015), one of the original creators of the study, explained the reasoning behind the impact of trauma and the discovery **of ACEs:**

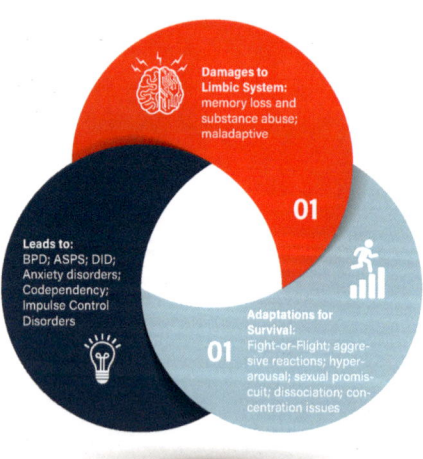

Figure 2: Relationship between the damages to the limbic system, adaptations for survival, and the non-exhaustive list of potential mental illnesses caused due to damages in the limbic system.

Life experiences that are lost in time and then further protected by shame and by secrecy and by social taboos against inquiry into certain realms of

human experience—that those experiences play
out powerfully and proportionately a half century
later, in terms of emotional state, in terms of bio-
medical disease, and in terms of life expectancy

—*Felitti, 2015).*

PTSD: The Past Doesn't Exist

Post-traumatic stress disorder (PTSD) carries a specific diagnosis with the medical community. As the only diagnostic classification in the DSM 5 based on etiology, a traumatic event must occur that severely overwhelms the person's capacity to cope successfully. Thus, instead of focusing on symptoms, clinicians can better understand how to resolve the person's distress, and it focuses on *what happened* to the person instead of *what is wrong* with **the person.**

As a trauma and stressor-related disorder, PTSD symptoms must persist for over a month in order to be considered a diagnosis. Sufferers re-live the trauma through nightmares, flashbacks, and intrusive thoughts, while behavioral changes force them to avoid certain situations and environments reminiscent of trauma, hypervigilance, or hyperarousal, such as: avoidant behavior marked by a loss of interested in one's favorite activities; feelings of detachment or difficulty thinking about the distant future; increased arousal or anxiety; increased vigilance against perceived dangers; trouble concentrating; exaggerated responses to being startled; and anger outbursts (Osmosis, 2016; Swann, 1998; Sparks, 2016).

According to the American Psychological Association, 5.2 million Americans aged 18 to 54 suffer from
PTSD; moreover, findings from the National Comorbidity Survey Report (NCS) revealed that women are twice
as likely as men to suffer from this disorder, and about
8% of Americans will experience PTSD at some point
in his or her lives (American Psychological Association,
2013). When children experience trauma, especially if
it were constant and repetitive, their natural instincts
kick in to protect them by developing self-protective
coping strategies, such as hypervigilance, disassocia-
tion, evasiveness or substance abuse as a way to numb
their thoughts, feelings, and emotions. These coping
strategies are either developed on their own, through
modeling by a parent or other authority figures, or as a
result of professional intervention.

There is a problem: coping mechanisms are only
patches and will oftentimes interfere with the survivor's
ability to live the life of their dreams. Because those
coping mechanisms were the only tool they had, I do not
want to suggest they have never had a purpose. However,
we now have a better solution. Through advancements
in neuroscience, the Inspired Performance Institute has
discovered methods that eliminate the issues and once
again empower trauma survivors to not only leave the
past behind, but also break those blocks that hinder
their performance. Does it not make better sense to
fix the problem instead of managing a **temporary
workaround?**

Trauma during childhood development will have a
major impact on a child's beliefs about his or her world,
disrupting even the basic developmental skills necessary

to succeed in life. As a result, childhood trauma survivors tend to see the world as unsafe and full of distrustful people, overwhelming, and disorganized, looking to outside sources––either good or bad––for some self-soothing and comfort. The developmental tasks and life skills disrupted during trauma happen so early in life the disruption will manifest somewhere in adulthood, and in response, doctors and mental health professionals will reccomend medication and psychotherapy in order to manage the trauma. However, there's no reason to relive the trauma. For this reason, the Inspired Performance Program provides quick relief, most times within one session and very little time re-exposing the person to the traumatic events. In fact, we will not spend any extended time recalling painful details.

DEPRESSION IS ANGER

The relationship between depression and anger is a complex endeavor, but it reveals how depression may arise from unresolved anger. In most of my clinical experience, in fact, depression comes from unresolved anger. Because of this, depressed people are stuck, unable to move forward because the mind has dissociated itself from future emotional damage. This complicates recovery since the mind can not solve the problem over an extended period, so it shuts down and perpetuates the anger by adding a sense of hopelessness, loneliness, or grief to the trauma (Scheve, 2012). As Busch (2009) explained regarding the relationship between anger and depression, depressed people cannot manage "angry feelings" and oftentimes indulge in hostile emotions that turn to an unconscious wish for self-harm. Additionally, anger serves as an "adaptive response to threat[s]" that shakes the sufferer's status quo and aims to expose other points of stress (McManamy, 2016).

In essence, depression is the absence of emotions or feelings, conceptualized as a form of self-directed anger (Sahu, Gupta, & Chatterjee, 2014). The subconscious mind has unsuccessfully attempted to fix the error messages operating for such a long time. Frustrated, disempowered, and discounted by a lack of results, the mind feels resigned to dwell in failure (Silver, 2017). Even 40% to 60% of unipolar or bipolar depression sufferers struggle with "anger attacks," and a 2013 study concluded that irritability and anger are associated with poor impulse control, substance abuse, and antisocial personalities, among other consequences (Preidt, 2013; Judd, Schettler, Coryell, Akiskal, & Fiedorowicz, 2013). Here is an example of how depression, combined with anger, becomes "insidious" to manage and hard **to understand:**

> Your mind cannot fully define your pain. The mind can only comprehend pain to a limited extent, and then it simply lets the body react. So you hit and kick, tear hair, throw pillows and tantrums. You feel like you have lost control of yourself, your life and of everything. (Farkas, 2014)

The long-term solution is to fix the error message, to update the mind and let it know that the event no longer requires its undivided attention. When the subconscious mind receives the update, the anger is resolved, and depression will lift at the same time. The depression has already run its course; why would anyone need to *manage* depression when you can *eliminate* it? Our mind can heal from living with unnecessary and unproductive problems. There's no need to trade one problem for another and fool ourselves into believing we have solved anything. There's a better, faster, and painless way to **overcome depression.**

THE STORY OF YVETTE AND THE ROLLER COASTER OF EMOTIONS

At an Orlando leadership conference, I sat beside a lady who was crying, overwhelmed with emotion while the speaker encouraged listeners to get in touch with his or her emotions. Softly and without interrupting the gaze of other listeners, I said to her, "I see you're crying a lot." She replied, "Yeah, I'm a very emotional person." In her mind, it was okay to be emotional.

I replied, "I can see you're very emotional. Have you experienced a lot of trauma in your life?"

She answered, "Well, yeah. I had a very traumatic childhood." *Now* I understood why her emotions came out so strong in the midst of the seminar.

I offered, "How would you like to clear that up, so that you don't have to feel that all **the time?**"

Skeptical and afraid, she responded, "Well, I've been like that for as long as **I remember.**"

"I understand. Would it be better for you not to be

dealing with that all the time and having those, y'know, roller coaster emotions?"

This became her point of motivation: "I'd **love that!**"

I immediately set up the plan: "Okay, so what we're going to do is during one of the breaks, I'm going to ask if we could get permission to take a longer break and we'll go through and do a session for you."

I followed through with my end of the bargain––I asked permission, requested a longer lunch time, and set up a private place to have my session with Yvette. When we sat down, I learned she suffered from sexual abuse and abandonment issues brought on from her mother's negligence.

From what she can remember as a four-year-old, she was sitting in the living room, watching TV, waiting for her mother to come home until three-o'-clock in the morning. As a child, this type of physical and emotional abandonment was a *very* dangerous threat to her survival. In her immature mind, she internalized for her protection: "What if Mom never comes home?" As a result, any relationship reminiscent of the one with her mother breeds codependency: "When parents are critical, dismissive, invasive, or preoccupied, they're unable to empathize with the child's feelings and needs. The child will feel misunderstood, alone, hurt or angry, rejected, or deflated" (Lancer, 2015). Yvette definitely felt overwhelmed with these emotions every time she approached **a relationship.**

From that moment on, she struggled with

abandonment issues, which came to a head when her first husband told her he was leaving her. In her mind, negative, internalized values of shame resurfaced, such as, "I'm not loved," "Nobody cares about me," and "They're willing to leave me." When she remarried, her husband was also put off by her codependency and severely low self-esteem. Unconsciously, she never felt safe in the relationship, but could not consciously vocalize it. Her codependency grated her husband's patience, causing friction in the relationship. Such an unfortunate outcome was named by Beck (2010) as "toxic shame," the result of years of "chronic loss" and "internalized fear" without parental guarantees of **psychological protection.**

Even though Yvette appeared to be a well-functioning and successful adult in every measure––she owned her own home; she was financially stable; she retired from a profession that guaranteed her a decent pension; and she stayed away from drugs and alcohol––she was depressed, lonely, vulnerable, and deeply unhappy. She sustained physical damage to her autoimmune system due to repeated years of trauma and stress: she developed thyroid issues, a physical response to the trauma. She used more makeup than needed in a vain effort to feel better and hide parts of herself. Even though she was an attractive and generous woman in her mid-fifties, she could not appreciate herself the way I could, as an outsider.

No wonder she reacted so strongly during the workshop: because the session involved discussing personal problems and offering ways to overcome them, every time somebody came with a problem that resembled her abandonment, her mind would pull at those childhood images, in order to produce a reaction. Once the mind truly learned that the event was over, there wasn't a need for the emotions to return.

As I helped Yvette clear through her repetition compulsion and past abandonment, she unblocked the internal glitches and freed her brain from chronic fear. Finally, she could see herself as a whole woman with an improved self-image. She sat through the end of the seminar without any **negative triggers.**

REPETITION: SHOPPING SOMEWHERE ELSE?

I always tell this story to my clients in order to understand the role of repetition into our distress:

"You walk two miles every day to get food, and along that two-mile trip there were snipers and landmines, but every time you got there, you come back, eat, and manage to survive. One day, somebody says to you, "Why are you walking two miles? There's a store with lights in three-quarters of a mile. It has a road, lights and it's very safe. It's all paved." You may feel very tempted to take up on that offer, but in the end, your mind would still choose to walk two miles because it knows it can survive that gauntlet, but it doesn't know if walking three-quarters of a mile is really safe. Your mind won't simply take someone's word for it unless something radically changes between the road or traveling down that road is your **only**

option."

The concept might sound silly at first glance—if perhaps a bit extreme—, but keep in mind this is a reality
in war-torn nations. These somewhat lopsided choices
are also the ones sufferers of repetition compulsion face
in his or her daily lives, from staying in abusive relationships and continuously eating junk food to making the
same mistakes at your job and even misplacing common
objects. Repetition triggers the basal ganglia, the part
of the brain geared towards survival. The basal ganglia
learns through repetition; it's how we learn to ride a bike,
hit a golf ball, and become drug addicts or alcoholics.
By repeating stimulating concepts, you teach your brain
that these things are important and necessary to your
survival. (That's why I say there's nothing wrong with
an addict or an alcoholic; their mind did exactly what
it was designed to do—survive, although it's not the
safest or **best route.)**

Repetition works to change your past, oftentimes
reliving negative emotions from parents, spouses, and
other loved ones (or perhaps even strangers) in an
attempt to create a new, personalized ending in the
present, making things right or as they should be in
our mind (Diamond, 2008; Ceccoli, 2012). The repetition
compulsion is both *preventive* and *novel* in its form and
intent—preventative because it protects us from "potentially traumatising experiences," and novel because
understanding *why* repetition compulsion occurs will
redefine the way we perceive our past (Kitron, 2003). By
understanding the circumstances leading to repetition
compulsion, we can alter our neural pathways to more
favorable conditions to the point that "we can replay the

trauma and, *this time*, triumph and grow to the process" (Holmes, 2014; Howard, 2017).

CONNECTING THE DOTS BETWEEN CHILD ABUSE AND SEXUAL TRAUMA

Child abuse and trauma create various social, emotional and spiritual problems in a person's life and oftentimes lead to addiction. Trauma in any form violates a child at his or her core: shattering personalities, distorting the past from the present, and fragmenting their sense of self. But childhood sexual abuse is perhaps the most heinous physical crime a person can commit—the ultimate act of betrayal and abandonment, wounding and scarring every fiber of their being. Left untreated, survivors will carry the trauma with them for a lifetime. How does this affect our society? Because they become our children's teachers, coaches, government officials, law enforcement, and clergy. As LaPierre (2013) stated, "We water down and minimize [sexual assault] because we are sickened to imagine what so many children experience. [...] As we struggle to make progress in prevention and intervention of substance abuse[,] we overlook the frequently underlying dynamics of surviving childhood sexual abuse." Even if most sexually abused children *will not* perpetuate the abuse, 38% of rapes in children ages 12 and older were reported, and most cases involved strangers rather than non-strangers or relatives (Division of Criminal Justice Services, 2014).

When sexually abused children grow up, they carry feelings of inferiority, worthlessness, hopelessness, inadequacy and deep shame, leading to a lifelong struggle against low self-esteem, self-worth, aggression, or depression and anger control issues. His or her social and coping skills are severely affected, and they struggle with trust, intimacy, and relationships. Adults who were sexually abused as children experience a constant state of internal deprivation with deep feelings of loss, isolation, emptiness, and shame in a competitive and individualistic world. Thus, it shouldn't surprise you that they turn to addiction as a coping skill; what other motivation they need to do what's healthy for their mind, body, and spirit if the easily inevitable way to seek temporary relief involves sex, drugs, and alcohol. These substances are used as coping mechanisms: it makes them feel courageous when afraid; accompanied when lonely; in control when powerless, and numb when pain keeps memories of the trauma at bay.

How Survivors of Childhood Sexual Abuse Cope

In 1995, researchers have identified two main types of coping responses to neurophysiological, physical, or mental threats on a *hyperarousal*, or *dissociative* continuum, and its shift between one part of the continuum to the other depends on the child's age and nature of the threat. The hyperarousal continuum includes the fight-or-flight and, in certain circumstances, a freeze mechanism, while the dissociative continuum is divided into avoidant behaviors––those that signal an avoidance from a problem, like dissociation and compartmentalization––or reframing behaviors––those that involve mentally changing the perceived danger of a threat (Blue Knot Foundation, 2017). Additionally, childhood sexual assault survivors may gain personal control by other coping methods which may or may not be interchange-able through a locus of control or a combined form of hyper-arousal and dissociative continuums.

Trauma and abuse have a very negative impact on neurotransmitters. Nurturing is a necessary component to survival and provides healthy stimulation to neu-rotransmitters. The effects of child abuse and trauma appears, on the surface, to be emotional and spiritual; however, the trauma is deeply interconnected with the physiological aspects of our bodies and exasper-ate the disturbing cycle of damage to brain chemistry. For instance, when a trauma survivor is addicted and has not addressed the effects of their childhood trauma on their adult life, they are at high risk of relapse or bouncing back and forth between different addictions. As soon as the addict becomes sober, all these feelings and memories they've numbed suddenly bursts into consciousness. As positive as sobriety is, it does not mean the person magically develops self-esteem and will stop feeling worthless, ashamed, and inadequate, etc. In fact, with drugs and alcohol out of the picture, all these negative feelings are still active and need to be addressed and eliminated. Overcoming trauma is a process; it takes time and work. However, healing is a possibility. It's important to note that not all trauma survivors become addicted and experience life the same way. It is possible to function at a high level even when these disturbances are active.

How to Restore Their Identities

In addition, the person will not know how to success-fully handle anger, build healthy intimate relationships, or even develop positive social skills. Because a trauma survivors' identity has been shattered, his or her identity has never fully developed and is deeply attached to their substances for relief. In sobriety, they do not really know their true self or how to find their place in the world, leading them to feel more fragmented, disconnected and lost, which furthers a vicious cycle of confusion. Identity must be both learned *and* restored to achieve true healing. On the other hand, if survivors are no longer under the influence of drugs and alcohol, they may still engage in harmful behaviors. Those behaviors are programmed over long periods of time. The survivor has a difficult time trying to understand why this is happening and this incites more feelings of shame and guilt, possibly leading them to drink or indulge in drugs in an attempt to cope.

How They Ask So Many Questions

I believe many social issues take root to childhood events and experiences. A young mind is facing the world without any experience as to what or why things are happening to them. This lack of experience causes their minds to search for reasons and then those reasons become facts with which they start to define who they are. Unfortunately, the reasons are flawed because a young mind is incapable of truly understanding why most things are happening at all. By answering questions that attempt to decipher these experiences without any underlying knowledge, you can see why a belief forms about who they are. Even when a child is brought up in a loving and nurturing home error messages can be created for the same reasons. Unfortunately, they have no outlet to safely explore the extension of their identity.

I believe that the most primitive part of our brain is engaged in everything that happens to us throughout our life. Let's examine one belief: "If Mom and Dad leave each other and stop loving me, I could die without them." Thousands of years ago, if for some reason Mom and Dad did disappear, you would die. That survival part of the brain is always active and, with a young mind, fear becomes a common emotion to experience. The more nurturing the home, the better a child handles these fears. When a child is abused or neglected, the fears are magnified and intensified. The long-term effects lead to some of the social issues we see in our society today. As a result, flawed beliefs of their identity are formed, and such a belief will follow them until they actively change that error message. That is what our Inspired Performance Program helps **to do.**

THE CONNECTION BETWEEN ABUSE AND ADDICTION

Statistics on childhood abuse and trauma are sketchy at best, since both data collection gaps and the victims' privacy complicate how researchers compile data in order to draw the most appropriate conclusions. Statistics demonstrate that as many as two-thirds of all people in treatment for drug abuse report that they had suffered physical, sexual, or emotional abuse during their childhoods (Swann, 1998). Because "memory is subjective" and unreliable to gather enough accurate qualitative data, researchers also look at court records and cases so as to create a complete image to study so, in the words of Dr. Cora Lee Wetherington, National Institute on Drug Abuse's (NIDA) Women's Health Coordinator, we can determine whether child abuse is caused by drug abuse or other factors (1998).

Despite the odds, in 1998 Dr. Lisa M. Najavits and her colleagues at Harvard Medical School in Boston examined 49 studies with drug-abusing women suffering PTSD and created an "innovative" treatment program designed to help women abstain from drugs and alcohol, reduce self-destructive behavior and establish support networks to manage both health problems simutaneously (Najavits, et al., 1998). Statistically speaking, 30% to 59% of drug abusing women also have PTSD, and 55%-99% reported "a history of [repetitive] physical or sexual trauma" occurring before age 18. (1998). Another study from NIDA's Collaborative Cocaine Treatment Study reports that PTSD-impaired patients suffered their first trauma at 8.4 years, instead of the 13.1 years reported for non-PTSD sufferers (Navajits, Weiss, & Shaw, 1997). Still another NIDA-funded study revealed that 61% of female rapes occurred before age 17 (about age 11), and these victims were more likely to abuse drugs than other women (Kilpatrick, Edmunds, & Seymour, 1992).

It's a no-brainer that trauma and substance abuse are closely related. As previously established, victims who experience symptoms of traumatic distress may resort to drugs, alcohol, or risky behavior as a panacea from stress. Unfortunately, it barely works, even on a temporary basis. Additionally, avoiding trauma becomes a witchcraft of sorts, and any suppressed memory only rejuvenates the memories of the event every time in their minds. The issues of addiction and trauma can be broadly explained using three theories; the *social learning theory, vulnerability theory*, and *betrayal trauma theory* (**Table 2**).

Social Learning Theory

Crafted by Albert Bandura, the social learning theory is pegged on *what* one learns and from *whom* they learn. The theory takes the position that when we see other people engaging themselves in certain addictive behaviors, and how they react to the use of the addictive substances, it can lead the individual into a behavior pattern which leads to addiction. As Heflick (2011) argued, "if parents are aggressive they are more likely to have aggressive children if they show that aggression to their children." Under the original Bobo doll experiment modeled by doctor Bandura, "Exposure to aggression modeling is hardly cathartic [...] and increased attraction to guns, even though it was never modeled" in the famous experiment (Everyday Psychology, 2008). More so, Bandura's approach has four principles: *attention* (the level of novelty or attention brought by a situation); *retention* (the amount and quality of information retained in memory); *reproduction* (the physical and mental practice of learned situations) and *motivation* (the degree of punishment and/or reward necessary for an action) (Wheeler, 2014).

For instance, if a child's mother comes from work every evening looking exhausted and drinks alcohol, this observation creates a connection for a developing mind. If the child observes that, after drinking, the mother's happier, the exhaustion suddenly stops, and her mood improves, the child is likely to view the use of alcohol as a very efficient and effective way of getting rid of stress and becoming happier. As the child grows, this impression is not erased and therefore in their adulthood, the child is likely to be a frequent user of alcohol to rid stress, just as they learned from their mother (Horvath, Tom, Misra, Epner, & Cooper, 2013).

BETRAYAL TRAUMA THEORY

As suggested, this theory refers to the extent to which betrayal by a person or an institution that one trusts leads to a negative, traumatic event, which determines how vividly the victim will process and remember the event. This happens when the source of the victim's physical and emotional dependence "betrays" his or her trust and threatens the person's wellbeing. For instance, when a child is molested by a father, the person the child depends upon for food, safety, and security, the child experiences betrayal trauma that severely affects the child's ability to trust others in the future, especially men, particularly those functioning in a similar role. It is also likely the child will remember the fateful event, or the meaning attached to it, more vividly than had the abuse been perpetrated by a third party, instead of a close relative (Freyd, 2008). As Kahn (2006) argued, love and betrayal are tantamount in understanding the source of betrayal theory: "The child both longs for the love of the parents and fears it. The child, and later, the adult, [suffers] a compelling ambivalence: seeking and desiring love with closeness while simultaneously dreading and **fearing it.**"

Moreover, the traumatic stress is likely to lead to the victims losing trust in certain people. For instance, a child who has been physically abused by their father may lose trust in parents or authority figures. Trust is an important factor in building healthy relationships, and trauma survivors typically have problems connecting to people with whom they need to develop trusting relationships. A lady who has undergone trauma because of sexual abuse, for example, is likely to lose her trust in men with a probability of generalizing men as unsafe people, or possibly, even as rapists. The traumatic stress may also result in the decline of the victims' academic performance, lead to frequent flashbacks, thinking of committing suicide and even indulging in drug and substance abuse as a coping strategy (Strand, Sarmiento, & Pasquale, 2005).

VULNERABILITY THEORY

This theory discusses the vulnerability of an individual who is involved in substance abuse or addiction. The theory summarizes that individuals affected by addiction are likely to become traumatized again at higher rates compared to individuals who are not addicted. For those people who are addicts or who use various drugs and substances, they accumulate significant toxins in their bodies and brains. The toxins can consequently cause damage to the body, and as a result, the body is likely to have a reduced ability or difficulty recovering from the traumatic event. The toxins also play a big role in inhibiting the recovery process of trauma in the body. Cortisol will be released into the bloodstream and eventually overwhelm the endocrine system, resulting in adrenal fatigue and systemic impairment. It is very common for women traumatized by sexual abuse as a child to experience hormonal issues related to improper thyroid functioning and autoimmune **disorders**Table 2:

Table 2: Types of trauma theories with respective examples.

Type of Trauma Theory	Definition	Examples
The extent to which betrayal by a person and/or institution one trusts leads to a negative—and oftentimes traumatic—result.	Individuals affected by addiction are more likely to be re-traumatized at higher rates.	A woman traumatized due to sexual abuse may lose all trust in men and generalize that all men are not good people and merely rapists.
Vulnerability Theory	Individuals affected by addiction are more likely to be re-traumatized at higher rates.	A traumatized adult may use cocaine to numb the emotional pain of being sexually abused in his youth as a coping skill.
Social Learning	Vocal learning and engagement of intellect and addictive behaviors reinforces a connection to addiction.	A child who observes his/her parent drinking a glass of wine to relieve stress may learn and associate that wine is an important stress reliever

Note: Adapted from "Betrayal trauma, " by J.J. Freyd, Encyclopedia of psychological trauma, 2008, eds. G. Reyes, J.D. Elhai, & J.D. Ford, John Wiley & Sons; and "Social learning theory of addiction and recovery implications," by A. Horvath, T. Misra, A.K. Epner, & M. Cooper, 2013.

Is the Abused Child Supine?

Temperament is another concept that can address the

role and likelihood of child abuse, even though this is contested in research. Temperament is defined as "the individual characteristics that are assumed to have a biological basis and that determine the individual's affective, affectional, and motor responses in various situations" (Rothbart, 2012). That being said, it is important to make a distinction regarding temperament. While research shows the child's temperament alone *does not* determine the propensity of abuse, parental reactions *to* temperament determine the extent of physical discipline on other grounds (Law, 2004; Jaffe, et al., 2004; **Table 3; Table 4**).

Instead, researchers consider both the child's inner temperament and the parents' reactions to it through a set of *risk factors* for child abuse on a wide spectrum including socioeconomic status, education levels of both parents, integration to society, cultural differences, and other aspects. Engfer (1992) noted that difficulty in dealing with a child's temperament is only problematic when parents lack the proper resources to address the child's unique needs, more so when organized under a collective, four-system framework detailing the potential circumstances surrounding the child, the parents, the community, and the society. In addition, a 2014 study concluded that individuals with greater temperamental sensitivities face a higher risk of becoming abusive parents, yet also benefit from nurturing environments that allow them to overcome major obstacles (Voorthuis, et al., 2014).

Table 3: Dimensions of temperament.

Category	Definition	Considerations
Activity	Refers to the child's physical energy.	Is the child constantly moving, or does the child have a relaxing approach?
Regularity (Rhythmicity)	Level of predictability in a child's biological functions	oes the child have a set routine in eating and sleeping habits, or are these events random in nature?
Initial Reaction (Approach or Withdrawal)	How the child responds to new people or environments	Does the child approach people or things in the environment without hesitation, or does the child shy away?
Adaptability	Length of adjustment to change over time	Does the child quietly adjust to environmental change, or is the child resistant?
Intensity	Level of a positive or negative response	Does the child respond internally to a situation, or does the child respond calmly and quietly?
Mood	Refers to the child's innate tendency or demeanor	Does the child frequently smile or feel optimistic, or is the child crying or throwing tantrums?

Category	Definition	Considerations
Sensitivity (sensory threshold or threshold of responsiveness)	How easily a child is disturbed by environmental changes	Is the child easily distracted by external stimuli like noises, textures, or light, or does the child seem to ignore them?
Distractability	Child's tendency to be sidetracked by other surrounding events	Does the child get easily distracted by the environment, or can the child concentrate despite the interruptions?
Persistence and Attention Span	Child's length of time on the task and ability to handle frustration	Can the child stay with an activity for a long time, or lose interest quickly?

Note: Adapted from "Betrayal trauma, " by J.J. Freyd, Encyclopedia of psychological trauma, 2008, eds. G. Reyes, J.D. Elhai, & J.D. Ford, John Wiley & Sons; and "Social learning theory of addiction and recovery implications," by A. Horvath, T. Misra, A.K. Epner, & M. Cooper, 2013.

THE SANGUINE

The sanguine is lively, optimistic, buoyant, and carefree; an adventure lover who tolerates high risk. A sanguine cannot tolerate a boring environment; as a result, they seek out variety and entertainment, which may negatively affect relationships. Pleasure-seeking tendencies open the sanguine to issues associated with addiction, ranging from drugs or alcohol to sex, overeating, and weight problems. In other ways, this makes the sanguine look "shallow, enjoy peripheral relationships, [and] go along with majority convictions regardless of [personal] concerns" (Elyot, 2008). Sanguine personalities are full of creativity and many become successful artists and entertainers––which, to a point, explains why so many famous entertainers and celebrities struggle with addiction.

THE PHLEGMATIC

A phlegmatic is a people person who believes interpersonal harmony and close relationships are important. Phlegmatics are traditionally loyal spouses and loving parents, and maintain and preserves relationships with old friends, distant family members, and neighbors. They tend to avoid conflicts and are natural-born mediators attempting to restore peace and harmony. As Elyot (2008) suggested, phlegmatics are contemplative and thoughtful, while others perceive them as detached and aloof. In addition, phlegmatics are also charitable and willing to help others.

THE CHOLERIC

A pure choleric is goal-oriented, savvy, analytical, and logical. Since many are practical and straightforward, a choleric is not necessarily a social companion; they enjoy deep and meaningful conversations and avoid small talk. Cholerics are considered "zealous [...] quick to anger, and impatient and disgusted with those who didn't see his way or [are] less intelligent than himself" (Elyot, 2008). They would prefer to be alone or associate with like-minded people as opposed to being around or surrounded by shallow, **superficial people.**

THE MELANCHOLIC

A melancholic loves tradition, chivalry, and the old-fashioned. Unlike the sanguine, a melancholic is not looking for novelty and adventure; in fact, they will go out of their way to avoid it. Considered "both an idealist and a doubter with little use for rules," the clear majority will socialize and marry within their race and culture (Elyot, 2008). It would be unusual for someone with a melancholic temperament to marry a foreigner or leave their homeland for another country. They are extremely social and want to give back to *their* **community.**

THE SUPINE

This leads us to the discussion on the fifth temperament, the supine, discovered in 1983 by doctors Richard and Phyllis Arno. Considered a balanced mixture between Melancholic and Sanguine temperaments, the supine may be either introverted or extroverted. Supines want to be considered useful and are driven to serve a higher cause other than their own self-interest, which may appear subservient and even deferent when it comes to satisfying personal needs. However, when it comes to their passions and interests, they will be fiercely assertive. At their best, a supine is caring, gentle, dependable and loyal. At their worst, the supine can be insecure, weak-willed, manipulative, and hold severe grudges.

When young, the supine is bullied or tormented by others, including children and adults. They do not fight back and learn to internalize their anger and pain, eventually believing that such a treatment is well-deserved.

A supine offers contradictions within relationships: they may not express a need for social contact, but desire such contact. With this, I conclude the supine is a morphing of these personalities due to abuse and trauma; by hiding their needs so well, they expect others to read their minds—and if someone fails to take their (unspoken) needs into account they will become offended and hurt. Some see the supine as being too sensitive and easily-offended, slow to make decisions and operating at an annoyingly slow pace, which can be construed as indifference or uncaring about life when in reality, supines have strong feelings and opinions but are unwilling to assert themselves. . This is common in abused children.

Should supines make decisions, they will seek others for advice, feeling inadequate and dismissing themselves as capable of making good decisions on their own. They will seek out advice from many people and then become confused if they receive differing opinions. Because they have such a strong desire to serve others, so they often become "natural born victims" and "injustice collectors," someone who "nurses resentment over real or perceived injustices" and "will never forget or forgive those wrongs or the people he or she believes are responsible" (O'Toole, 2014).

Supines can be difficult to work with because they like to be involved in the decision-making process—even if they say or respond to nothing—and will be deeply offended when left out, even though they are not comfortable in making the final decision or assuming responsibility for them. As a result, they harbor anger, resentment, and (perceived) rejection. While others see the supine as dominating, they are manipulating others to take care **of them.**

For this reason, the supine fits the profile of a victim of abuse. In each of the stories highlighted in this chapter, all their temperaments coincided with that of a battered supine, one driven by fear manifested through people-pleasing, codependency, lack of assertiveness, and a lack of clear boundaries. Most of these react negatively to the lack of structure in their lives, or the lack of financial stability and constant violence within their homes.

The advancements in neuroscience are now shedding light on how trauma affects us on a biological and hormonal basis, including the psychological and behavioral effects. Research has demonstrated how interruptions in childhood development affect the autonomic systems which in turn has a profound effect on how the brain is hard-wired during childhood. In fact, this only touches the surface of the extent of neurological damage from child abuse and neglect. So much has been written on this subject that explaining it in brief paragraphs can be overwhelming. There are numerous treatments, medications, diets, and even scams that play on the pathos of abuse without recognizing how the body-mind connection helps or hinders the progress of trauma. Learning more about the consequences of abuse, trauma, and sexual assault can help you or your loved ones run away from a confusing and undesirable world of hurt and be *Out of Your Mind* to reap the benefits of looking towards a brighter future.

Table 4: Summarized profiles of "ancient" personality types.

Personality type	Characteristics	Strengths	Weaknesses
Sanguine Driven by attention and charm	• Lively, optimistic, buoyant, and carefree • Loves adventure and has a high-risk tolerance • Optimistic by nature	• Enthusiastic and cheerful • Able to express and receive large amounts of love and affection	• Pleasure-seeking personalities may open a door to addiction • Prone to exaggeration and may lack responsibility in order to be with people • Needs constant reassurance
Melancholic Driven by fear of rejection and the unknown	• Enjoys time with friends and family • Loves tradition and will go to any lengths to avoid changing it • Task-oriented rather than relationship-oriented	• Family oriented individuals • Loyal and self-sacrificing • Empathetic and deeply committed	• Perfectionistic attitude • Rigid and inflexible • Afraid of failure and the unknown
Phlegmatic **Driven by lack of motivation**	Preserves relationships with old friends, distant family members, and neighbors	• Consistent • Charitable • Not plagued by emotional outbursts	• Slow-placed and stubborn • Becomes an observer rather than a participant • Procrastinator

Personality type	Characteristics	Strengths	Weaknesses
Choleric **Driven by goals**	• Decisive • Prefers solitude instead of being surrounded by shallow, superficial people	• Goal-oriented • Efficient and well-disciplined • Expresses love and affection to a select group of people	• Excessively controlling • Has a tendency to overwork and is prone to burnout • Self-centered
Supine	• Great capacity for service • Balanced personality between Melancholic and Sanguine temperaments	• Inborn gentleness • Loyal • Useful and serve for a higher cause	• Dependent • Unable to initiate love and affection • Little ability to express innermost needs

Note: Adapted from "Linking trauma to addiction will provide the treatment solution," by Wood, D. 2016

CHAPTER THREE

How Your Mind Works

One key element in the Inspired Performance Program's success is the education of *how* the mind functions and *why* it functions the way it does. It is not our intention to present our program as magical, mystical, or exclusive to our clients––rather, everything boils down to science, and people's natural curiosity to learn of a clear, direct, and concise answer to their problems. As opposed to diagnosing problems the conventional way doctors do while in session, I will explain the reasons *why* this concept works as I ask for clients' input at the same time. If there is anything clients feel uncomfortable or disagree with, I encourage them to let me know. That way, we engage in a collaborative mood that empowers them to succeed and motivates them **to grow.**

The Four-Hour Session

During my practice, I have received many questions about the logistics of the Inspired Performance Program, including the techniques I use, the length of a session, the cost of the program, the personal commitment, and so on. However, there's also an important aspect that radically transforms the Program: the four-hour session.

One problem in conventional psychotherapy is the extensive, bureaucratic, and time-consuming recovery process for clients. In 1967, a study on the average length of psychotherapy revealed a positive relationship existed between treatment length and patient success in psychotherapy, meaning patients who stayed in therapy longer would benefit more (Errera, McKee, Smith, & Gruber, 1967). However, a 1975 study countered that the average length of psychotherapy was estimated at eight sessions, and 80% of clients left treatment before receiving 25 sessions (Koss, 1979).

On the other hand, a study by Hawkins (2015) and Lambert (2013) stated that half of dysfunctional patients could achieve recovery in about 20 psychotherapy sessions, and three-quarters of patients could improve after 50 sessions, respectively. In addition, one must consider the two value models of psychotherapy and its effects on the counselor's perceptions within treatment: the "illness model," where therapy is used in order to "alleviate a disorder or treatment" and resolve symptoms; or the "wellness model," where therapy attempts to improve a client's life through personal empowerment (Howes, 2014). The program understands both models, but, ascribes to neither––we refuse to accept clients as inherently "sick," nor do we coach or improve a "brand." Instead, the Inspired Performance Program aims to become the primary stop in relieving people's distress. Our experience has shown it is unnecessary for a client to endure weeks, months, or years of suffering, waiting for an illusory breakthrough or feeble insight, when a simple, four-hour intensive session––arguably the length of a morning seminar––can provide better, long-term results. As Mager (2014) explained the author's philosophy on recovery, "Recovery is about reclaiming one's humanity and reconnecting with one's **true self.**"

Here is a breakdown of the typical program's four-**hour session:**

- The first hour of a session serves to educate the client on how their minds work and why they are experiencing such emotional distress.

- The second hour involves discussing the solution to the problem and the many details for success, like brainwave states, the symbol, and the alpha state, among major concepts to resolve.

- In the third hour, I will help the client clear distortions in their life.

- Lastly, I will help clients do something that I call a "sweeping," where the mind will automatically sweep out anything that was not cleared in the third hour while I bank their personal highlights and successes.

Now that you have a better understanding of the four-hour session, let's begin by learning how your brain works and how past errors and glitches play into your **current distress.**

THE BRAIN IS EXCEPTIONAL

As far back as Aristotle's time, a myth persisted that because our brains were larger, we were more intelligent. However, he was a cardiocentric who believed that the brain was a "bloodless, cooling radiator from the heart" that had some involvement in sleep (Jarrett, 2014). There is no question that our brains are special and unique. This uniqueness has created the world we live in and, at the same time, many emotional problems that only humans constantly encounter. In fact, no other sentient animal faces the trials and tribulations humans endure through them––or fail––masterfully. Our minds are far more complicated than the mind of the animal. Because of this, they are also prone to developing many error messages that only take up space and damage our internal functioning.

We now know a lot more about the brain and how it works than ever before, yet we still have a long way to go before we truly understand how powerful and amazing this apparatus sitting on our shoulders really is. In fact, "it is hard to pin down what makes the human brain exceptional among mammals––neither brain size, relative brain size, nor number of neurons is unique to humans" (Koch, 2016; Gonzalez, 2012). That being said, can you consider the human brain as an exceptional element in our body? Absolutely! Not because our brains are bigger––in fact, size is not a relative factor when measuring the amount of neurons in our brains against that of other animals in the world. The relationship between brain and body size is not an efficient benchmark to determine or assess cognition.

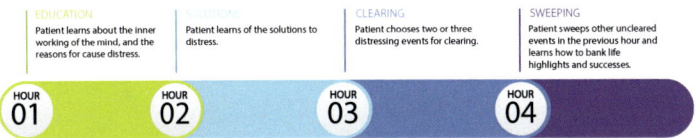

Figure 3: Graphical description of the Inspired Performance Program's Four-Hour Session.

However, a significant factor that can be used to measure the functioning between species is the total number of neurons that a species possesses. The average-sized human brain contains 86 billion neurons, which is unexceptional to some extent and, based on a scaling rule for primates, it would compare in line with that of a chimpanzee. That calculation would assume an increase in size for the chimpanzee, equating to a comparable number **of neurons.**

When you buy a computer, you assume its operation will be complicated and you will need to take care in how you handle it. If you drop your computer, you would expect it to have some damage. The same can happen with your brain, but with a slight difference: our brains can heal. So, how can we correct these error messages? Correcting the error message is not as complicated as you believe, but it takes some creativity. Brains can't be bought, refurbished, nor replaced; while the easiest way to deal with a broken computer is to simply buy another one, or you *can* get *new* programming and update it. Just as a computer's software can be easily updated and needs certain downloads in order improve its functioning, our brains carry outdated or misplaced messages from the past, occupying a needless amount of space. Thus, these error messages need to be updated with new ones if we aim to feel relief from any emotional distress. After they are cleared up in almost the same way error messages are fixed on a computer, the mind operates faster, clearer, **and smarter.**

BRAIN OR MIND?

Before we continue, it is important to understand the difference between the brain and the mind. We tend to use both terms interchangeably. We do not realize the different processes both take in our life. Instead,

> The brain is an organ but the mind is not. The brain is a physical place where the mind resides. It is a vessel in which the electronic impulses that create thoughts are contained. [...] The mind is the manifestations of thought, perception, emotion, determination, memory [and reason], and imagination that takes place within the brain." (Control Mind, n.d.)

Whereas the brain contains the *physical* electronic impulses, the hormones, and the many alarm systems within our body that signal natural things like hunger, panic, and desire, the mind reflects the *spiritual* manifestation of these impulses. When the brain signals hunger, I feel my stomach rumble within my belly; at the same time, my mind craves a certain type of fatty, salty, and sugary food because I had a bad day. Thus, the brain can reflect both physical *and* emotional circumstances based on what I've learned from the past. If my brain's functions want me to cry, the mind will let me know *what* to cry about. Instead of looking at the brain and the mind as opposites, I believe it's better to look at them as companions. The physical is "neurobiological" and the spiritual "psychological," to which improving at one will invariably enhance the other (Satel, 2013). Another way to distinguish the difference between the brain and the mind is the one Zhu (2015) espoused: "Brain is the hardware and the mind is the software with the totality in action, so the brain with mind is the hardware **plus software**."

How Our Minds Process Incoming Data

As you read this, your brain is hard at work in the nervous system, making sense of this sentence. To read and understand this sentence, the nerve cells in your eyes calculate the letters and their shapes and then transmit that input to your brain. It makes sense: approximately one-quarter of your brain's activity involves the processing and recording of visual data. You see, your mind receives the data from all your senses and records it for future reference, since visual processing and recording is higher than any other sense; even so, if the sense of vision is missing or atrophied, the brain will adapt and reconfigure itself to rely on other senses for processing and recording. For example, if a blind person reads Braille, nerves in their fingers will send the data the skin is sensing through the spinal cord to the brain. This is done at lightning speeds, all at a subconscious level.

When you read, your brain and the nervous system uses a series of electrical impulses that move through your body connected to a network of nerve cells called neurons. Neuroscientists are studying how these groups of neurons interact and affect our behaviors. Are we *choosing* to act or behave in a certain way, or are our connected neural pathways *over*-reacting from the patterns the brain has been recording and learning from? These neurons are firing in such a rapid process we must ask: do we have any conscious thought at all in this process? In our bodies, the individual nerve cell or neuron is the building block of our nervous system, communicating through a series of chemicals or electrical signals where they connect. These connections are referred to as *synapses*. Synapses are important because

Synapses are what allow you to learn and remember. They're also the root of many psychiatric disorders. And they're basically why illicit drugs––and addictions to them––exist. Pretty much everything in your experience––from euphoria to hunger to desire to fuzziness to confusion to boredom––is communicated by way of these signals sent by your body's own electrochemical messaging system (Green, 2015).

WHAT IS THE MIND?

We have established earlier that the mind is where the spiritual and social connections of the brain reside. It goes beyond synapses and neurotransmitters and becomes "the seat of human consciousness" *separable* from the body; thus, the mind cannot be discovered through conventional means (Henriques, 2011; Reuder, 2004). The mind serves to optimize self-organization, one that is "flexible, adaptive, coherent, energize, and flexible," and integrates many ideas of oneself. In a sense, the mind extends beyond our physical perception (Goldhill, 2016b). Even then, the mind can be a mystical, yet grossly misunderstood part of the body, one we normally treat with distrust and contempt:

> To laypeople in Western Culture, the unconscious mind has been viewed as an enemy, a murky power that swooped in to sabotage our conscious desires. It became the scapegoat for every failure, mistake, or unwanted action. More recently, people have thought of the unconscious mind as a tool they can consciously use to get where they want to go. They bludgeon the mind with affirmations and then wonder why they aren't working. (James M. , 2013, par. 4).

You see, our minds are complicated and prone to errors, but this does not mean that change is too lofty or impossible. Allow me to explain: human and animal minds are both similar and unique due to the way the mind processes error messages. The animal mind is fully present and focused on the now. This is the same advice you'll find in self-help books as the often touted, all-consuming key to peace and happiness. But how? A wolf has no problem living in the present, yet the "smarter" human mind struggles with it—and both are mammals. The reason this occurs is that our mind, our brain, is unique.

Perhaps you are not aware of it, but our subconscious mind operates in fashion similar to the animal mind. Our subconscious mind is fully present, submerged in the moment, focused on its surroundings, and operating through various survival-based actions focused on keeping us alive; that is why processes like our heartbeat, digestion, and our breathing are happening automatically and without any conscious effort. The same is true for an animal like the wolf, but only with the caveat that the wolf need not be fully aware of *every* attempt **to survive.**

You see, our conscious mind is brilliant. Our conscious mind uses reason and logic to figure things out. It created the world we live in. Planes, trains, automobiles and a host of other technological trinkets like smartphones and computers arise from the human ability to figure things out. Our consciousness adores convenience, and the ability to reason is (no pun intended) the reason our society advanced at such a breakneck speed. We are definitely getting smarter, even if oftentimes visible and hopeless actions may make us feel and look dumber. We cannot levitate yet, but now we have the power to imagine doing things we have never expected, as we are cognizant of our neurological development. However, as brilliant as our conscious mind is, it only runs about 5% of everything happening for you on a daily basis––the rest is happening on a subconscious level, below **your awareness.**

Animals do not need to figure out complex tasks; they either do something or they do not. For instance, the wolf cannot do anything other than what he or she is capable of. For example, if a wolf is hungry and looking for something to eat and sees a bird flying overhead, the wolf can't think for itself, "*I wish I could fly and catch that bird.*" Since the wolf can't fly, the wolf can't even conceive the possibility of flying and catching the bird. Therefore, the wolf moves on looking for easy and vulnerable prey on the ground. Humans, instead, are capable of shooting a projectile into the air and knocking the bird out of the sky to eat it, even if we have never done that before. Like I said, our search for convenience entitles us to look for conscious ways to fulfill our subconscious desires, be it power, hunger, **or lust.**

If you want to teach an animal to do something new, then you need to repeat the new task over and over until it becomes programmed. Eventually, the program will become an automated response to a particular situation or experience. The same holds true for the human mind: this is the same process we use in order to learn to ride a bike, drive a car, or use a computer. Once we repeat the action enough times, the pattern is programmed, automated, and run by our **subconscious mind.**

EMOTIONS: YOUR MIND REQUESTS AN ACTION

What is the purpose of an emotion? The answer is simple: your mind requests an actionInterface. Emotions are important tools for communication, be it "voluntarily or involuntary" (Furnham, 2016). Emotions tell us how other people are experiencing their environment. They provide a continuous commentary on how others––and ourselves––see meaning in the world. First used in the 16th century and coming from the French word émouvoir, "to stir up" or "to excite," an emotion is defined as "a complex psychological state that involves three distinct components: a *subjective* experience, a *physiological* response, and a *behavioural or expressive* response [emphasis added]" (Hockenbury & Hockenbury, qtd. in Cherry K., 2016a). In a nutshell, emotions reflect three aspects of the body: a *personal* aspect, which depends on individual's range of emotions; a *physical* aspect, which depends on the individual's bodily composition and health; and a *behavioral* response, which depends on the person's course of behavior in the situation. For some, anger reflects sadness; for others, they

Figure 4: "Grey Wolf (Canis lupus) Portrait" by hkuchera, 2017, https://as1.ftcdn.net/jpg/00/51/69/94/500_F_51699465_hvdWz7J0kRDWfF-wDSNKA5bsXiVTXi8rG.jpg

express sadness through anger. Because of this, emotions can be as volatile or as measured as **the beholder.**

THEORIES OF EMOTION

There are three ways to group the nature of emotions: *physiological*, where bodily responses trigger emotions; *neurological*, where brain activity leads to emotion; and *cognitive*, where thoughts play an important role in developing emotion. In fact, there are six theories that attempt to explain the root of emotions and its role in psychology (**Table 5**):

- **Evolutionary Theory:** First proposed by English naturalist Charles Darwin, Evolutionary Theory extends the realization that emotions were adaptive and important for survival and reproduction. For example, fear signals a rapid intention to run away from danger, while happiness suggests company with other like-minded individuals who would collaborate and increase their chances of survival (Cherry, 2016b). This motivates individuals to respond quietly to **environmental stimuli.**

- **James-Lange Theory of Emotion:** Proposed by researchers William James and Carl Lange, this theory suggests that *visceral experiences* (more commonly known as "gut feelings") trigger and label emotional experiences, allowing us to respond quickly to environmental stimuli in order to survive. This means that instantaneous changes of emotion are guided by instinct and do not account for other bodily processes, which is considered a major drawback into the theory. As James summarized his theory in 1890, "We feel sorry because we cry, angry because we strike, afraid because we tremble" (Feldman, 2011).

- **Cannon-Bard Theory of Emotion:** Countering the James-Lange Theory of Emotion is this one proposed by Walter Cannon and later expounded by Phillip Bard, who believe that certain physiological responses can be experienced without triggering *any* emotion (e.g.: a person could feel like crying because of yawning, not because of sadness or joy). Instead, they proposed that both physiological *and* emotional responses come from nerve signals in the thalamus, who receives the stimulus and then transforms it into emotion for the whole brain to trigger the appropriate commands (Cherry, K. , 2016b; Feldman, 2011)

- **Schachter-Singer Theory of Emotion**: Also called the "two-factor theory" and proposed by Stanley Schacter and Jeremy Singer, this theory combines the James-Lange and Cannon-Bard theories of emotion through the notion that combining physiological and cognitive responses offers emotion. Because of this, labels are needed to confirm the physical experience, even though the same physical symptoms can happen in completely different circumstances. By this theory, a pounding heart on a dark alleyway can be interpreted as fear, while a pounding heart while watching an action movie may signal excitement. Both reflect different emotions even if they share the same physical and **cognitive symptoms.**

- **Cognitive Appraisal Theory**: Initially proposed by Richard Lazarus, cognitive appraisal theory believes that a thought must occur before an emotion; in other terms, a person's thoughts serve as the trigger for the emotion, which may or may not be different even if others experience the same situation, depending on the person's environmental cues and ingrained error messages. An example could be a promotion: whereas one person may feel happy because such colleague was promoted, another person may feel bitter and jealous, and their emotions will be reflected throughout the body.

- **Facial Feedback**: The facial feedback theory proposes that six emotions are basic in every culture—happiness, anger, sadness, disgust, fear, and surprise—and any other secondary emotions are a combination of two or more of the basic emotions through facial recognition. In facial feedback, someone who smiles more is likely to be happier than someone who does not smile frequently, because emotions are tied to changes in facial muscles that signal different changes according to unique situations.

In the end, no one theory accurately explains the true purpose of emotions: to request an action. Fear, for instance, prepares you to run. Your body changes, you become faster and stronger. Anger prepares you to fight. Happiness prepares you to interact with others. Desire prepares you to mate. So, what's the point of feeling fear when thinking about something that happened 20 years ago? I can tell you why: it's an error message, a glitch in your brain's operating system. Have you ever heard that before? Why is your mind asking for an action about something that's **not happening?**

Table 5: Theories of emotion

Type of Theory	Prosper (s)	Characteristics	Role
Evolutionary	Charles Darwin	Emotions evolved because they were adaptive, allowing both humans and animals to survive and reproduce.	Motivation to respond quickly to environmental stimuli. The correct interaction of emotions ensures safety and survival.
James-Lange	William James & Carl Lange	Emotions occur due to physiological reactions to stress.	The brain interprets bodily changes as emotions.
Cannon-Bard	Walter Cannon & Phillip Bard	Emotions result when the thalamus sends a stimulating message to the brain at the same time it receives signals triggering the emotional experience.	Physical and psychological experiences are simultaneous.
Schacter-Singer	Stanley Schacter & Jerome E. Singer	The physiological arousal comes first, then the individual must label the reason and the emotion.	The situation and cognitive systems define the emotion.
Cognitive Appraisal	Richard Lazarus	A thought must occur before any emotion or psychological arousal.	Cognition is essential to emotions.

Type of Theory	Prosper (s)	Characteristics	Role
Facial Feedback	Charles Darwin & William James	Facial expressions are connected to emotions since emotions are tied to changes in facial muscles.	Social interaction is necessary to form emotions.

Note: Adapted from "What are emotions and the types of emotional responses?," by K. Cherry, 2016a, https://www.verywell.com/what-are-emotions-2795178; "What are the 6 major theories of emotion?," by K. Cherry, 2016b, https://www.verywell.com/theories-of-emotion-2795717; "What are emotions for?," by A. Furnham, 2016, https://www.psychologytoday.com/blog/sideways-view/201606/what-are-emotions; and "Comparing the 5 theories of emotion," by B. Micallef-Trigona, 2014, http://brainblogger.com/2014/10/22/comparing-the-5-theories-of-emotion/.

We have been taught by most mental health professionals, pop psychology and self-help books that emotions like depression, anxiety, anger, or fear must be managed. We learn various coping mechanisms, positive or negative, or learn to develop our own that only manage to further or deepen our self-imposed misery. How refreshing is it to know that there is a better way; managing and coping is a *patch*, providing some temporary relief that does not solve the problem. The answer is to address the root cause of the emotions: the events and experiences throughout a person's **life.**

MEMORIES, IN THE CORNER OF MY MIND

The other unique difference within our brain is our ability to record, store and recall billions of bits of information. You see, everything you have ever heard, seen, smelled or touched in your lifetime has been recorded and stored into what we know as *memory*. This memory is amazing, useful, and at the same time a major contributor to the error messages we encounter throughout our lives (**Table 6**).

Short-term memory is the "temporary retention of acquired information" (Seitbert, 2016). It lasts longer than 20 seconds, and is useful to recall speech during discussions or arguments. Short-term memory has three components: *trace life*, or the number of times the information can be retained in memory without further processing; *storage capacity*, where memory "chunks" information to remember more efficiently than if it were pieces of information;" and *code nature*, where form is used to understand and store information (Seitbert, 2016).

There are two types of long-term memory: *implicit* or *non-declarative*, which requires a person to learn by rote or memorization; and *explicit* or *declarative*, which requires a subconscious knowledge of procedures one can memorize or articulate. For instance, learning the procedure to bake a cake can be considered *implicit* memory, while learning the *facts* of baking a cake, such as the temperature it takes to bake it, the exact measurements for each part, and the minutes to cook it, can be considered *explicit* memory. Whereas implicit memory is procedural, explicit memory can be either *semantic* (related to factual knowledge) or *episodic* (recalling factual events). Returning to the cake, recalling numerical facts of baking a cake is semantic, while remembering the time of day and circumstances that led you to bake a cake is episodic (Corayer, 2017).

Table 6: Types of memory.

Type of Memory	Description	Examples
Implicit (non-declarative)	Requires a person to perform a task and master it. Depends on trial and error to establish the stimulus responses conducive to learning.	Driving a car. Playing a video game. Explicit (declarative)
Explicit (declarative)	Requires the conscious grasp of specific knowledge of procedures that one can memorize or articulate. Can be episodic (recalling life events) or semantic (non-biographical)	Remembering your Social Security number Remembering yesterday's lunch

Every day, our experiences are being recorded and, since they are usually mundane enough not to be perceived as any threat, they are recorded as simple images and sounds in low resolution (lo-res). These images and sounds are stored in our memory. So if I asked you to close your eyes as soon as you finished reading this sentence and recalled right now what you ate for breakfast yesterday, what did you experience? Did you see images of what you ate? Did you remember the color of the dish? Did it have enough salt to satisfy your tastes? Perhaps you saw where you ate it, but you may not have even the vaguest idea of how the dish was served. The images aren't bright or intense because your senses were operating normally when the event occurred. The images have been stored and are easy to recall with little effort. Now, if I asked you what you ate last year at this time, however, it would be a little more difficult or consciously impossible to retrieve. However, the image is still stored and archived within your brain because the meal was not perceived as any threat. The need to recall that data about the event is not as simple because of its attributed importance.

You see, our subconscious mind is fully present, operating in the same real time as the conscious mind. When traumatic or disturbing events occur in our lives, the details of the event are recorded in high resolution (hi-res) because our senses are operating on high alert. Your eyesight is sharper; your hearing is acuter, and your sense of smell increases. That's why research confirms smells evoke a sensation or feeling from an earlier time in our lives (and can exhibit completely different emotional responses even if their chemical composition is identical), be it comfort, amusement, or trauma; as an example, a 2011 study on painful memories trigger by smell revealed that smell can indeed induce stronger unpleasant memories than sound (Gaines-Lewis, 2015; Collins, 2012)

When you recall a traumatic or threatening event, these high-res images create a response as the subconscious sees these images as real, something that is happening now. If the event were *actually* happening, it would make sense to experience the emotion, be it random mind-chatter or a sudden trigger. But if the emotion still shows up when you think about the event, then that is the error message. What can you do about the event now? Nothing!

Remember, what is the purpose of the emotion? To request an action. If you are experiencing fear, then your mind is preparing you to run and escape the threat. If you are experiencing anger, then your mind is preparing you to attack and eliminate the threat. Are you hiding from events that happened ten years ago? If so, then that is an error, a glitch. The solution is simple: re-process the hi-res images into low-res, and the mind will no longer respond to the request for an action. Is it that easy? Absolutely. That way, you'll be out of your mind, free from the self-imposed prison your mind is operating from. That is the target, and we can absolutely get you there. Staroversky (2013) noted regarding the subconscious mind's information storage, "You can become aware of [the subconscious] information once you direct your attention to it. Think of this as memory recall [...] You can easily bring to consciousness the **subconscious information**."

Right now, is your energy being drained by these error messages? It's quite common for us to feel that an overwhelming portion of your energy is drained by the way the mind is currently operating. What would it be like to have your mind with *all* of its energy focused on what is happening *right now*? So now, doesn't it make sense that the reason you are struggling with your relationships, your business or career is because you have so little energy available to be present? If so, you may be asking, how do we address and fix that?

Advancements in neuroscience have brought about the changes we have available. The Inspired Performance Program compiles improved cognitive techniques discovered and developed through research and experience. When the error messages are updated and corrected, you can improve your mind's performance and they will no longer influence the processing of current incoming data; in the end, the mind can focus on being present, producing thoughts that are *always* beneficial, appealing and possible to you. Your mind will be clearer, calmer, peaceful, and enhanced.

WHAT IS CONSCIOUSNESS?

An important concept to understand in the Inspired Performance Program is awareness. With awareness comes the ability to understand ourselves and our environment, to break through subconscious desires, and to even take greater control of our bodies. The goal to complete awareness comes through consciousness: "Consciousness is the awareness of sensations, thoughts, and feelings we experience at a given moment. Consciousness is our subjective understanding of both the environment around us and our private internal world, unobservable to outsiders" (Feldman, 2011). Consciousness is a personal endeavor, since our conscious experiences are unique to us and are dependent on our many physical, mental, spiritual, or emotional states. Our awareness during our waking hours is never the same as that in our sleep. More so, it changes through events such as drug use, exercise, **or meditation.**

We tend to look and study our senses separately when they all work in tandem to record, trap and categorize our experiences into awareness. In fact, consciousness has a twofold role: it codifies "potentially vast amounts of information" into the body and combines the conscious memories into a single narrative thread (Barras, 2013; Myers, 2011). More so, the awareness of your thoughts, experiences, and listening entail the value of consciousness (Stevens, 2012).

ANCIENT CONSCIOUSNESS

In the third century B.C., the Abhidharma Buddhist school developed a theory that consciousness is not stuck in one moment, but is rather continuous and shares multiple layers flowing like puddles in the water. This cognition that carries both thoughts and emotions, of which many "thought-moments" pass by in rapid succession, exists even when the thinker lacks notice. In fact, "The rapidity of the succession of such thought memories is said that within the brief duration of a flash of lightning, or in the twinkling of an eye, billons of thought-moments may arise and pass away" (Therabada Buddha Sasana Organization Mahasi, 2015). For Abhidharma, consciousness is divided into four mayor layers (Hanh, 2006):

- *Mind consciousness,* our "working consciousness" where the both the body and the mind complement each other in a person's waking moment, engage in judgments, worries, and activate prediction and analysis **in time;**

- *Sense consciousness*, where the senses serve as "doors" of perception in a three-fold process relating the organ, the object, and **our experiences;**

- *Store consciousness,* the deepest point of consciousness that keeps and preserves every type of information, attached to its trove of stored memories; and *manas* or *cogitation*, where it embraces or stores consciousness and attempts to appropriate it as **its own.**

The complex philosophy of Abhidharma served as an important comparison to one of the most recent breakthroughs in understanding the role of consciousness and psychology––and a revolutionary way to get you out of **your mind.**

THE TIME-SLICE THEORY

How do our modern glitches start? Why is our subconscious viewing these images as dangerous memories? When I began the research leading me to establish the Inspired Performance Program, I discovered an important scientific advancement titled the *time-slice theory* that

Note: Adapted from "Explicit memory," by GoodTherapy.org, 2015a, http://www.goodtherapy.org/blog/psychpedia/explicit-memory & Implicit memory, by GoodTherapy.org, 2015b, http://www.goodtherapy.org/blog/psychpedia/implicit-memory.

aligned with the program's goals, making it clear that our subconscious mind is aware of the images and sounds we are currently experiencing 400 milliseconds before our conscious mind even receives the data. In most cases, we are not conscious of *most* of what the subconscious mind is viewing. The incoming data is being processed at such a rapid rate, our conscious mind can't handle such an inordinate and exorbitant amount of processing detail. However, your subconscious mind, looking for any threats to your survival, will multi-task and attend to more than several things at once.

That's the reason why you'll oftentimes drift off: your conscious mind is aimlessly wandering, while the subconscious takes the seat, looking at every piece of data it can collect within its surroundings. Have you ever driven somewhere and when you arrive it's difficult to remember the trip? You may even think to yourself, "How did I get here?" Your conscious mind zoned out because it stopped perceiving danger, and your subconscious mind became completely focused on what was happening on a consistent and continual basis. Plenke (2016) explained the concept using the analogy of frames in the movies:

> Think of when you watch a movie at the theater. To the naked eye, the movie is seamless. But in reality, it's a series of storages flying by at 24 frames per second [fps]. Similarly, your brain is actually translating new information from the world around you...hundreds of milliseconds after you **experience it.**

Using the time-slice theory, as your subconscious views an image or listens to a sound, then takes that data and compares it to related data about past life experiences, its purpose is to compare and see if there is anything similar or the same that it needs to know about to protect you. In other words, your subconscious asks itself, "Does this image look familiar, or is it the same as a past threat?."

THE GOOGLE SEARCH

The image is viewed 400 milliseconds before it may be made available to your conscious awareness, then your subconscious mind does a quick Google search of its memory database. During the search, your subconscious views billions of bits of information to look for information onhow to respond *should* there be a threat——any image, sound or smell that looks or sounds similar to the past——it begins to look at events and experiences embedded within the memory data bank to determine if a response is warranted. This is where the glitch happens: as soon as the subconscious views these sounds and images from memory data storage in hi-res, the subconscious data reacts to them as if the threat is happening now, its brightness and intensity confuses the survival-based subconscious mind to respond, for it cannot discern between the real or imagined. Keep in mind that only your conscious mind relates to time. Even if your subconscious mind is physiologically prepared for fight-or-flight, you may not be consciously aware of what is happening within your body. You may sense the rising emotions within you and have no idea why. You see, your subconscious takes the incoming data and at the same time views the old data from memory. That is the glitch, a unique feature of the human mind.

Now, does knowing this help explain much of what you have experienced in your life? Whenever you

consciously think about a traumatic or disturbing event
and feel emotional, there is an error message operating.
Remember: the purpose of *any* emotion is to request an
action. You know what the sensation of hunger feels like.
What is the purpose of the sensation? It is a call for an
action. What does your subconscious mind want you to
do? Eat! Why does it want you to eat? To survive! Now,
what happens if you try to ignore this call for action?
The sensation grows stronger and intensifies. You may

Figure 5: Graphical description of the process of emotions.

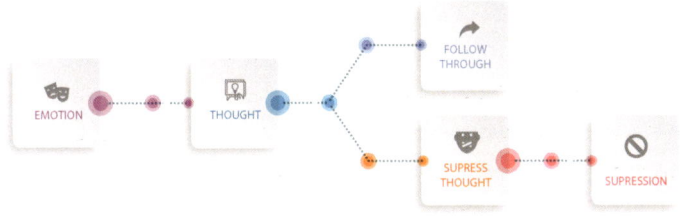

Note: Adapted from "The four layers of consciousness" by
T.N. Hahn, Lion's Roar, 2006, https://www.lionsroar.com/
the-four-layers-of-consciousness/.

even feel shaky, irritated, or have a headache. The message grows stronger just as an emotion does when a
(perceived) threat is not handled properly. As soon as
you eat, the sensation goes away. In essence, an action
initiated is a message received; the sensation turned on
when it was appropriate, then turned off when finished
(**Figure 5**).

MEDIATING THE SUBCONSCIOUS

Currently, the medical community uses medication as a catch-all tool to *manage* emotional disturbances. Medication works because it blocks the subconscious mind from accessing the images during the Google search. However, this solution is *not* and *should not* be the long-term answer; instead, we must address the error that is occurring. Because the Inspired Performance Program allows the mind to update, reboot, adjust, and refresh, the high-res images are converted into a low-res format the same way as the information about what you ate for dinner yesterday. Once that is complete, the mind has no other reason to call for any action since the image no longer observes the necessary intensity to warrant it. The subconscious mind reboots the information into a format that the mind perceives as non-threatening. When there's no threat, there is no need for action. The best part: it's **fast!**

Our minds are brilliant and are designed to heal on their own. However, when the mind has so much energy being drained by these error messages, calling for actions that cannot be done or undone, it has little energy available for maintenance or to focus on more pressing issues. When there is a (perceived) threat from old data stored in memory, all the energy is required to eliminate the danger. It makes sense why our minds do this because the threat, even if a threat is simply perceived, is seen as a life-or-death situation. Even though the perceived threat is not dangerous in reality, your subconscious mind does not view it that way without the benefit of reason and logic. For this reason, the fight-or-flight system is an automated process that requires no thinking, as we shall see in future chapters.

So, now you have a better understanding of how and why your mind is operating the way it is. You also now know that it could not operate any differently, based on the science behind how our minds work. Does knowing this help you to see that the guilt or shame you may have experienced about events in your life were simply the product of error messages? Your mind has accumulated these error messages and they have been hindering the way your mind operates. The thoughts produced by your mind are based on faulty intelligence and distorted thoughts. With this new understanding, you can take greater responsibility for your actions, and make clearer, better decisions that are no longer interrupted with error messages, or faulty intelligence. By understanding how these glitches affect your subconscious mind, you will feel empowered to get *Out of Your Mind* and into enjoying your life with greater peace, clarity **and focus!**

CHAPTER FOUR

ATMOSPHERIC CONDITIONS; OR, YOUR MIND COULD NOT HAVE DONE IT EVERY OTHER WAY

THE STORY OF TWO SISTERS TALKING UNDER A TREE

I learned of this story from Dr. John Connelly, a brilliant trauma therapist and the founder of Rapid Resolution Therapy (RRT), who used this story to explain to his clients how things could not have happened every other way:

> Two sisters were walking through their neighborhood, and as they come up to a neighbor's house, the biggest branch of a neighbor's tree––a big, beautiful oak tree they climbed all the time as kids––had fallen. Saddened and surprised, the little sister said to the bigger sister:

"Oh, it's so sad! Why did the biggest branch have to fall down from our favorite tree?"

The big sister replied, "Well, don't you remember last night? There was a storm, and a storm created the wind, and the wind blew really hard and broke the branch off **the tree.**"

So the little sister asked again, "Why did there have to be a storm?"

The big sister responded, "Well, there were atmospheric conditions, and the atmospheric conditions created the storm, which created the wind and broke **the branch.**"

Still unsatisfied, the little sister asked again, "So why did there have to be atmospheric conditions?"

The big sister, knowing she'd ask again, replied, "Well, there were other atmospheric conditions that created those atmospheric conditions, and that created the storm and the wind, and that's why that **branch broke.**"

So the little sister said, exasperated, "Yeah, and I'm sure you would tell me there were other atmospheric conditions that **created those.**"

The big sister, nodding with understanding, returned the answer: "Right; there were. However, there is another reason that the branch broke, and it's genetics."

Confused, the little sister asked, "what's *genetics*?"

The big sister explained very carefully, "Well, that tree grew from a seed, and that seed was blown off from another tree that landed exactly at that spot, where there was enough water and nutrients in the soil to allow the tree to grow exactly the way it did.

Interested, the little sister replied, "well, does that mean the tree could've been any bigger? Could the tree have been **any stronger?**"

The big sister agreed: "Right! That tree couldn't even have had one more leaf; that tree couldn't have been any different than what it was, and the atmospheric conditions happened exactly the way they did, and the storm couldn't have happened every other way, and the branch couldn't have broken any other way, based on all those factors."

Nodding in agreement, the little sister said, "Okay, I get it; **I understand.**"

The big sister said: "Well, let me tell you another story: A man was traveling through a small town. Suddenly, his car broke down in the middle of the road. So, he walked all over town in order to get help for his car, when he suddenly heard a lady screaming, 'Save my baby! Save my baby!' He realized her house was on fire. So, this guy runs into the house and rescues the baby, darting right out and saving the baby's **life.**"

Beaming with joy, the little sister said, "I love this story! This guy's a hero!"

The big sister wisely responded, "You're right; he *is* a hero! Now the fire department and the police and the news agencies are all there, and a reporter comes up to this guy and asked, 'We heard about what you did. Can you explain why would you run into a house that's on fire, risking your life to save a baby you've never met?' He responded, 'Well, I heard the mother screaming and the house was on fire and I thought to myself, 'If I don't do something, a baby's going to die. So I ran in and found the baby.'"

Excited, the little sister replied, "'Cause that's what **heroes do.**"

The big sister acknowledged her response by saying, "you're right; it is what heroes do, but let me tell you what happened right before the fire: The mother was talking on the phone in her front yard, arguing with the person on the other line, 'I can't believe you forgot to bring me my cigarettes! I really need a cigarette, but I don't want to wake the baby from a nap just so I can get some cigarettes. I'm going to run to the store and I will be back in five minutes.' She left to the store to buy some cigarettes. What the mother didn't know was that there was a man listening and watching her, and when she left to go to the store, he set the house on fire."

So the little sister said, "I don't like this story anymore; that's a *very bad* man."

The big sister acknowledged, "You're right; he is a bad man. However, the reason I'm telling you the story is for you to understand that our hero, who ran into the house to save the baby, couldn't have done it any other way."

For the hero of our story, all the atmospheric conditions in his life combined in perfect harmony so his mind could produce a thought that led him to save the baby. His mind *could not* have produced any other thought. Society would judge the mother—*why* would a mother leave her baby *alone* just so she could by a box of cigarettes? It wasn't her best thought, but do you think she would have left the baby alone if she knew the man was around? I don't think so. There is no reason she should be spending the rest of her life feeling guilty for something about which she had no knowledge. It doesn't absolve him of any responsibility for his actions, but could you imagine *what* could have created such a dangerous mind that produced a thought to set a house on fire when there was a baby inside? So, the whole purpose of that story is to understand that our minds can't produce any thoughts other than those based on life's experiences. Atmospheric conditions are automatic. So doesn't it make sense that the better the atmospheric conditions are, the better the thoughts will be?

This story helps clients understand the value of learning the whole picture. It becomes such a liberating tool to them because it takes away all the guilt and shame of all the things they've done in their lives by realizing they could not have done things differently. Like I said, it doesn't mean that we'll let the arsonist get away with his actions out of pity and mindless compassion—he still must respond to the law for his nefarious actions. However, now we understand that his mind could not have done it any other way. In the end, if you have an experience, it will be very hard to get your mind to produce a different thought.

"Why?" is Pointless

There is no "why," because there is no need to question every action. "Why" only exists because that's the way your mind produces the thought at that moment in time. As an example, think of any embarrassing event you've gone through recently. What happened? How did you react? How did everybody else react? Was it thrilling, exhilarating, or perhaps mortifying? Did it break any self-imposed boundaries? Would you do it again? Most importantly, did you ask yourself *why* it happened? It may not be a comforting statement, but had I gone through your life the exact way you have lived it without changing a second, my mind would have produced the same thoughts.

Even though my wife grew up in such a traumatic household, her sister ended up becoming angry and bitter while my wife only turned out afraid and unassertive. Why? Because they did not experience life the same way, there were other atmospheric conditions in their lives that led them to change their perceptions. Her grandmother convinced my wife that there was a God looking out for her, filling her with hope, and that there was something else to live for, since "the essence of psychological trauma is the loss of faith that there is order and continuity in life." Spirituality helped her reduce unhealthy habits through changes in lifestyle, expanded her social support, enhanced her coping skills, helped her to relax through prayer and meditation, and made meaning of trauma (Daniel, 2012, p. 2). On the other hand, my sister-in-law did not have this type of spirituality, so that her life story was radically differ-ent—and, to a point, was much more painful. Is it something to question the world about? No. Is it something to lose sleep over? No.

SELF-JUDGMENT IS POINTLESS

Because our conscious mind can find reason and logic in everything, it attempts to analyze the world surrounding us. Your subconscious mind doesn't; it takes everything literally. Our conscious mind finds reason where there shouldn't be—that's where cognitive distortions come into play. These distortions try to answer questions such as, "What does this mean about us that this person did *this* and said *that* to us?," or "What did I do to deserve this?"

This is why I believe the over-analysis in traditional psychotherapy can be harmful to clients: it may work towards justifying their negative behaviors. Instead, why not provide the important solutions to solve our clients' problems instead of providing feeble insights? Certain events need not be understood. What is important is to accept the events and move towards a new perception of them (Stark, 2014). As Kilgore (2016) explained, "The reason you are the way you are—the reason you've taken on the behaviors, failings, and limitations you've taken on—is because those behaviors were the best ways to navigate whatever difficulties you faced in your childhood." Instead of asking questions that internalize clients' frustrations, I will ask something like, "What do you think it means about *you*?" These questions allow them to realize that their attackers' or providers' minds produced a thought and you happened to be there, at the wrong moment and the wrong time. The behaviors of the other person was never about *you*, or *your* thoughts, or *your* actions; it's about *them*. Watch and see how their guilt will decrease.

Self-punishment serves as a protective buffer against negative emotions––namely, "rejection and failure;" by preemptively taking the role of judge and accuser against oneself, a person encourages a false belief that (s)he will be saved from others' negative judgments (Paul M. P., 2015). In addition, self-criticism's "proclivity for experiencing failure and guilt" exposes how vulnerable one's identity and definition is to others (Chui, Zilcha-Mano, Dinger, Barret, & Barber, 2016). If your mind uses its intelligence to create an action and afterward, second-guesses your actions, it is unfair to do so because there is no way you could have done things differently if the faulty intelligence in your mind only created actions based on the way your mind produced such thoughts. Could you have done it differently? No! It is impossible to do so until those atmospheric conditions are cleared, and those events no longer overwhelm your choices and potential in life.

As discussed by Akin (2014), "People who have [a] high level of self-doubt experience themselves in danger of being undermined by their poor judgment and approach crucial decisions in which they are likely to find themselves wanting or to be found wanting by others." This means that self-doubters' uncertainty and ineffectiveness in determining the outcome of their actions and judgments only fosters a fear and attitude of dependence. That is why the Inspired Performance Program has been so successful: by teaching you to update your mind, increase your performance, and empower you to confidently assess your peak performance. How better would you feel when you know that your mind is filtering clearly and in **the present?**

Choice is Pointless

Did you choose to read this book today? What made you choose this book over others in the same section? What were you looking for in a book? Perhaps you liked the cover, read some reviews, and found a title that promised you knew things to learn and apply to your daily life. Perhaps somebody else who read this book or successfully completed the course recommended this book to you. Still, maybe you wanted to try something new that suddenly popped up as a best-seller and you clicked away?

All these questions may seem odd, dumb, or downright invasive. You may dismiss them at first, saying it was a random choice you made at a bookstore. For you, choosing a book takes almost no precedence over other choices, for example, such as choosing a shirt, which in turn is not as serious or consequential a choice to make, as choosing a well-paying job or a partner would be. The fact is, choices are made by your mind filtering through what we know. Did you choose the thought of picking a book from millions of thoughts darting through your mind at the same time? Not really. Your mind focused on that one thought that invaded your attention the most, and that one thought led you to buy **this book.**

Your mind only produces thoughts based on what little or how much it knows. It knew you wanted to buy a book. It knew you had to get dressed to buy a book or, if you wanted, your mind led you towards a Google search or a click on an app. It even knew you needed to get gas or check the balance on your credit card. When the mundane steps in your life were done, your mind looked at itself and asked, "What do I have to do *now*?" Then it produced a series of thoughts, and the purpose for those thoughts was to get an action. If you knew it was cold outside your mind would produce thoughts based on the knowledge that it is cold, like wearing something warm, heating up your car, or buying the ingredients to make hot chocolate with marshmallows at the store. If you knew it was hot outside, your mind would step in and get you to buy more water, wear something loose and comfortable, and turn on the air conditioner.

Your mind can only offer so many options to you. If your mind has limited data to deal with, it will produce different thoughts. If your mind has more data to deal with, it will produce different thoughts. Remember: thoughts are created by our mind in order to conceive an action. We do not *choose* the thoughts; they are *presented* to us in the form of choices. In fact, thinking can be defined as "mental exertion aimed at finding an answer to a question or the solution to a practical problem" (Handel, 2012). Even though it feels like we are consciously making an effort to assert our choices, our minds are simply trading thoughts for actions. Now, you could reject the thoughts. You could say, "No; that's not the book I'm looking for," or "I prefer my book to be a hardcover, not a softcover." You could suppress your thoughts, but be warned that should you *really* desire to buy a book, there can only be so much suppression your mind can handle in a short amount of time before it suddenly invades your consciousness (Wagner & Erber, 1992). Thus, your mind will only present you with so many choices based on experience.

People judge themselves by his or her choices: "How did I make that choice? Why did I do that? Why did I allow that to happen?" Because of the way the mind filters life's experiences, their judgments will depend on their experiences: If their life was dark, their thoughts will be dark and will be presented with many choices until they no longer have an effect on the way their minds produce thoughts. You could not do it every other way, because your mind is narrowing down those choices for you. As MacKinnon (2016) explained, "We too often treat reality as an immovable fact. It is as if the world were ice and we were unable to see the liquid state inherent in its form. Reality is as flexible and as plausible as the mind we use to perceive it." That is why the "illusion of choice" is somewhat troublesome to grasp. If you believe that you have *control* over your actions and are suddenly *forced* to choose the same course of action you wanted to take, you would still be resentful because of that when, in fact, it is the need for *control* that drives your choices (Kennon, 2010).

IRAQ: A STORY OF (FAULTY) INTELLIGENCE

Let me help illustrate the concept of faulty intelligence in another, albeit more politically-charged, way. Let's take politics, ideologies, or even our personal perceptions of morality out of the picture, and look at a story of faulty intelligence during the **Iraq War.**

When President George W. Bush was given military intelligence stating that Sadam Hussein had weapons of mass destruction, he needed to make a decision quickly. Reeling from the tragedy of 9/11, he had to respond to a grieving nation. Other Western powers shared the same intelligence, as the United States agreed with President Bush that he needed to take drastic action in order to safeguard the nation—and Iraq's future. There were reports of weapons of mass destruction (WMD), biological warfare, nuclear warheads and even records of oppression of the Iraqi people. Given the circumstances and the information available at the moment, there was no choice for the Americans but to attack Iraq using all our military strength.

After attacking, however, America soon discovered that Hussein never *had* the weapons our intelligence believed he had. This was *not* a good situation. So, what happens next? How does the American government—and its people—receive reassurance of its actions in Iraq? Everyone second-guessed the decision to attack: President Bush was accused of warmongering, and attacking Iraq only to line the pockets of oil tycoons and cronies. Private contractors were accused of war profiteering with our taxpayer dollars at work. Intelligence officials were accused of gross incompetence and negligence, and political finger pointing and infighting ensued during the Iraq Intelligence Commission of 2004. Politicians drew swords with shoulds, coulds, and woulds at each other's throats. However, based on the faulty intelligence he was presented with, how could he have made any other decision? If the intelligence were accurate and

Hussein actually used those weapons to attack Israel, would we discuss the consequences (Pillar, 2006)?

You see, the faulty intelligence created by the built-up error messages accumulating through your life have affected your thoughts and actions. Nevertheless, your mind could not have produced any other thoughts based on the information it was using. So what makes us feel guilty when we think about the things we have done and then realized they were mistakes? The reason is that like every other emotion, the mind creates guilt in order to provoke an action on your part. The mind wants you to seek punishment for our actions and point towards reparations, ammends, or an apology. The mind also wants you to hide from the world and suffer in silence (Baumeister, Stillwell, & Heatherton, 1994). Now, what does your mind want you to do about that event from ten years ago? Your mind wants to change it. Why is it requesting that action? Because it still views the disturbing high-resolution images of the event in real time and is attempting to change the memory and avoid making the mistake. Is that possible? No! It's only a pesky glitch.

THE STORY OF COLIN, THE ATHLETE

I once worked with a sixteen-year-old athlete named Colin (not his real name). He was a committed Christian who did everything right and exactly what was expected of him. Nonetheless, there was a problem: every time he played sports, his father confessed, "He gets so angry we don't know where it's coming from," which begs the question: why or what would cause such a well-adjusted child to fly off the handle, punch holes in the walls, smash rackets and cause so much distress within the family?

Contrary to what is expected—and particularly nothing traumatic happened during his childhood—it came down to the way his mind perceived frustration in childhood. When he was eight years old, he built a Michael Jordan avatar on an NBA video game. After painstakingly grinding his avatar through continuous gameplay, he eventually developed the player to a 97% efficiency rate. In a sense, he was cleaning up in the game; every time he shot, he scored, and such efficiency led him to win, win, win very easily.

The next year, he bought the newest NBA game and once again rebuilt his Michael Jordan avatar to peak efficiency. Suddenly, as part of the random events that occurred during gameplay, Michael Jordan was injured and could not play for 30 games. Before the injury, Michael Jordan won eight straight games; through simulation, his team was suddenly losing 8 to 30. In other words, he could never reach that level of success again. The situation sounds illogical at first glance, but his mind continued to filter through such a frustrating childhood event in such a manner that whenever something went wrong, he saw all the frustration he had playing these video games. Who knew that video games could be an exercise in frustration?

Richard Lazarus explained that frustration "always arises from a threat to the ego" in which "something must have happened to challenge or unsettle a person's sense of self" (Krueger J. A., 2015). For Colin, the frustration he felt when losing his favorite game bruised his ego and manifested, even years later, into aggression. The frustration and subsequent aggression turned into a vicious cycle, where the anger greeted by frustration generated more aggression, which also generated more anger, and so on. Colin's expectations were locked in the past, which caused problems whenever he did not perform according to his own self-judgment (Myers, 2011). He exhibited the phenomenology of anger, including emotional experiences, varying from annoyance to rage, as well as behavioral patterns varying from social withdrawal to physical aggression and cognitive phenomena, such as attributions of blame and rumination (Sukhodolsky, Kassinove, & Gorman, 2004).

After Colin finally cleared his mind from past frustration, the aggression suddenly stopped. He could go back out and play without making a scene or destroying anything. His father was both shocked and surprised at such change for Colin. Several days later, he sent me a text message expressing his gratitude at his son's transformation: "Holy smokes! What an amazing weekend! It's so exciting to see Colin free of that torment! Thank you!" Now, a note: had Colin never fixed this now, this may have developed into depression, because his mind would have attempted to fix the solution to his problem from when he was younger and prevent Michael Jordan from injury, so that he would not lose.

CONFIDENCE IS NOT YOUR FRIEND

During my session with Colin, we discussed an important outlook that challenged his views on confidence. I remember asking him during the session, "Do you think you need to be confident to be a good basketball player?

He answered, "Yeah."

I replied, "… because everybody told you that you need to be confident. What if I told you that confidence is not your friend?"

He was surprised at hearing that. "Well, how couldn't confidence be your friend?"

I responded to his curious question, "Because confidence is a predictor. Let's use golf as an example: When you say to yourself, 'I'm confident I'm going to win the game. I'm confident I'm going to make this shot.' Well, there are so many other factors that are not in your control that when you say, 'I'm confident of the result that's going to come,' your mind is predicting success—but you can't predict success. You can only do so much in the moment; if the wind blows after you hit the shot and it pushes your ball into the water, what happened to your confidence? It's shot!"

"Instead, I want you to develop an attitude of optimism that no matter what happens, if the wind blows and knocks my ball in the water, you can say to yourself, 'I'm optimistic that I can make a good shot and recover. No matter what happens to me, I'm prepared to handle it. I've got the skill level. You've hit tens of thousands of balls. You know that you can hit pretty much any kind of shot you need to hit. You do not have to be confident about it. You just need to be optimistic that no matter what happens, you'll be optimistic that you can adjust to the next shot."

For this young athlete, listening to those words blew his mind away. He said, "Oh my God! That's so good!" That was the exact reason playing sports had created so many problems for him: he had tried to predict outcomes from past childhood successes. Suddenly, there was a change in the way things were operating and he could not control them. However, even if you can't control everything, you can control your actions. That is why the idea of mindfulness is so key. In the words of psychologist Martin Seligman, "The optimists believe defeat is not their fault: circumstances, bad luck, or other people brought it about. Such people are unfazed by defeat. Confronted by a bad situation, they perceive it as a challenge and try harder" (Popova, 2012). Only this time, the challenge is a self-imposed friend named *confidence*.

How do you define confidence? It can be a feeling of having little doubt about yourself and your abilities. However, can you notice the many problems with confidence? If conditions outside of your control affect your outcome, what does that say about your abilities? Nothing—it doesn't mean that your skills are hopeless or that you are a failure. Because people tend to be overconfident and overestimate their judgments, confidence is only "adaptive" as a feel-good mechanism enabling people to attempt to do things they would not have done otherwise (Griffin & Tversky, 1992).

DO YOU NEED CONFIDENCE TO SUCCEED?

Most people would agree in a heartbeat. I say, no you do not—in fact, I believe confidence is more harmful to your performance than you would think possible.

How could this be? The reason is because confidence is a zero-sum predictor of an outcome. If you are confident, you'll win. If you are not confident, you'll lose. However, there is a problem with that logic: you are conforming to self-imposed and other-imposed expectations that only serve to reinforce your need for confidence in order to succeed. That, in and of itself, is a vague, simplistic, and unsustainable argument by any logical construct.

As a result, confidence is NOT your friend; it works against you because it distorts how the mind will operate. For a professional golfer who was also a client of mine, he first found this concept unbelievable. Since learning about the problems with confidence, he is not afraid of anything because he has learned to let whatever happens, happen. For instance, a professonal golfer I worked with in the past answered the same question the way anybody else would. Then I said to him, "After you hit your shot, can you control a gust of wind? Or how about the terrain when the ball hits the side of the green and bounces right into the bunker? What just happened to your confidence? The result wasn't what you predicted."

If this situation continued for our golfer throughout the round, his confidence would suddenly crumble, and his performance erode. Why did this happen? It happened because he told his mind he could execute a shot within his (very small and self-imposed) margin of error, but the wind changed by blowing the ball a bit to the left, the right, or to the side. Through this example, you can see that confidence relies on (incorrectly) predicting outcomes and treating them like facts, and when they do not line up, brining our confidence into question. This also relates to the illusion of control, as expectations of an illusion of control "create fantasies of wielding more influence" in personal actions. However, maintaining the illusion of control makes sufferers insensitive to feedback and unable to learn from mistakes (Sanger, 2011; Dean, 2013). In addition, even if meeting expectations provides an illusory sense of happiness, reactivity to events is *never* the best way to enjoy life's circumstances (Sanger, 2011; James, 2015).

That being said, why do some people appear to be so confident? There is no clear-cut answer—for instance, some are pretty good at what they do and seldom make mistakes. This could be true in a situation with very few variables in the outcome. Alternately, these people could just be looking at mistakes and failures in stride and seeing them for what they are—small steps to assure success. Still others are comfortable in his or her own skin. Can you identify with either *one* of those perspectives? Or, like most people, do you feel confident when things go *your* way and lose it when *something* inevitably goes awry?

For example, a golfer has a shot that is measured at 150 yards to the pin. Water is at the 130 mark, and a bunker is at the 170 yard mark. A professional golfer has a plus or minus range with each of his clubs. So now, if the professional golfer knows that he can hit his pitching wedge between 145 and 155 yards, why would he care about the water and sand? By focusing any attention on the water and sand, he tells his mind that there is a danger at 130 and 170 yards, but his subconscious mind will focus on danger. Instead of letting the subconscious do all the work undermining his confidence, he can assure himself that there is a way out and into hitting the hole without expectations.

Why was Tiger Woods the greatest golfer of all time? If you look at Tiger Woods' stats, he hit a lot of balls into trouble: he would hit balls into woods or bunkers or the sand. He wasn't the most accurate golfer. However, he knew that, no matter what, he could respond. If he hit the ball into the woods, or close between two trees, or right of the green, instead of panicking, he went to the next shot and said to himself, "I can do this." In golf, they call him a *scrambler*, and despite his many personal scandals, Tiger Woods was considered the best scrambler of all time. Learning about this changes peoples' mindsets and empowers them to perform their best: fully present, in the moment, and using their skills at maximum efficiency.

TRADE CONFIDENCE FOR OPTIMISM

Optimism will change your life if you allow it. Optimism can be defined as "the tendency to be hopeful and to emphasize or think of the good part in a situation rather than the bad things" (Cambridge Dictionary, n.d.). There are three important words to point out when you break this down: *tendency*, meaning you are more likely than not to do something; *emphasis*, meaning to strongly exert influence; and *hope*, meaning that you hope that good things are more likely to happen than bad things. For this reason, optimism creates a positive tendency to change, never emphasizes a demand for an outcome, and stays hopeful that the odds are in your favor—and even if the odds aren't in your favor, there's always an opportunity to make things work; that better things are coming, meaning that optimists accept whatever happens without resignation and wisely push through Obstacles. Doesn't it make more sense to be optimistic rather than confident?

Hampton (2015) exposed the hurdles of positive thinking if done wrongly: by attaching one's expectations to our outcomes, we're setting ourselves up for disappointment. However, if we can consider other "potential outcomes" or "courses of action" *without* attaching any outcomes to our thoughts, then positive thinking would be more successful. As a result, an outcome-blind approach takes away all the expectations of our decisions and focuses on the process, learning what works well and what doesn't along the way (Beidacki, 2015).

Staying present and in the moment is the key to staying optimistic. If our "confident" golfer makes a bogey or hits a ball in the water, he will begin to question *why* this happened and *what* went wrong. For others, they may even realize the wind blew, but then they see this as a mistake on their part because they did not calculate how much wind there was. They will not account for the wind gusting right after they hit their shot. Instead, they identify *their* share of the mistake and do not blame everything on themselves or the world. In my experience, people who rely excessively on confidence experience a lot of internal turbulence. Whereas confidence becomes a constant internal check, optimism looks at failures as only necessary steps **for success.**

LOSE, A LOT!

I learned an important lesson from a tennis professional named Vic, who played at a club I belonged to when I was about thirteen-years-old. Vic was the best tennis player I had ever seen——he easily beat every pro at every club he played. Even in his early forties, I always admired Vic's Buddhist mentality: peaceful, calm, and completely in control of his emotions. One day, as we were sitting on a bench at the tennis club, Vic said something to me that to this day has a profound effect on my **life outlook.**

He asked me, "You want to be a great tennis player, don't you?," I replied with an enthusiastic "Yes!" He then responded cryptically, "I'm going to tell you the secret," and looked around to make sure no one else was listening. Would he tell me the key to fame and untold riches? Would he reveal his deepest, darkest secrets to me, a teenager who idolized his and wanted the quick and easy secrets to success? Was he humoring me with **his wit?**

He said, "Lose, *a lot!*"

"What is he *talking about*!? It makes no sense!" I thought, "Losing takes the glory out of competition! Losers get *no* **respect!**"

He then explained that I would never improve unless I played better players and took away a lesson from each loss. If I were willing to take that risk, I would improve faster than any of my competition. He wanted me to be humble, and never challenge better players, because that would put them in a defensive position. Instead, he suggested I ask the players if they would be willing to hit balls with me for ten minutes before competing, because I would like to learn from them. I would complement them on the skills and techniques I wished to emulate. I learned that this type of graceful losing successfully conveys one's "honorable and impressive and respectable" character (Tenner & Tenner, 2011; Lubin-Katz, 2014).

Vic said they would pour the knowledge into me in a few hours that would take years for me to learn on my own. Then, if I played a few games and lost, I would study the techniques that helped them win the match. That's what I first understood about optimism: I would need to stay optimistic that their strengths would soon be mine through hard work and persistence. Had I used confidence as my guide, I would only travel as far as my pride and ego would allow me to go.

Even the great Arnold Palmer had a similar piece of advice and an interesting approach to a bad shot: he expected to make *seven* bad shots per round, which was just a part of the game. Whenever he hit one bad ball, he simply counted it as a part of the process to success. That, I believe, reflects true optimism. While most would argue that Arnold Palmer was confident, I believe he stayed present and in the moment, accepting any outcome in stride understanding the next shot provided a new opportunity to succeed. Ball in the bunker, no problem. Ball in the woods, no problem. Any opportunity is perfect to amaze the fans with a shot around or through, adding to his already **legendary status.**

By developing an optimistic attitude, the mind looks at the future through beneficial, appealing, and possible ways, keeping the mind centered, peaceful, and fully present. Science demonstrates that optimistic people are healthier and live longer, promoting good health through proper nutrition and exercise, reducing any major health risks and chronic diseases. Even more so, a 2008 study conducted by British behavioral economists Andrew Oswald and David G. Blanchflower discovered that our happiness declines from our teenage years and bottoms out at around age 40, then improves when we grow older—even when accounting for social, economic, and cultural differences: "We start off life with high hopes, which we gradually realize are unlikely to be fulfilled [...] Middle age brings a new sense of realism; a determination to enjoy life as is; and thus an increase in happiness" (Freeman & Freeman, 2015; Oswald & Blanchflower, 2008; Sharot, 2012).

An optimisttic attitude empowers you. When you know that anything is possible and move towards that direction, your brain is programmed to cross paths and avoid harm along the way. On the other hand, a pessimistic atttiude deflates you because you believe you will not grab *any* opportunity. Your brain will not avoid harm or learn from adversity and, despite many Google searches from memory, will be adamant that change of any scope is hopeless. While the optimist will be aware of potential danger and understand that when it arrives—if it ever does—will handle things with as much care and tact as possible, the pessimist will only be stuck through victimizing, self-imposed choices.

Can you learn to be an optimist? No, never! (That was for the pessimists reading this book.) Of course you can! Practicing optimism will improve your thought process immensely—but you must be ready to put in the work and overcome your atmospheric conditions if you want to be *Out of Your Mind*!

CHAPTER FIVE

GETTING YOUR MIND INTO ALPHA STATE

The brain is a living, electric organ. Researchers believe that 10 watts (W) of electrical power can be generated from a fully functional brain. In addition, the electrical signals running through your brain are fast, allowing for a nearly instantaneous response to control messages (Layton, 2008). Should every nerve cell discharge at one time, five-millionths to fifty-millionths of a volt would course through your brain at the same time (Hermann, 1997). In fact, your body is an amazing electrical conductor. With electricity, your blood vessels easily transport blood through the body, your muscles contract, and your brain activates your responses to thoughts, emotions, and dreams. Still, even though your body produces small portions of electricity, you can't use your body's electricity to charge electronics such as phones, tablets, and computers, or as an alternative energy source––at least, **not yet.**

However, we *can* use all that energy in your brain to develop Alpha state relaxation. By learning the important tricks about brainwaves and becoming one with the pulse of the natural environment, you can get yourself out of your mind and **into success!**

WHAT ARE BRAINWAVES?

Also known as *neural oscillations*, brainwaves can be defined as a "combination of synchronized electrical activity in the brain," named as such because the structure of a brainwave resembles that of waves (Bergland, 2015). A brainwave, in fact, is a *pattern* representing the brain's physical and electrical activity by "synchronize[ing] electrical pulses from masses of neurons connected with each other" (Berman, 2015; Brainworks NeuroFeedback, n.d.) These can also be compared to musical notes, where the high frequency brainwaves tend to be "subtle" and "high-pitched," while low-frequency waves are "deeply penetrating" and deeper to understand. Whether awake, asleep, or everything in between, the different parts of your brain form unique "functional networks" that swing back and forth in synchronicity, and which produce different types of brainwaves for different types of situations within your body (Cellvideoabstracts, 2012).

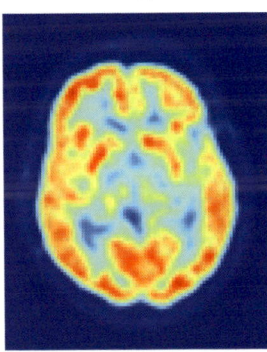

Figure 6: PET scan of a healthy brain by Jens Maus, 2010, https://commons.wikimedia.org/wiki/File:PET-image.jpg. Public domain.

While there are only five brainwave "types," these serve as a convenient way to describe changes in brain activity. For instance, you may prominently exhibit alpha and theta activity when sleeping, but *all* five brainwave types are still present in minor degrees. In fact, two things are necessary in order to produce the appropriate brainwaves for success: *flexibility* by "shift[in] your brain activity to match what [you] are doing"; and *resilience* from negative events (Shue, n.d.; **Table 7**).

BETA BRAINWAVES

The Beta brainwave state is between 15-30 Hz. It's your normal waking state, where your conscious mind is significantly active (**Figure 7**). An extraordinary amount of data is flowing to and from your brain, and you are engaged with others in work or social settings These are also emitted when you are "agitated, tense, or afraid" (Heyrman, 2010). As a result, beta waves are important for concentration by mental stimulation, motivation, and language and reading entrainment (or synchronizing your brainwaves to an external rhythm), and serve as an important treatment for children with ADD that helps restore their natural Beta wave activity (Cvijetic, 2017; Mager, 2014). However, remaining in a Beta state for too long will harm a human being, since other brainwaves (such as Alpha) are produced in too little amounts. On the other hand, "stress, [lack of] concentration, and [...] depression" are common to those suffering from too much Beta brainwaves (Gorbea, 2016, par. 5).

ALPHA BRAINWAVES

Alpha brainwaves are present at that perfect moment when your mind is performing at its best. Alpha waves were discovered by German neurologist Hans Berger through the use of his invention, the electroencephallograph (EEG), a test that measures and records your brain's elecrical activity, by noticing the brainwave differences between opening and closing the eyes. (**Figure 8**). Due to his discovery, the Alpha wave was originally known as the "Berger's Wave." Even though Berger published his findings in 1929, he was met with skepticism and criticism and did not gain widespread

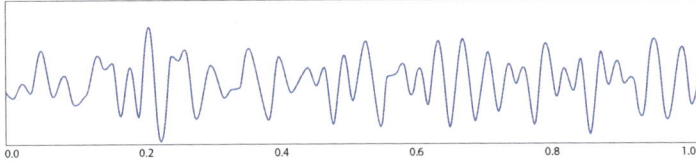

Figure 7: EEG diagram filtering Beta waves by Hugo Gamboa, 2005, https://commons.wikimedia.org/wiki/File:Eeg_beta.svg. Used under the Creative Commons Attribution-Share Alike 3.0 Unported license, https://creativecommons.org/licenses/by-sa/3.0/deed.en.

acceptance until 1937. However, during the early sixties and the creation of biofeedback, the interest in Alpha waves resurfaced in experimentation at the University of Chicago by Dr. Joe Kamiva. Dr. Kamiva discovered that some individuals were capable of controlling their ability to raise or lower their Alpha brainwave activity. In addition, evidence suggested through Alpha wave biofeedback that there was the possibility of suppressing seizures and depression in humans. For this reason, "Alpha oscillations are now associated with inner focus and suppression of distracting stimuli," and are the easiest waves to reord on an EEG (Frölich, 2016). Moreover, inducing Alpha brainwaves improves relaxation and introduces a sense of well-being (Gorbea, 2016).

THETA BRAINWAVES

Theta brain waves occur during light sleep, including important during the Rapid Eye Movement (REM) dream state where you experience vivid visualizations and receive inspiration, creativity, and personal insight (**Figure 9**). As you move from Alpha to Theta, you begin

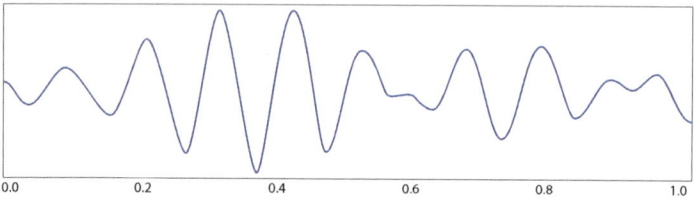

Figure 8: EEG diagram filtering Alpha brainwaves by Hugo Gamboa, 2005, https://commons.wikimedia.org/wiki/File:Eeg_alpha.svg. Used under the Creative Commons Attribution-Share Alike 3.0 Unported license, https://creativecommons.org/licenses/by-sa/3.0/deed.en.

to sleep lightly and dream. Ranging from 4Hz to 7Hz, your mind consolidates the data about everything that happened during your waking state and prepares your mind to begin a relaxed and deep sleep so your mind and body can perform its maintenance programs. These waves also act as a "docking mechanism" for the hippocampus, allowing the organ to make time-tracking and memories easier to process (Frölich, 2016).

DELTA BRAINWAVES

Delta frequency brainwaves are the slowest of the brainwave frequencies at less than 4 Hz. These brainwaves are experienced in deep, dreamless sleep where your mind and body go through healing processes (**Figure 10**). Also, people who practice transcendental meditation achieve this state of conscious, yet detached, awareness. Therefore, it is important for people to get into this deeper state since not having a deep sleep will have a detrimental effect on a person's health in more ways than one. This points out how abuse and trauma keep the mind from reaching this state due to the mind's frequent exposure to fight-or-flight. If the body and mind cannot reach this level for an extended period, maintenance will be affected. In addition, Delta state helps slow and reduce the aging process in our body, rejuvenate various bodily functions, help produce empathy

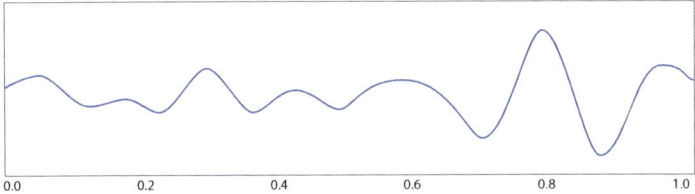

Figure 9: EEG diagram filtering Theta brainwaves by Hugo Gamboa, 2005, https://commons.wikimedia.org/wiki/File:Eeg_theta.svg. Used under the Creative Commons Attribution-Share Alike 3.0 Unported license, https://creativecommons.org/licenses/by-sa/3.0/deed.en.

to others, and improves learning, among other advantages (Fournier, 2016). Conversely, "When people have too little Delta activity (including from traumatic brain injury [TMI] and ADHD), sleep will be more restless and [people] will be unable to feel refreshed and rejuvenated upon waking (Pedersden, 2016, par. 4).

GAMMA BRAINWAVES

A newly discovered brainwave frequency, Gamma brainwaves are the fastest type of brainwave frequency at above 40 Hz (**Figure 11**). Studies have shown that Gamma brainwaves improve neural synchronicity, which helps your brain's neurons fire at the same time, improving your system's consistency (Walton, 2014; J.C.,

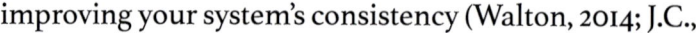

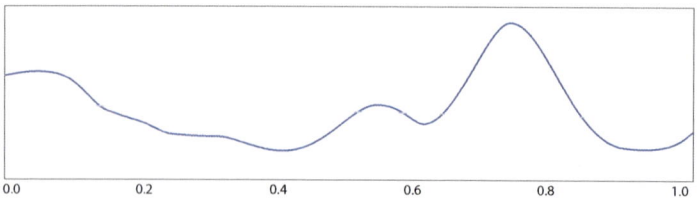

Figure 10: EEG diagram filtering Delta brainwaves by Hugo Gamboa, 2005, https://commons.wikimedia.org/wiki/File:Eeg_delta.svg. Used under the Creative Commons Attribution-Share Alike 3.0 Unported license, https://creativecommons.org/licenses/by-sa/3.0/deed.en.

2016). During this state, there is also increased mental activity and cognitive enhancement, clearer focus, improved information processing, learning, and preventing migraines, among others ("Gamma", n.d.; Karakaş & Başar, 1998). As Migliore (2012) stated, "Gamma activity indicates a constellation of neurons binding together for the first time in the brain to create a neural **network pathway.**"

Table 7: Types of brainwaves

Type of Wave	Common State	Charateristics
Beta (15-30 Hz)	Waking State	Alertness, attentiveness, and problem-solving.
Alpha (7-14 Hz)	Awake and resting state	State of relaxed, effortless alertness, important for creativity and peak performance.
Theta (4-9 Hz)	Light sleep	Includes REM state: vivid dreams and extreme meditation.
Delta (less than 4 Hz)	Deep sleep	Dreamless sleep. Body begins internal healing process.

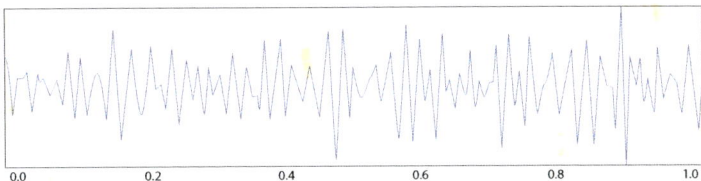

Figure II: EEG diagram filtering Gamma Brainwaves by Hugo Gamboa, 2005, https://commons.wikimedia.org/wiki/File:Eeg_gamma.svg. Used under the Creative Commons Attribution-Share Alike 3.0 Unported license, https://creativecommons.org/licenses/by-sa/3.0/deed. en.

Type of Wave	Common State	Charateristics
Gamma (more than 40 Hz)	Active mind and heightened perception	Simultaneous brain processing information.

Note: Adapted from "If we're going to talk about brainwaves, we should know what they are," by R. Berman, 2015, Big Think, http://bigthink.com/robby-berman/if-were-going-to-talk-about-brainwaves-we-should-know-what-they-are; "What are brainwaves?," by Brainworks NeuroFeedback, n.d., "Brainwaves", http://www.brainworksneurotherapy.com/what-are-brainwaves; by H. Heyrman, Dr. Hugo Heyrman, 2010, http://www.doctorhugo.org/brainwaves/brainwaves.html; and "The 5 brain waves and its connection with flow state," by C. Wilson Meloncelli, C Wilson Meloncelli, 2015b, https://www.cwilsonmeloncelli.com/the-5-brain-waves-and-its-connection-with-flow-state/.

WHY ARE ALPHA BRAIN WAVES IMPORTANT?

The optimal time to prepare and train your mind for success is in Alpha state because it heightens your imagination, memory, learning, visualization, and concentration. Alpha state allows your subconscious mind to perform all the necessary and beneficial functions for performance, peace, and relaxation. Your subconscious mind functions at its best when most of your brain oscillations are in the range of 7.5 Hz. That being said, our hectic lifestyles are forgoing the value of staying in Alpha state, which increases the change of suffering "stress-related disorders and diseases" and "lower[s] the strength of the immune system" (Naik, 2011; **Figure 12**).

IMPROVED PROBLEM SOLVING

Have you ever struggled with test-taking? Everyone has suffered a fair share of struggles when testing, because information has a more difficult time flowing when stress is involved. In fact, most people attempt to solve problems in a Beta state, making problem solving significantly more difficult. Instead, by improving communication in a relaxed state, information is accessed easier. Alpha state clears stuckness. From writer's block and brain teasers to engaging in critical thinking with limited time and resources, Alpha brain waves help you get back the flow state provided by the Alpha state: "An individual has increased abilities to [...] vividly recount past experienes, and critically analyze situations" (Gardner, 2015).

RELAXED THOUGHTS EQUALS A RELAXED BODY

When in Alpha state, your body calms down. Your parasympathetic nervous system, the section of the nervous system that controls your automatic body functions like breathing and digestion, is operating through homeostasis. When your mind is in Alpha state, your body will experience no stress, no tension, and no anxiety. As a result, targeted meditation and deep breathing exercises, along with the tools you will learn to use in the Inspired Performance Program will significantly improve your stress levels. To this point, a 2009 study on Alpha brainwaves revealed that such waves are more abundant in the posterior parts of the brain during meditation (The Norwegian University of Science and Technology (NTNU), 2010).

CREATIVITY

Research has also shown that creative individuals like writers and painters exhibit more Alpha brainwave activity than others with "logical and unoriginal" means, since they enjoy looking at the world from various points of view (Bergland, 2015; Meyer, n.d.; Positive Minds Psychotherapy, n.d.) In addition, creativity in Alpha states allows "new possibilities or new alternatives" to improve your flow, including "super learning," which involves remembering and recalling information with less effort due to hemospheric integration (Positive Minds Psychotherapy, n.d.).

PEAK PERFORMANCE

When you stay in an Alpha state, your mind will be

calm and peaceful, centered and present. Our process has proven very successful for both novice and elite athletes, whose sporting experience affects their presence in Alpha state by performing at an "optimal and most innovative" phase: "When Alpha waves are prominent, sensory impact is minimized and your mind is generally clear of compulsive thoughts" (Bergland, 2015; Meyer, n.d.; Mindvalley Academy, n.d.). For this reason, most artists and creative persons display better Alpha state connections than others (Austin, n.d.).

IMPROVED HEALTH

The longer your mind and body are in a relaxed state, the better your immune system will perform. Your brain will learn how to produce cells that will protect you from immune diseases, create serotonin, and stabilize your emotions. Additionally, as Alpha brain wave activity functions as your brain's natural antidepressant, thereis no need to rely upon medication as a crutch as a result. Your neurotransmitters produce and function much better when stress is reduced. You feel connected, and your sense of peace and calm changes the chemicals and hormones used by **the brain.**

HIGHER BUSINESS PERFORMANCE

Have you ever heard of the term "business trauma?" This is a term most people have never heard of, but is a is a very real phenomenon affliction affecting a growing number of business owners, entrepeneurs and venture capitalists. Both internal and external factors, such as customer relations, employee productivity, or failed investments can spur this unique type of trauma. Of course, every businessperson can improve personal perceptions by entering into an Alpha brainwave state. There is no reason to allow failed business experiences to be used to your detriment when focusing on new business ventures. This is not to say that these experiences aren't important learning tools; the experience has taught you a lesson about what to avoid. With the Alpha brainwave state, your mind is not focused on past outdated glitches. As an end result, our experience proves that executives, CEO's, sales personnel and professionals have experienced increased performance through the Inspired **Performance Program.**

In addition, Alpha brainwave biofeedback has been used to treat mental conditions such as anxiety and depression. So do you recognize the importance of maintaining an Alpha state when life stresses you out?

WHAT IS FLOW?

Do you remember a time when you were doing your work, or you were crafting a hobby with an intense level of concentration? For those brief moments, you were not thinking of anything else in the world except for that activity in front of you? You felt productive, recharged, and refreshed. You were not only learning from your most creative moments––you executed them with precision. There's an ecstatic feeling that stays long after completing the activity, and there is an even greater desire to continue the next time by raising the stakes. Composers, athletes, singers, and surfers have reported experiencing this state of altered consciousness performing their most passionate activities with gusto and *flow*––in other words, "the performer is totally connected to the performance" (Jackson & Marsh, 1996). You too may have experienced this on your own. As Jamie Wheel (Silva, 2013) questioned in the creation of his Flow Genome project, "What if we could use those peak experiences to make us whole, to render us *holy* [emphasis mine]?" "Holy" is the perfect word to explain

Figure 12: Graphical display of the benefits of promoting an Alpha state.

the experience that goes with patching up all those gaps in the self, and maximizing your potential **with flow.**

Flow is a state of consciousness where "all aspects of performance are incredibly heightened," where our performance is at peak levels and our many selves disappear (Kotler, 2014). In this state, both skills and challenges are at an optimal level, allowing our focus to meld into our activities without any interruptions or frustrations. Learning is both practiced and enhanced, and it becomes an opportunity to go further beyond self-imposed challenges and develop new ideas for future flow states (Csikszentmihalyi, 1997). Hungarian psychologist Mikhail Csikszentmihalyi (1990) described how many experienced the power of flow for the first time:

> Yet we have all experienced times when, instead of being buffeted by anonymous forces, we do feel in control of our actions, masters of our own fate. On the rare occasions that it happens, we feel a sense of exhilaration, a deep sense of engagmenet that is long cherished and that becomes a landmark in memory for what life **should be.**

Because the skills and challenges are balanced, flow state occurrence is "essential" and "dependent" on structuring consciousness (Russel, 2001). This means that

Figure 13: Surfer on Blue Ocean Wave in the Tube Getting Barreled by Epic Stock Media https://as2.ftcdn.net/jpg/00/56/21/77/500_F_56217796_MOvQQCsbfYXSSgaDNogkERBjbL74nrrz.jpg

objects like money, task completion, and material possessions aren't necessary to determine the success of a flow state. Instead, happiness is considered the *ultimate* achievement of flow—a natural and elusive "high" of sorts. On the other hand, happiness is very hard, if not outright impossible, to reach when you do not enjoy your job or constantly doubt your performance. Even if flow is a desirable state to be in, only 29% of adults can reach flow while working, and less than 5% of the average population has successfully "hacked" the flow state (Gotzler, 2014). For this reason, there must be a positive engagement to the task at hand for flow to occur (Csikszentmihalyi, 2004). As Schilling (2013) explained, "Flow occurs near the summit of ability, the level of mastery."

HACKING THE FLOW CYCLE

To "hack" the flow cycle, you must understand there are four important requirements Csikszentmihalyi outlines in order to enter the flow state: *clear and defined goals, immediate and unambiguous feedback, balance between one's perceived skills and those perceived as necessary for the task, and uninterrupted concentration* (Matthews, 2015; Fábrega, n.d.; Jackson & Marsh, 1996). As a result, proper preparation is necessary if you wish to achieve flow which, unlike a straight line, is a four-part cycle (**Figure 14**):

- **Struggle:** In the beginning, there is a loading and overloading of the brain with information. For the person attempting to reach flow, it's an unpleasant sensation that produces "extreme frustration, tension, stress, and anxiety" as the body pumps up adrenaline and cortisol (Wilson Meloncelli, 2015a). Even if struggling is obviously unpleasant, it can determine what information is necessary to solve the challenge, while strengthening its awareness to the subconscious at the same time (Ammons, 2015). To prevent "agitation and anxiety," it is important to meditate and observe deep breathing (Schilling, 2013).

- **Release:** In this part, the Beta waves transform to Alpha, and you learn to accept the struggle and tackle the challenge by taking your mind off the problem and calming down for as long as necessary before tackling it. Like a puzzle, "your brain is organizing the problem and subconsciously and forming connections between the pieces loaded during struggle" (Ammons, 2015). Beta waves are transformed into Alpha waves in preparation for flow. In addition, release flushes out stress hormones, avoiding burnout. (Wilson Meloncelli, 2015a).

- **Flow:** The body releases a "cocktail" of five neurochemicals to activate your flow: norepinephrine (for concentration); endorphins (to make you "feel good"); dopamine (for "cognitive alertness"); serotonin (for mood-boosting); and ananide (for a sense of "bliss") (Wilson Meloncelli, 2015a). Every neurochemical improves muscle relaxation, and three major problem-solving skills: attention, pattern recognition, and spatial thinking (Kotler, 2014). During flow, "the challenge provided by the activity is high enough, but the skills of the person can still cope with the situation" (Mauri, Cipresso, Balgera, Villamira, & Riva, 2011). The brain is between the Alpha and Theta brainwave states, with a spike in Gamma wave activity. Time dilation occurs, and your brain transforms into a distraction-free zone, with full immersion to the task at hand. The self disappears and the person is "one with the activity" (Jackson & Marsh, 1996).

- **Recovery:** After flow, your brain and body reset, for enough time as necessary to recharge: "The down time is the best time for integrating our experience and committing to long-term memory" (Matthews, 2015). This is an important time to reflect on the process and look at ways to better improve the next access to flow state. On the other hand, if a sufficient recovery period is not maintained, there is a risk to short-circuit the process automatically by filling the body with excess cortisol and processing immediately to the struggle phase.

Csikszentmihalyi (1990) placed five important recommendations to achieve body-induced flow and gain the important skills you need to improve and extend your **flow states:**

1. Set an overall goal, and as many sub-goals as are **realistically feasible.**

2. Find ways of measuring progress in terms of the **chosen goals.**

3. Keep concentrating and making finer distinctions in **involved challenges.**

4. Develop the necessary skills to interact with available opportunities.

5. Raise the stakes if an activity becomes boring—but do not raise it too much such that achieving the goal becomes frustrating.

By achieving flow, you are engaging in a trance-like state of meditation where your awareness is maximized while working in your most creative or powerful ideas. However, for flow to occur, it's important to understand the value of Alpha brainwaves and how improving their

Figure 14: Graphical description of the flow state cycle.

activity will improve **your focus.**

Note: Adapted from "Hacking enlightenment with flow states," by K. Matthews. Elephant Journal. 2015. Elephant Journal. https://www.elephant-journal.com/2015/05/hacking-enlightenment-with-flow-states/.

THE SCHUMANN RESONANCE: THE HEARTBEAT OF THE EARTH

As you read these words, try to remember a time you were outdoors, enjoying your time in nature, and you felt a deep sense of peace and awe come over you. Where were you? What do you remember experiencing? Were you walking? Were you gazing at the stars? Were you swimming in a lake or sunbathing at the beach, listening to the frothy sound of the waves crashing towards the sand? When you experienced that sense of peace and excitement, you were centered and balanced. You became aware of your center. You see, that is peace and power: you at your best with all your resources available. I'm very sure that wasn't the first time in your life that you experienced such a powerful moment.

What you experienced in that special moment is an intimate connection with the Earth. As I developed this program, I stumbled upon the discovery of an important measurement, the Schumann resonance, which explained the remarkable changes I have witnessed with my clients as they worked through our program. What is the Schumann resonance and how does it apply to brainwaves and your well-being?

You see, the Earth is protected from the Sun's deadly rays due to an electromagnetic field that surrounds the Earth, sustained by the energy created by the 2000 or so thunderstorms that produce about 50 flashes of lightning around the planet every second (Hoffman, 2016). At the same time, the electromagnetic field has us grounded to the Earth, carrying electric charges inside our bodies and creating fields of our own. This helps us become receptive to the Schumann resonance's influence and attune ourselves to nature (Miller, 2013). Volland (1995) provided an accurate description of this important **atmospheric phenomenon:**

> Like waves of a spring, they are not present all the time, but have to be "excited" to be observed. They are not caused by anything internal to the Earth, its crust, or its core. They seem to be related to electrical activity in the atmosphere, particularly, during times of intense **lightning activity.**

In 1952, German physicist W.O. Schumann began to work with his students on electromagnetic waves in the atmosphere while teaching about the physics of electricity. He predicted there was a frequency connected between the inner and outer surface of the earth, for which he asked his students to calculate that frequency. Schumann calculated a frequency of 10 Hz. Later, Schumann and student colleague Herbert Konig detected a main resonance frequency of 7.83 Hz. Due to this groundbreaking work, a number of properties and characteristics dealing with electrical frequencies, more so, as the association of the Schumann Resonance with human bioactivity–– were established (Hoffman, 2016). (It is noteworthy that physicist and inventor Nikola Tesla was perhaps the first person to discover the Earth's resonance frequency when he carried out experiments fifty years earlier in Colorado Springs, Colorado, but his discovery wasn't taken seriously at **the time.**)

While significant research and dialogue have

occurred regarding the Schumann resonance, very few have knowledge of its value on human life. Notably, the frequency established by Schumann and the Alpha brainwave state have significant connections to human behavior. Is it possible that the advancements in our technology are interfering with the natural frequencies of the Earth and, as a result, we are witnessing an alarming rise in emotional disturbances experienced by so many people today? As a result, if we can train our brains to achieve peace and stability by slowing down the frequency to Alpha state, this may be a clue to resolving a growing number of emotional disturbances like anxiety, depression, and anger on a broader scale. For instance, a 2009 Japanese study recognized that "exposure to low-frequency" and "low-intensity electromagnetic fields can produce biological effects," such as the ones exhibited in the Schumann resonance (Mitsutake, et al., 2005).

Physician Anker Mueller read Schumann's research and drew the connection between the Schumann resonance and the Alpha rhythm of brainwaves. In 1979, Herbert König, one of Schumann's students and disciples, also compared human EEG recordings with natural electromagnetic fields in the environment, and discovered there was a correlation between the Schumann frequency and the human brain's Alpha rhythm. Likewise Dr. Wolfgang Ludwig discovered that manmade city electromagnetic technology operating made it difficult for him to record accurate measurements, so he took measurements in at sea and at underground mines where he could be assured of good electrical conductivity and stronger Schumann waves. In effect, Ludwig took measurements both above and below ground. But did he stumble upon this himself? Not really.

YIN AND YANG

In his later work, Ludwig came across the ancient Chinese teachings of the Yin and the Yang, which completed his research on Schumman waves. These well-known Taoist precepts state that to receive and align with perfect health, both signals––the masculine *Yin* and the feminine *Yang*––must be in balance. Yin looks at the world below, while Yang looks at the world above. It is also important to point out that there are three "basic themes" surrounding the Yin and the Yang: "[1] the coherent fabric of nature and mind [...]; [2] *jao* [interaction] between the waxing and waning of the cosmic and human realms, and [3] a process of harmonization enduring a constant, dynamic balance of all things" (Krentzman, 2015, Yang, n.d.).

Out of this, the associations made sense: Ludwig recognized that Yin represented the signal from below and Yang the symbol from above, meaning that he needed two environmental signals for accurate measurements. More so, research carried out by E. Jacobi at the University of Düsseldorf demonstrated through experimentation that the lack of either signal would cause serious health problems, even if the subject never had a compromised immune system (Martino, 2013; Dickerson, 2003). Now, doesn't it make sense that this earthly frequency is imperative to our health? With all our technological advancements, is the Schumann resonance being drowned out? The better the mind is balanced, the easier it is for it to heal the body. When we keep our minds close to the Schumann resonance, the stress levels decrease, and chronic illnesses like autoimmune disease, high blood pressure, inflammation, joint pain fatigue, heart palpitations, and lowered levels of melatonin production are relieved and even eliminated through the promotion of **Alpha brainwaves.**

THE SYMBOL

To help my clients remain in Alpha state, I will have them come up with a symbol that represents their centered mind. Symbols are important because they call the object they represent to our attention and recognition. They are the reason advertisers use logos, slogans, and other catchy marketing gimmicks. Every time you recognize a popular symbol, you know they've spent a considerable amount of money on consumer quality (or so you'd expect). If you studied at the University of Central Florida, you know that the Pegasus logo, the Knights image, and the black-and-gold motif add an emotional sense of value to your alma mater. In a way, those logos say something to you whenever you see them. Symbols serve as reminders of our limits, our future, and everything we stand for in our society (Routledge, 2010).

It's also important to clear up the distinctions between *symbols* and *signs*, as studied by Swiss psychologist Carl Jung:

> Whereas a sign just points to something (a green light is a sign we can go, for example) a symbol has far more resonance. We are familiar with the symbol, but it has layers of other

meaning for us to explore that is at first hidden. For example, a heart is an internal organ we all know. But it can also be about love, connection, and even life force (Jacobson & Blundell, 2016).

As Adams (2009) stated, visualization through mental imagery "enhance[s] motivation, increase[s] confidence and self-efficacy, improve[s] motor performance, prime[s] your brain for success, and increase[s] states of flow," while at the same time increasing your commitment to personal growth. This allows people to plan––*not* rehearse––their actions on a short- and long-term basis by increasing their confidence in their abilities to handle various complex situations without despair. More so, visualization through meditations helps exercise and secure neural pathways, develop a stronger cortex necessary for "abstract thought and introspection" and other complex tasks, and improves connections within the hippocampus (Jabr, 2013).

As a result, by conditioning his or her minds with a personal symbol of their choice, clients will be able to draw feelings of inner peace, which will center and balance their minds in whatever way it is needed. For instance, imagine you are going to a big meeting and you are very nervous about your part of the presentation. Your chosen symbol is a palm tree because that always gives you a peaceful feeling. So before, during, and after that work meeting, you would visualize or look at a picture of palm tree and watch how everything in your body calms down. You will perform better, and your mind will learn how to **relax naturally.**

However, keep in mind that whenever you venture out into nature, your mind is aligning itself with the energy of the Earth, which is why it becomes such a pleasurable feeling to have at your disposal. By connecting your symbol to the Earth's natural energy, you will learn to draw strength from within yourself, face challenges head-on without cheap aids or distractions, and use your brain to get yourself *Out of Your Mind*.

CHAPTER SIX

YOU MUST BE OUT OF YOUR ANXIOUS MIND

I am always amazed when people say they struggle with anxiety in a nonchalant voice, wearing it like a badge of honor, a thing of pride impeding them from achieving success. Some do yoga. Others take medication to solve the problem––but what does that tell you? The anxiety medication is not working. "Oh, but it would be worse if I wasn't on it." No! There's no need to submerge yourself in medications when you can eliminate the anxiety you feel on your own. In fact, a 2016 study published in the *Australian and New Zealand Journal of Psychiatry* revealed that a placebo treatment of "serotonin" and "oxytocin" sprays reduced depression and anxiety symptoms to patients who never knew it was only a placebo (Darragh, et al., 2016).

THE PHILOSOPHY OF ANXIETY

Think of psychologist Rollo May's words as you read through **this chapter:**

It always involves destroying the status quo, destroying old patterns within oneself, progressively destroying what one has clung to from childhood on, and creating new and original forms and ways of living. If one does not do this, one is refusing to grow, refusing to avail himself of his possibilities; one is shrinking his responsibility to himself (Popova, 2013).

Anxiety is a common emotion that in and of itself, functions as a boilerplate and disguises other primal emotions like fear and disgust. When we were children, we were afraid of the dark, so our parents might leave the door open or leave a night-light on to calm our fears. Growing up, our fears became more existential and surrounded us, pressuring ourselves to compete in order to survive. These anxieties have carried over and affect us today, even if we do not notice them on a daily basis. There is a reason we live in a so-called "Age of Anxiety," where the world is constantly *on edge* about something in particular, be it terrorism, finances, our work commute, technology, work, or anything else humanity can conveniently use as a scapegoat. Anxiety is only an emotion, but our overreaction or willful distractions to it only *empowers* it, and that leads sufferers to face such **debilitating distress.**

PANIC VS. ANXIETY

The main difference between panic and anxiety is related to the length and severity of the symptoms. When someone experiences a panic attack, the symptoms come suddenly and with extreme intensity. People describe the symptoms as coming "out of the blue," peak within minutes, and then subside, though there may be times when the attacks may last longer or recur. Should this happen, it is difficult to note when one panic attack finishes and another panic attack begins. The anticipatory anxiety only feeds and deepens the cycle (Rauch, 2017).

In order to fall into the category of a panic attack, there must be four or more of the following symptoms:

- **Heart palpitations;**

- **Accelerated heartbeat;**

- **Pounding heart;**

- Trembling **or shaking;**

- Chest pain or discomfort;

- Nausea or **abdominal distress;**

- Dizziness, lightheadedness, or faintness (though not necessarily fainting);

- Fear of dying;

- Choking sensations (though not necessarily choking);

- Excessive sweating;

- Numbness and tingling sensations in limbs and extremities;

- Shortness of breath or **difficulty breathing;**

- Feeling out of control or **going crazy;**

- Chills and hot flashes; and derealization, or the feeling of detachment from oneself (Ericson, 2014).

- Anyone experiencing a panic attack knows all too well what it is like, since even the most productive members of society suffer from panic attacks and panic disorder.

- A client of mine confessed she tried to hide it because she did not want to have people think she was crazy, even if she actually felt like she was crazy due to her panic attacks.

- Another person experienced panic attacks for over twenty years, and yet was on financially solid ground because he became an entrepreneur. This allowed him to call his own hours and duties. A panic attack could shut him down for anywhere between one to three days, so he would work extra hard to catch up after being decommissioned for any extended period. Even if he reinvented himself, he would still be under anxiety's grip, which threatened to destroy **his productivity.**

- Another lady I worked with is a supervisor at a large corporation, and suffered panic attacks on her commute to and from work. Even though she needed to drive her daughter everywhere, she attempted to conceal her panic attacks out of fear of losing her job or scaring her daughter––even though she already knew how much her mother struggled with trying to protect her. She was afraid that her daughter would somehow "catch" the disease––panic attacks are not contagious, though numerous studies have shown that genetics influence the propensity of panic and other anxiety disorders––and she desperately wanted to avoid that. She coped with a dose of strong coffee before the drive and chocolate for the commute, which perhaps exacerbated the anxiety due to the high doses of caffeine (Winson, Hardwick, & Jaberi, 2005).

Allow me to explain the role of heredity and anxiety: as revealed in a 2013 study, "certain anxiety traits correlated with panic disorder are evident by the age of 8" (Waszcruk, Zavos, & Eley, 2013). Personality traits may also preclude panic disorder. To explain, "low levels of sociability, high levels of arousal" and a neurotic and pessimistic temperament may be lead to the development of panic disorder (Na, Kang, Lee, & Yu, 2011). Lifetime prevalence of anxiety disorders is 28.8%, and its median age of onset is 11 years (Kessler, et al., 2005).

Anxiety is a very complex emotion whose sufferers are irrationally locked into fear despite not recognizing any trigger, because it represents "a sense of dread about something out there that seems menacing," even if the threat is minimal or nonexistent (Henig, 2009). Likewise, Strauss (2016) suggested another difference between fear and anxiety: whereas fear attempts to protect you from a "present threat," anxiety is much more complex in scope and is highly anticipatory of any future threats. More than a simple concern, anxiety is related to excessive worrying, dread, or anticipation about the future or an upcoming event. This is perceived by the subconscious mind as a threat, and it begins to kick into emergency mode to protect you, even if there is nothing actually there of threat to you. Although anxiety is viewed as being different from a panic attack, there are some similarities in symptoms. Symptoms may include: an increased heart rate; fatigue; restlessness; disturbed sleep; irritability; muscle tension; shortness of breath; dizziness; and difficulty concentrating or focusing (Winson, Hardwick, & Jaberi, 2005). Remember, however, that despite the differences, both anxiety and panic can be debilitating and isolating conditions if not treated accordingly, so you need to get out your mind as soon as you can.

Remember: if you feel anxiety, it's okay. You will not crash. You will not burn. You will not die. Anxiety is a normal and unpleasant emotion signaling an inconvenient feeling meant to trigger an action. This is neither the end of the world, nor the worst experience of your life––it's only an unpleasant feeling. Anxiety doesn't need medications or treatments to overcome.; The remedy involves a combination of discipline, rational thinking, and a **certain detachment.**

YOU MUST BE OUT OF YOUR ANXIOUS MIND

WHAT IS AN ANXIETY DISORDER?

If the anxiety you experience is too overwhelming and impedes your daily functioning, then you suffer from an anxiety disorder, as do one out of five Americans. Like other mood disorders, anxiety disorders are considered "internalizing disorders" or mood or emotions caused by "difficulties regulating negative emotions," oftentimes overlooked as natural temperament shyness making a person more likely to suffer from anxiety disorders, depressions, or both (Terzian, Hamilton, & Ericson, 2011; Shackman, 2015; Goldberg, 2016).

About 40 million Americans are diagnosed with at least one anxiety disorder, making them the most common mental illness in the country. Also, between 1996 and 1999, estimates regarding the economic cost of anxiety disorders ranged between $42 to $47 billion ($62 to $82 billion in 2016 when adjusted for inflation), and long-term opportunity costs would range in excess of $2,000 per year per person (Kessler & Greenberg, 2002). Let's take a look at some of the most well-**known disorders:**

GENERALIZED ANXIETY DISORDER (GAD)

For some people, anxiety is nothing but a mere annoyance. For others, the mere thought of *anything* going wrong triggers an endless, ongoing, and free-floating type of worry. For those who worry more days than not during six months about *everything* and *anything* surrounding everyday circumstances and events *excessively*, he or she can be diagnosed with Generalized Anxiety Disorder (GAD). Because the worry is chronic (as in long-lasting) and unfocused, it's simply tough to get rid of. The anxiety ebbs and flows according to life events, with it becoming stronger during stressful circumstances and during moments of conflict. Uncertainty, busyness, stress, and entertaining hypothetical "What If?" Questions, and ineffective worrying techniques that only further worries fuel the anxiety for sufferers. For sufferers, worrying "is a method of attempting to avoid future catastrophe" and "may represent an avalanche of affect in general or an anxious emotional experience" (Borkovec & Inz, 1990).

SOCIAL ANXIETY DISORDER

You may know people who are naturally jovial, charismatic, and easygoing. You may also know still others who enjoy their solitude and keep to themselves. Others are reserved, intimate, and have a tighter circle of friends. Still others are so irrationally anxious about judgment, rejection, or humiliation that they can't cope properly with every social situation. This condition is known as social anxiety disorder or "social phobia." From blushing and bodily sweating to nausea, rigid body postures, and alienation from crowded places, social anxiety can hamper a person's quality of life. As a result, social anxiety sufferers feel they cannot progress professionally, academically, and socially, and shun any social event out of fear of judgment or disinterest from others (Stein & Stein, 2008; Turk, Heimberg, & Magee, 2016).

SPECIFIC PHOBIAS

Everybody's afraid of something, be it snakes, airplanes, or even death. Remember that fear wants to request an action from you. Other individuals, however, are completely afraid of something that impairs their ability to function properly, even if the *actual danger* is arguably nonexistent. This is called a *phobia*, and it is oftentimes maintained by a cycle of avoidance of the anxiety-provoking stimulus, which only reinforces the irrational fear of such an object, animal, or person. According to the American Psychological Association, phobias are an irrational fear of something that appears discernibly dangerous, even if the threat is not proportionate to reality (Muris, Schmidt, & Merckelbach, 1999). The most common type of anxiety disorder, specific phobias are as numerous as the people who suffer them, and are divided into five types of fears: for animals (*arachnophobia*, or fear of spiders); the natural environment (*auroraphbia*, or fear of the northern lights [*Aurora Borealis*]); blood and needles (*hemophobia*, or fear of blood); situational fears (*aviophobia*, or fear of flying); or other fears not easily categorized (*coulrophobia*, or fear of clowns) (AnxietyBC, 2009).

OBSESSIVE-COMPULSIVE DISORDER (OCD)

Checking things once or twice is normal and sometimes warranted. However, if one can't leave the house without opening and closing the doors twenty times, or cleans every water faucet in the house every fifteen minutes, dresses in certain clothes that have "bad" colors or stays inside on certain days due to irrational and self-imposed superstitions, then that person may suffer from Obsessive-Compulsive Disorder (OCD). While no longer classified as an "anxiety disorder" in the DSM-5, this chronic condition has the sufferer go through "uncontrollable [and] recurring thoughts" which lead to compulsive behaviors that only temporarily keep anxiety symptoms at bay, aimed at "preventing or reducing distress or preventing some dreaded event." However, this behavior only serves to temporarily avoid the disturbing situations and strengthens the triggers (National Institute of Mental Health, 2016; Osmosis, 2016; Abramowitz, Taylor, & McKay, 2008). Obsessions can include germs, safety and the lack of certainty. At the same time, compulsions can range from cleaning to arranging or even checking and mentally counting numbers. OCD is common, chronic, distressing, and arises from a mixture of genetic and environmental causes, which are addressed by the Inspired Performance Program through certain time-tested techniques aimed to neutralize and clear the mind's **glitches**.

PANIC DISORDER AND AGORAPHOBIA

A common description for people suffering from panic attacks is to declare the event as the worst experience of his or her lives. As explained, the hallmark of the disorder is the *panic attack*, a "discrete episode of intense dread or fear" involving a strong urge to fight-or-flee the urgent threat, even if it is mental (Craske & Barlow, 2008). What makes panic attacks insidious is that the conditions mimic physical symptoms such as cardiovascular or gastrointestinal problem, which may be confused by the sufferer as a heart attack or another serious physical condition (Goodwin, et al., 2005).

Even when the panic attack is over, the person may continue to feel anxious for a time and fear another attack, which leads to panic disorder, as explained earlier. Because of this, it is very common for sufferers to modify their lifestyles in an attempt to fend off or control the onset of another panic attack. The behavioral changes caused by frequent panic attacks will complicate recovery and limit the ability to perform everyday routine tasks which then, if not treated properly, can develop into such phobias as *agoraphobia* as an avoidance technique. For this reason, the threefold relationship between pain, anxiety, and phobia can destroy a person's independence (Bouton, Mineka, & Barlow, 2001).

Someone suffering from agoraphobia is feeling afraid of "being in places or situations from which escape might be difficult (or embarrassing) or where help may not be available in the event of an unexpected or situationally predisposed panic attack" (Hara, et al., 2012). According to the Mayo Clinic, 1.8 million Americans over 18 years old suffer from agoraphobia without a history of panic disorder, while one in three with panic disorder will develop agoraphobia (Anxiety and Depression Association of America, 2016). Common fears for agoraphobics include loneliness, losing control, fear of leaving your home without someone else, and fear of going to places where escape may not occur during panic (Mayo Clinic, 2017).

AN IMPORTANT DISCLAIMER

It's very important for an individual to receive an accurate diagnosis of whether they truly are experiencing any type of anxiety disorder, since there are numerous medical and psychological disorders that mimic other symptoms. For example, people with recurrent abnormal heart rhythms may be misdiagnosed as having a panic attack. In addition, because the symptoms appear as physical distress, people will rush to the emergency room of the local hospital for assistance. For example, studies have shown that between 20% and 25% of all emergency room visits for chest pain are the result of a panic attack, and that these types of patients make between eight and ten visits per year for these symptoms.

Dr. Mohammed Memon, editor-in-chief of Medscape Reference, has cited that two out of five patients seeking emergency treatment due to chest pain are, in reality, suffering from a panic attack (Thomas C. , 2014; Huffman, Pollack, & Stern, 2002). However, a 2015 study has found that individuals with panic disorder are 36% more likely to suffer a heart attack and 47% more likely to suffer heart disease—even if these links remain controversial to address in practice (Whiteman, 2015).

It's imperative for people suffering any type of anxiety to receive help as soon as possible. Anxiety is not a feeling to live with or manage with costly and unnecessary medications and isolation. However, people avoid receiving the necessary help because they feel like they will be viewed as crazy, even though panic and anxiety can affect anybody. Instead, it is time to break out through the Inspired Performance Program and learn how to take back **your life!**

At the Inspired Performance Institute, we have developed a response to this using a process we call NEURO, standing for *Neuro Engagement Using Recall Optimization*. This process is part of the Inspired Performance Program, specifically targeted at reducing and eliminating the symptoms of panic attacks and anxiety. Combining psychological and physical elements, NEURO focuses on addressing the memory that begins the recall process and prompts the mind to reprocess and optimize mental data. Eventually, the alerts and breathing techniques will address the physical elements and calm the mind down.

In addition, we have added a wristband and application alerting the person that a panic attack is in process. You see, a panic attack starts up to an hour before the person realizes it is happening. Imagine not knowing a hurricane is approaching, something we take for granted today. By having this information ahead of time, before you have recognized any symptoms, you have a key to help in shutting them down and eventually eliminating them all together (Meuret, et al., 2011).

CORTISOL AND STRESS

Cortisol is a life-sustaining adrenal hormone released to balance and counter stress, which also maintains the body's homeostasis. Often referred to as "the stress hormone," cortisol modulates many of the changes that occur within the body due to stress, including glucose levels, autoimmune responses, anti-inflammatory actions, blood pressure, central nervous system activation, fats, proteins, carbohydrates, and our metabolism. Because of the way the human brain stores memory, if our minds stay highly aroused for too long, the stress response is activated so often that the body's homeostasis is disrupted, creating numerous health problems due to the excess of circulating cortisol in **the body:**

If a brain is triggered enough times for

survival, and the stress hormone cortisol is released, cell and neuron development are altered, and an excess of myelin, or white matter, develops. Communication slows between the amygdala (responsible for emotional process-ing) and the prefrontal cortex (responsible for memory, learning, decision-making, and the like), while it increases between the amygdala and the hypothalamus, where fight-or-flight begins (Zera, 2016).

When our body feels threatened, cortisol redis-tributes the energy in our body, but excessively high levels lead to high levels of fear and anxiety. Cortisol also damages the hippocampus, which as we learned is detrimental to memory and cognition, and may damage or alter the hormonal system. Severe damage to the hippocampus is believed to lead to dissociation, and in extreme cases results in Dissociative Identity Disorder (DID).

When the adrenal glands are exhausted, they no longer produce enough cortisol, which is crucial for maintaining body homeostasis. When there is not suf-ficient cortisol in the body, the individual is susceptible to autoimmune disorders, chronic pain, fatigue, asthma, allergies and more. Again, attempting to self-medicate the many symptoms that occur because of malfunction-ing adrenal glands, the abused individual often reaches for drugs **and alcohol.**

THE STORY OF ROBERT'S PANIC ATTACKS

In late 2015, Robert, a twenty-one-year-old, was introduced to me by a friend who had told her mother about the program. Robert's mother worried about him, because he lived at home and struggled to function. He wasn't getting along with his stepfather and she tried to mediate between the two. The stepfather tried to force-fully ingrain some discipline into him, but Robert wasn't accepting it. He wanted to move out, and any attempts at independence were stifled by panic attacks, which destroyed his quality **of life.**

The way his stepfather saw his panic attacks did not help, either—and his father saw Robert's struggle as lazi-ness and a moral failure. He was such a good employee, however, that his coworkers were more than willing to accommodate him. As life's demands piled up, Robert visited many specialists who only wanted to solve everything with medication. As a result, he self-med-icated with alcohol, marijuana, and pornography and became addicted to all three. I explained to Robert that he self-medicated because his mind was in pain and these substances temporarily numbed his mind, even if he knew they were addictive and would only worsen his anxiety. Within this, Robert identified abandonment and resentment issues with his father not being in his life since childhood. He was also bullied, so his step-father's threats of discipline triggered resentment. He also felt resentment against his mother because he felt unsupported by her when, in reality, her mother medi-ated between both men. As a result of the internal and external turmoil to Robert, thinking about them created emotional pain. Because his subconscious mind was aware of what was affecting it, it had a purpose: *survive*.

Knowledge is solving half the battle. Before going through the program, Robert assumed there was something wrong with him and resigned himself to the belief that there was no solution for his problems. After identifying several events that caused some error messages, he learned how to use our process to update his mind and clear the internal glitches. As Robert described these traumatic events for the first time, I could observe how the distress was lifted from his shoulders. In four hours, he was able to discuss any distressing event with no emotional distress. Shocked at how quickly it worked, Robert started laughing. Could it be this simple? Of course––his mind was rebooting on its own!

After rebooting, Robert listened to a series of audios best served to modify negative habits and behaviors. I started him on the *Walking Out Addiction* audios for 28 days, which addressed the way his mind coded the addictive substances and equated them to attempts at survival. Because the survival brain learns through repetition, the constant use of the substance told the survival mind what it needed, so it programmed it. The only way to stop the program was to to recode a new response that overrode the old neural pathways through repetition. By walking those negative behaviors out of the client's reach, he was finally ready to develop healthier habits.

Upon completing the first audio session, Robert continued with the *Walking in Gratitude* audios, which reinforced the positive changes Robert wanted in his life. Gratitude is an important value to develop in our lives, as the other-directed material or nonmaterial nature which stems from "the perception of a[n undeserved or unearned] positive personal outcome" because of someone elses's positive actions (Emmons & McCollough, 2004). Also, gratitude builds a sense of spirituality, fosters and improves friendships, and encourages people to feel appreciative for what others have done (2004). Behaviors like gratitude promote the "sedative and stress-reducing" effects of oxytocin, which plays an important role in social interactions such as "breastfeeding and sexual pleasure" (DeAngelis, 2008; Algoe & Heidt, 2009).

Robert became one of the most disciplined clients with whom I have ever had the pleasure to work.. He wanted to know exactly *why* and *how* things worked. He followed everything religiously, and would constantly follow up to make sure he was doing everything exactly right. That's why the program worked so well for Robert—his anxiety was eliminated, his addictions quickly dropped, and within two to three weeks he was living a normal life. In fact, one time he was with his friends, and one of them started smoking a joint, and he had no interest in it. He stopped drinking. He stopped smoking marijuana. He stopped watching porn. Due to his diligence, Robert was completely out of **his mind.**

One of Robert's friends asked him to visit his church, which he struggled with because he never considered himself as a spiritual person. While he did go to church, Robert was suddenly confronted with fire-and-brimstone preaching that overwhelmed him to the point of discomfort. Now he goes to church and is actively involved in youth groups. In the end, he has found God, and he has grown into the person he wishes **to be.**

PLAN, NOT PREDICT

In many cases, anxiety sufferers attempt to run away from anxiety-provoking experiences in a feeble attempt to control the future. Their thought process goes something like this: "I've got this important meeting coming up, but I do not like meetings because I do not speak very well in public. I do not want to be laughed at. I hope they accept me." This conundrum is known as "anxiety expectancy," where the "individual has learned that a given stimulus arouses anxiety and fear," such as the fear of a traumatic experience recurring in the future (Reiss, Peterson, Gursky, & McNally, 1986). This "fear of fear" is a mixture of negative experiences, biology, and personality that complicates any attempts at resolving the issue (1986). As a result, many predict how the event will unfold or what are the best words to say because, in their minds, the more control they (think they) have of this future event, the less likely are they to experience the shame and failure of the past. Writer and columnist Debbie Hampton explains how this type of predicting unfolds in your brain:

> Your brain has a natural composition to connect experiences, symbols, and ideas to make sense of its environment to ensure the survival of the species [...] This hardwired tendency has generally served us well, but it also causes a lot of unnecessary pain and anxiety as our brains jump to assumptions, make something out of nothing, and try to find a cause which leads to producing blame (Hampton, Your fortune-telling brain, 2014c).

Instead of predicting, I propose planning as a healthier and much less distressing alternative.

When you make predictions, you are set. That is why anxiety and panic reinforce predictions: if things do not go the way you expected them to, in the exact order of events within the exact time-frame, this experience reinforces the need to gain more control of the past. Instead of simple predictions, planning can provide the structure necessary to manage your expectations, but also offers you the flexibility to let go of control. If you suffer from anticipatory anxiety, you fear an anticipated, yet irrational, future event you believe is an "unpredictable threat" (Fristcher, 2017). In fact, anticipatory anxiety showcases five important facts (Seif, n.d.):

- The anticipated event is not a true predictor of how much anxiety we feel in **each situation;**

- the anxiety is real and **oftentimes misjudged;**

- the anxiety is quick to appear, but slow to disappear;

- the anxiety increases with indecision;

- the anxiety only triggers a sense of **disjointed restlessness.**

My wife had trouble avoiding fortune-telling for many years. For instance, if I had a big business meeting coming up, I would plan, sketch, and adhere to an extemporaneous list of talking points of the topics I wanted to discuss. She would worry about the outcome of the event, and she would be flabbergasted at my calm demeanor: "I don't understand; how are you so calm? You are going to meet them on Monday. It's the weekend. What if this goes wrong? What if they say that?" And I would always respond to the lines of, "Well, I don't know what they're going to say. When I get to the meeting, I will be prepared for what they say and I will respond accordingly. However, if I tried to predict every move, every thought, and every conversation, I would have built up anxiety. I have no idea what will happen. I only have to show up, be present, and then trust the fact that my mind can handle however they respond to me. If I don't have an answer, I will just say I don't have an answer."

As Peterson (2015) discussed, "When we automatically project [our innermost fears], we take our own thoughts of self-doubt [...] and assume others are thinking those very same things." Instead of allowing my feelings to build up and look at a simple business meeting as a threat to my survival, I will nip my thoughts in the bud and be aware of the atmospheric conditions any time my mind tries to forecast its own results. Planning does not mean that we will not show any concern for the future; it means that, whatever happens, we will be prepared to handle the consequences. One of the many tricks anxiety plays is destroying one's ability to manage life's circumstances. Planning means that you're giving yourself a chance to persevere and innovate––and this is something everybody who wants to be successful needs anyway (Zipp, n.d.). We must clear up the things that were creating it, and stop our minds from trying to forecast results.

THE STORY OF RITA, THE THERAPY JUNKIE

Rita learned about our program through a friend and contacted me because she was interested in our radically different approach. She was a *bona fide* health nut: she did yoga: she had a personal coach, various therapists who diagnosed her with different illnesses, and took at least five different medications. However, Rita was all over the place, and these things merely served as distractions (and pocket-burners) for the problems that hindered her. Yes, Rita wanted to look healthy, feel healthy, and be healthy. However, the things that she attempted to help herself hurt Rita even more, because she could not stop searching for reassurance.

In fact, she was a very beautiful woman in great shape, but childhood torment continued to affect her relationships. She was in her middle age, so she felt that her biological clock was ticking. However, because of a nasty and bitter divorce, Rita felt inordinate amounts of anxiety when meeting other guys, and that anxiety resulted in her inability to build relationships with people because she was projecting her thoughts and actions to them. All of this led to her feeling "a sense of meaningless and absence" in her frantic need for self-improvement (Cushman, 1900).

Rita's trauma came from childhood, when her own mother lost her parents in a tragic accident. Because that event happened during her pregnancy, Rita's mother could not process her grief and depression and connect with her daughter as soon as she was born. Rita carried that pain for many years. Abandonment issues also colored her relationship with her divorced father, who wasn't in the picture as he moved on with a new family of his own. While her parents loved her, Rita never felt attachment or attention from them, leading her to face a childhood riddled with self-imposed isolation and loneliness. For this reason, relationships were a very important and a time-consuming affair for her, and she attempted to control every aspect of her relationships by projecting her fears and unattainable expectations on her partners. She believed that having a mental script would afford her control, but at the time I met Rita, her most recent relationship was falling apart.

During her session, Rita would predict every conversation with her partner, telling me in excruciating detail what she would say and how he would react. If the conversation inevitably derailed from Rita's well-entrenched predictions, panic would ensue. The play that she scripted became an improv. In this case, the key to solving her maladaptive projection was to clear the atmospheric conditions and teach her mind how to plan, and not predict. As Paul (2016) reflected upon anxiety and the need for certainty, "The anxious mind often spins in overdrive as it looks for a guarantee that the relationship will not end in failure."

Rita's fortune-telling undermined her ability to handle things, because it never worked out the way she wanted it to. o. Whenever the mental script she wrote was thrown out the window, the result was a reinforcement of her powerlessness. The more she tried to control it, the more she realized she had no control. The problem with her mind-reading was accuracy, as it was impossible to recognize other's emotions, and she automatically assumed that others were thinking negatively of her when she never even challenged *if* that was what people actually thought of her (Covin, 2012). To solve her distress, Rita needed to understand that she doesn't need to be in control, only in the moment.

Through the program, Rita learned how to live and be present in the moment. She finally discovered that she was smart, beautiful, and would meet someone who would love her for who she truly was. She slowly tapered off her medications. She improved her relationship with her mother by understanding the circumstances surrounding her depression. Also, even though she always had a good relationship with her kids despite their own hurts due to the divorce, Rita now felt reassured of her skills as a mother, and understood she was a much better mom than she realized. Before the program, Rita was very anxious and insecure; now, the real Rita, hidden in the deep recesses of the subconscious mind, flourished into her new and **improved self.**

THE LOTTERY

One of the stories I used with Rita relates to the lottery:

> When you buy a ticket for the lottery, do you assume that you are winning a lottery, or do you understand that it is a chance? If you *think* about winning the lottery, but you never *buy* a ticket, you'll never give yourself a chance to win. If you choose to try your luck, you'll buy the ticket and see what happens. If you win, you win it, and if you don't you don't. You can't predict with absolute certainty you'll win the lottery,

because the odds are always stacked against you. In this case, it's important to understand the difference between planning, and predicting: I *plan* on buying the ticket and fulfilling my wildest dreams with it, but if I don't, then it's simply a waste of time and two dollars. If I want to buy another ticket, I'm free to do so for the next drawing; if I don't want to, then I don't need to.

By understanding how planning can detach you from anxiety, you are empowered to course through many options that predicting will not allow. In Rita's case, she would be crushed if, say, her boyfriend suddenly called and could not fulfill a certain event in time due to sudden work obligations. Rita's life would fall apart in a mixture of anxiety, panic, and powerlessness. After completing the program, she learned the value of flexibility in her life, which led her to shed anxiety from her plans without any emotional investment.

THE STORY OF RHONDA AND TRICHOTILLOMANIA

Rhonda lived through a lifetime of trauma: she suffered through sexual abuse and molestation; she had breast cancer, which lead to a double mastectomy; and she suffered from panic attacks and anxiety, which severely impaired her daily functioning. I learned about her heart-wrenching story through Dr. Alexander Gimon, a recognized neuropsychologist, who asked me to assist him in this special case. However, there was a catch: instead of a the one-time, four-hour session accustomed by the program, I worked with Rhonda through eight weekly sessions as she committed to the program in between sessions.

Separate incidents of rape and child molestation by relatives caused Rhonda an extraordinary amount of distress. The silence and dismissal of these sexual assaults as a young child led her to develop trichotillomania (hair pulling disorder) as a way to cope with stress. Much like self-mutilation in any form, this serves the sufferer as a away to feel better: "Pulling hair reduces feelings of anxiety and frustration, anxiety, boredom, and sadness and this issue is the reason why hair pulling seems to increase with stressful live events" (Rehm & Slikboer, 2015). She felt ashamed and embarrassed due to her hair pulling, which she attempted to disguise from friends and family by the use of wigs. You wouldn't notice it, but wigs protected her from relationships, as relation-ships were cumbersome because she was afraid her wigs would come off—which then furthered her anxiety. During our sessions, Rhonda informed me that she went as far as using tweezers to **remove hair.**

She also suffered from anxiety and panic attacks, where she would think her car was falling apart as she was driving, pulling the car over to make sure the wheels had not come off the car, even having her children reas-sure her. Reassurance-seeking is addictive, demanding, and reinforcing in its own right, because the sufferer superstitiously believes that reassurance is gratifying enough to avoid future pain (Ferenciak, 2015; Osborne & Williams, 2013). Instead of interacting with them like any mother would, Rita's anxiety only created a distance between her and **her children.**

It did not help that she lived with her mother-in-law, who was dismissive as the rest of her family towards her sexual trauma. Rita was enraged over the dismissal, because she never felt protected by her mother. The dysfunctional relationships Rhonda experienced throughout her life further escalated her anxiety, to the point where she became overprotective with her children, constantly worrying something could happen to them.

Within a minute of meeting Rhonda, she began to cry even though we had not discussed anything. You see, Rhonda felt crazy and wanted to be reassured she was crazy. In fact, when she said she was crazy, I calmly replied, "I don't think you're crazy."

She was stunned. "Don't you think it's crazy to be pulling out all of my hair on my head with tweezers?"

I replied, "No; I think you have been trying to feel better." That was something new to her ears. For the first time in a long time, she stopped looking at herself as "crazy." I calmly understood her plight: "I bet you started feeling better when you start pulling the hair." She stopped crying. So, then I said, "your mind has been in pain from some events and experiences throughout your life and the only solution available up until today was to pull out your hair. It's not the best way to cope with overwhelming feelings, but now we know why you're doing it." I had her undivided attention. "There's nothing wrong with your mind. Your mind is fine. It's trying to survive the best way it knows how. Today, I'm going to show you why your mind has been doing what it's been doing and provide a new solution.

How does that sound?" She smiled, beaming full of pride and hope.

Harbeck (2016) explained that "[Crazy] is used to describe something that people with some kinds of anxieties are afraid of becoming or being seen as." For instance, a person suffering panic attacks suffers the "fear of going *crazy* [emphasis added]," or a person with social anxiety fears being judged as "crazy" by his or her peers. Defining some*thing* or some*one* as "crazy" because of uncommon or unorthodox experiences does not necessarily merit such a label (Field, 2014). Even Muhaiyaddeen (2007) considered every desire as tantamount to being considered crazy. Everybody experiences life, and the effects it has on the way our minds work is profound. Many people experience emotional pain and are still looking for a way to feel better. Some use substances while others turn to depression and shut down. Still others strike out at the world with a proverbial chip on the shoulder, with anger and rage. Rhonda's solution was pulling out her hair. What does that say about her or any of the other people attempting to stop their emotional pain? *Nothing!* Her distress is only a sign that we're all human and wish to be out **of pain.**

By following through the program, I am pleased to report that Rhonda's life has improved dramatically. Her panic attacks no longer affect her quality of life. She can drive her children to school without believing the wheels will fly off the axle. The kids are saying, "I like driving with you now!" when before going through the program, they wouldn't even like being in the car with her due to her panicky episodes. Her eldest son, a ten-year-old, came with her to one of her sessions, so Dr.

Gimon, Rhonda, and I could explain to him his mother's improvement. In a matter-of-fact way, he said, "Yeah––I can see it." This program also improved her relationship with others and allowed her to feel more confident in her own skin, without a wig. She was finally out of her mind, and her anxiety no longer took power over her.

Let these success stories inspire you to get you *Out of Your Mind* and break through the anxiety that hinders you. Do not let anxiety determine your future––it's time to kick anxiety to the curb and move towards **the future!**

CHAPTER SEVEN

TRAUMA, CHRONIC ILLNESS, AND BEING OUT OF YOUR MIND

My wife has a thyroid malfunction: she suffers from Hashimoto's disease (also known as *chronic lymphocytic thyroiditis* or *hypothyroidism*), an autoimmune disorder that attacks her overactive and partly burned out thyroid, a small gland at the base of your neck below your Adam's apple. This gland affects many hormonal functions within the body, as it controls and balances the body's energy, regulates gut motility (how fast nutrients are moving through the gut), affects skin hydration, and regulates the body's temperature (Wentz, 2015). Long-term stress causes the adrenal glands to over produce hormones, resulting in our bodies responding with inflammation and disease, along with fatigue, weakness, dry skin, and weight gain. Medicine has just recently started to recognize the occurrence of thyroid issues and stress, so not one physician she visited asked her about her childhood trauma—except her family doctor.

As a child, only her family doctor asked with tact

and wisdom about her trauma. Yet her response was typical of children in abusive situations: nothing was wrong, nothing happened, and everything was okay. This flabbergasted him. Why would his patient say that nothing was wrong, even within the constraints of doctor-patient confidentiality? There is only one circumstance that could severely hinder getting the help she needed: *fear*. She was afraid of retribution and that her confession would tear her family apart. She feared becoming a scapegoat to her family, especially to a father looking for any signs of weakness. She feared losing the only source of survival for a young child. That, in and of itself, is a major problem; most people refuse to talk about their trauma, and shame keeps them from admitting it later. Had Bridget been aware of the terrible aftermath of trauma earlier in her life, there is no doubt she could have done something about it, especially if the Inspired Performance Program were developed earlier. Only now is the strong connection between a woman's stress response and her thyroid function recognized by the medical community when, at no time during Bridget's earlier life, had a doctor made that link.

Our concept of pain tends to be limited to the physical. However, as Krane (2011) suggested, pain is persistent and easily mutates into other diseases. The idea of pain being a permanent fixture in someone's life is unfathomable––no human can withstand so much bodily punishment. Unfortunately, chronic illnesses are damaging, extensive, and growing at an alarmingly high rate in American society. Many causes are attributed to the growth of chronic diseases: our fast-paced, convenient, sedentary lifestyle; an overabundance of cheap, mass-produced foods; our neurotic attitude towards exercise; technology; our broken healthcare system; our bad posture, and so on. The list continues, the blame games rage on, and people get sicker and sicker. What's lost with preventable diseases is two-fold: first, we lose productivity for the sake of our health; and secondly, we lose our health itself when most of these preventable diseases are *completely avoidable*. Even when struggling with a chronic disease, however, there is still a chance to be out of your mind and enjoy a happier and **healthier lifestyle.**

"Disease" or "Illness?"

In previous paragraphs, I've used words like "disease" and "illness" interchangeably. Even though they have similar approaches, their definitions may differ according to the beholder. For Eisenberg (1977), "patients suffer *'illnesses'*" and "doctors diagnose and treat 'diseases'." Whereas *disease* reflects any abnormalities in proper bodily organs and systems, *illness* suggests the perceived experience in a patient's "state of being." In other terms, a disease is a *medical* term, while an illness is *social and psychological*—a person can *feel* ill when there aren't any *medical* indicators of a disease (**Table 8**).

It is noteworthy to understand that both terms are not mutually exclusive. Both can occur in the absence of illness. A patient can have a disease without feeling an illness—for instance, someone can be diagnosed with cancer without experiencing any symptoms until much later. Likewise, a patient can have an illness without feeling a disease, as is the case of health anxiety, formerly known as hypochondriasis, where people worry excessively and irrationally about their health, constantly seeking reassurance of their illness even if nothing provides a logical cause or reason for their **perceived illness.**

WHAT IS A CHRONIC DISEASE?

Now that you understand the differences between both terms, it is also important to understand how many organizations define *chronic disease* and how that impacts a person's chances for access to treatment. According to the U.S. National Center for Health Statistics, a chronic disease is defined as "a disease lasting three months or longer" (National Health Council, 2014). In turn, the World Health Organization uses the term "noncommunicable diseases" (NCOs) that are "not passed from person to person [and] are of long duration and generally slow progression" (World Health Organization). There are four types of chronic diseases: cardiovascular diseases like stroke and arrhythmia; cancer; chronic respiratory diseases; and diabetes.

Chronic diseases in the world represent 63% of all deaths worldwide. In the United States, seven out of ten deaths are caused by chronic diseases, 133 million Americans live with at least one of the four main types of diseases, and 75% of rising healthcare costs are attributed to chronic illnesses affecting people of all ages and lifespans (Shim). Additionally, racial and ethnic, rural and urban, and socioeconomic disparities further the troubling circumstances surrounding chronic diseases (Shim). As a result, comorbidity (the simultaneous presence of two chronic diseases or conditions within a patient) is high for mental disorders and chronic conditions. Chronic diseases hinder independence, even if some believe that freedom from disease means that symptoms are simply not visible (Illinois Public Health and Disability Program, 2012).

Table 8: Table displaying the differences between the terms "disease" and "illness."

Disease	Illness
• Structural and functional abnormality of bodily organs and systems	• Patient's subjective response to feeling unwell
• Pathological process undertaken on a cellular or a subcellular level	• Social/psychological phenomena directly influence by disease
• Can occur in the absence of illness––patients can learn of their disease despite feeling no symptoms	• Can occur in the absence of disease (e.g.: hypochondriasis/health anxiety)

GRIEVING A CHRONIC DISEASE

Even with the amount of studies and information available, diagnosing a chronic disease for a patient can be troubling and––if not handled properly––traumatic. Learning there is enough time to successfully reverse or even eliminate the threat can be a watershed moment in a patient's life. Alternately, this can be the moment where the patient is resigned to despair, regret, and remorse. It all depends on the patient's resilience, motivation, and family support aiming in unison to good health, which can be defined as "not only the absence of disease, but a condition of perfect physical, mental, and social wellbeing"––and grief, oddly enough, can be

a picture of health (Schiavon, Marchetti, Gurgel, Busnello, & Reppold, 2014).

Grieving the beginning of a chronic disease is radically different from losing a loved one who has passed
away. While grieving a loved one, there is always a light
sense of relief and knowledge that the pain will eventually pass. With a chronic disease, however, the image
of illness must change in order to reflect the sufferer's
reality. There may be new limitations to consider. There
may be a loss of personal autonomy. Grief, like the rest of
life circumstances, is not linear nor should it be rushed.
Instead, it can be divided in six interlocking phases that
target one's actions and beliefs (Jamie, 2010; Kübler-
Ross, n.d.).

CRISIS

This stage is full of frantic energy and fear, since
the sufferer cannot understand the cause and origin of
the illness (Jamie, 2010). Meeting normal physical and
daily demands becomes impossible due to mental overwhelm. In addition, denial of the chronic disease's new
reality may occur, because it eases a person's emotional
overwhelm and displaces the irrational constraints of
grief with something else beyond the person's control
or comprehension (Kübler-Ross, n.d.).

ISOLATION

In this stage, a realization if the illness' chronically
occurs, resulting in a major shift in the patient's experience. The ill person may feel resentment towards friends
and family, and may isolate him- or herself, if they do not

encourage good communication. . Since "nobody but the patient can fully comprehend the devastation of their losses," friends and family may slowly withdraw from the patient's life, even if some mean no ill will (Jamie, 2010). Isolation becomes harder if the patient used to be a caretaker or a provider and must now be taken care of and provided for due to **the disease.**

ANGER

Because of the strain on the family's financial resources, the sense of loss, and the lack of control, anger brews in the patient's life. This doesn't mean that the patient was feeling angry before the diagnosis. Rather, the circumstances attract a helplessness and worthlessness that can oftentimes be compounded by anger. That said, there is an important societal dimension to anger, more so in our society where anger is treated as something to be feared. Thus, to avoid a furthering of anger to dangerous levels, the patient needs structure in life (Jamie, 2010; Kilpatrick, Edmunds, & Seymour, 1992).

RECONSTRUCTION

Reconstruction involves re-evaluating a person's identity. At this point, the patient feels increasingly empowered to enjoy remissions and find personal strength in setbacks. Skills and hobbies, spending time with friends and family, and setting proper boundaries allow the patient to affirm his or her personal identity despite the disease. Adapting reconstruction to the general stages of grief model developed by Kübler-Ross and Kessler, a *positive bargaining* occurs, even as the patient learns to come to terms with the chronic illness

(Kübler-Ross, n.d.; Jamie, 2010).

INTERMITTENT DEPRESSION

However, the patient's self-reinvention is incomplete. When the patient remembers the simplicity of the past before suffering chronic illness, the patient can fall into despair and depression by nostalgia (Kübler-Ross, n.d.). Because depression can be "unnatural" to the patient, guilt is compounded because such grief needs to be resolved as quickly as possible. A dual awareness of function and loss triggers depression.

RENEWAL

In the end, the hopelessness of depression and new-found abilities, the patient enters into a stage of renewal within him- or herself. New relationships are formed, connections are created, and the person proceeds in awareness and self-growth. Awareness and self-growth helps for the patient to learn to be proud of accomplishments, however small may be. Acceptance and recognition of the trauma of chronic illness helps the sufferer maintain a sense of peace and grounding, lessening emotions such as denial, obsessive thoughts, and rage (Seifter, 2010). In addition, this optimism serves to motivate the individual to take greater strides in improving their health overall (Schiavon, Marchetti, Gurgel, Busnello, & Reppold, 2014).

THE STORY OF JENNY AND CROHN'S DISEASE

Jenny was referred to the Inspired Performance Institute by a therapist who learned of our program. She suffered from Crohn's disease, and the debilitating flare-ups forced her to become a self-employed entrepreneur, because keeping a regular job would be significantly difficult for her and her future employers, as her illness would lead to hospitalization and countless days of sickness. However, what was so shocking about Jenny's case is not the fact that her chronic illness would force her to sit out on life; but rather, it was where it came from: a traumatic experience when she was ten years old, witnessing her father's **death**.

One day, Jenny came home from school and saw an ambulance taking her father away. That image was burned in her mind, and she never felt any resolution of her pain as the adults surrounding the scene tried to hush her and move away—even though as a ten-year-old, she knew what was happening. Even today, if she would saw an ambulance and its flashing lights, and she would re-live the moments of her father's death. The error messages stuck within her mind wanted her to make it different: Get in the ambulance. Say good-bye. Have some closure. Her mind said she could do it differently, because her mind continued to register the past as if it were still happening in the present.

She loved her father, and she shared a beautiful childhood with him. He was very important to her. Her mother never wanted to talk about the pain, because her mother would become emotional if anybody talked about her husband. To complicate matters, Jenny's mother suffered through financial struggles that forced her mother to lose any sense of security. Since she internalized grief as something unacceptable, the resulting stress may have triggered her Crohn's, as carrying her pain internally compounded **her stress.**

Within her session, Jenny returned to the traumatic event and allow her mind to reprocess it through a different lens, without any emotions involved. She also understood the adults around her weren't trying to actively *keep her* away from her father. Instead, they wanted to protect her from further trauma. Maybe her father had already died, or maybe he was too horribly disfigured to be recognizable for a child––who knows what condition he was in at that point? All are well-intentioned responses, even if they unknowingly caused more trauma for Jenny by completely shutting her out from the grieving process. Her resentment against her mother subsided, allowing her to find peace and resolution. If you remember from past chapters, you could say that Jenny internalized that event in such a way because she did not have any life experience to counter her judgment. As an adult, you'd probably think it was a good idea to keep a young child insulated from death until the appropriate time arrived to allow a safe grieving process.

To date, Jenny has stopped having any flare-ups. Once she resolved her trauma, her relationship with her mother improved because a lot of the anger she had about the circumstances resulted from only looking at one side of the story. Now she had greater compassion at the atmospheric conditions surrounding her mother's grief. In the end, Crohn's no longer became a threat to her survival, and she could finally live a **peaceful life.**

Fight-or-Flight!

As mentioned, chronic disease has the power to destroy lives––if people allow it. The mind and body have a significant connection and interact on every level. There is a ripple effect from early childhood trauma, and that ripple can cause more than psychological issues. Our brain biology and immune functions are influenced. However, we need to know *what* is damaged due to the onslaught of **chronic disease.**

First described in 1914, the fight-or-flight response is a complex physiological response that prepares the body for fighting or fleeing. Stressors cause a response from the sympathetic nervous system, in effect suppressing the calming effect of the parasympathetic nervous

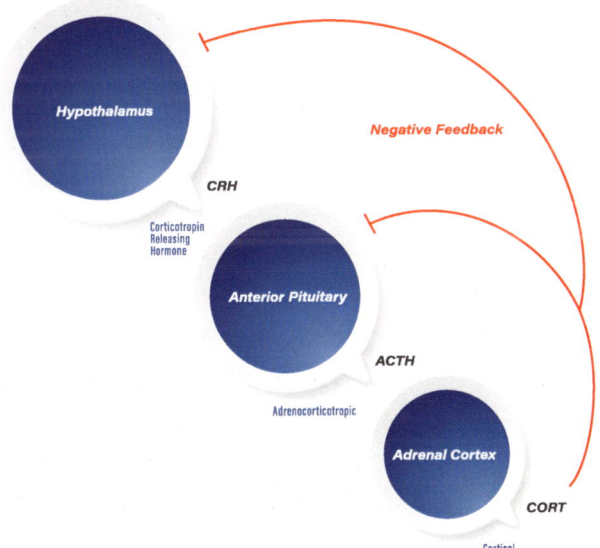

Figure 15: Basic hypothalamic-pituitary-adrenal axis (HPA) summary, Brian M. Swells (2012), via Wikimedia Commons. Used under creative commons Attribution 3.0 Unported license, https://creativecommons.org/licenses/by-sa/3.0/deed.en,

system. The hypothalamus secretes hormones that will in turn influence the kidneys and the brain. This flooding of secreted hormones ripple through various bodily systems, including the cardiovascular, gastric, respiratory, endocrine, and immune systems. These hormone secretions have a direct correlation to brain function, and affect the immune system in particular. When the hypothalamic-pituitary-adrenal (HPA) axis becomes involved, there is a significant influence on physical and psychological functioning **(Figure 16)**.

The problem with fight-or-flight is not about responding to threats. It is a perfect design that works extremely well, as our survival depends on our body's ability to protect us.. However, there is a timing issue in the human brain––we need this system to turn on when it is appropriate, and turn off when the threat is over or nonexistent. That is exactly what happens in the animal mind.

THE STORY OF A RABBIT AND A HOUNDING WOLF

If a rabbit experiences a hunger sensation, the rabbit will look for something to eat. If the rabbit finds some

Figure 16: Hase im Gallop by Alexande o]Oberst Cecchetti, 2016, https://stock. adobe.com/84810170

carrots to eat and suddenly looks up a sees a wolf, what will happen to the hunger sensation? It will shut off immediately and be replaced by a more appropriate response to the wolf – fear. So now, the rabbit's body is being prepared to run. Its heart rate increases, its breathing accelerates, all to make the rabbit stronger. The rabbit doesn't choose to do this; it is a programmed response to a threat happening in milliseconds, without the rabbit even realizing it. So now the rabbit runs away and makes it safely to its rabbit hole. The system worked successfully to protect the rabbit. When the rabbit can no longer see the wolf, smell the wolf or hear the wolf, what will happen to the emotion of fear? It shuts off, exactly as it should. The senses work as a perfect system designed to protect animals from the harsh realities of the world.

Humans exhibit the same operating system as the rest of the animal kingdom. However, if the human system turns on when it is appropriate, and then stays on or is reactivated by the memory of the event, it becomes a perpetual wolf. For Jenny, the threat to her survival––the death of her father––continued to play over and over in her mind. The sound of a siren, the sight of an ambulance, a hearse or hospital could cause her mind to look at the hi-res images of those traumatic moments when she was ten years old. Viewing these subconscious images in real time, her mind engineered a response to the threat. It released hormones, creating a physiological response to the threat. For Jenny, this process continued over and over. In her case, the stress on her immune system was overwhelming, and led her to suffer Crohn's disease when her body could not handle that stressload.

Nonetheless, the flight-or-fight response only works as an *emergency* system, not as an *operating* system. The system's design is perfect and works extremely well for the animal world. However, the advancements of the human brain, memory and conscious awareness have created the serious psychological issues we are being faced with in our society. So can you see why abuse and trauma survivors suffer so many physical health issues? This is the same reason soldiers returning from war struggle when they return to their regular life in society. Their emergency system was turned on for such an extended period it overwhelmed the body's normal everyday functioning systems. Our bodies just aren't built to handle that kind of stress.

This extension of the normal fight or flight process is the root of the emotional distress many people are experiencing, which in turn, is caused by the storing data from traumatic or disturbing events in high resolution. Have you ever seen someone explode with anger in a situation that seems benign at best, or annoying at worst? Rather, they overreact to past real-time images, which become overwhelming when recalled by the subconscious, so that the threat appears to be much larger than it really is. It never ends well because resentment can build from unpreedictable situations like random outbursts of anger, which makes no sense because the words or actions from the other person shouldn't evoke such a response. To both parties, that combative and defensive stance doesn't work either. It's only an automated response to threats, and understanding that can be very healing for all parties. Fixing the error messages is the *only* **answer.**

INFLAMMATION

When we have a physical injury to the body, we

expect it to become swollen and inflamed. Did you know the same holds true when an emotional or psychological injury occurs? The inflammation is, what I believe, creates a lot of the illnesses and diseases we are experiencing. Allow me to explain: It is quite common for a client to tell me he or she suffers from an autoimmune disease like lupus, and I'll immediately find out there have been some disturbing and traumatic events in her history. Researchers are discovering there is a correlation found in blood samples taken from women who have a history of trauma and biomarkers of inflammation are found in the blood. As a result, people are much more prone to disease when their immune system is affected by the trauma or **disturbing event.**

In 1978, Dr. Ryke Geerd Hamer, an oncology internist at the University of Munich, got the shocking news that his son had been shot, who died several months later. Within a few months, Dr. Hamer also learned he had testicular cancer. He connected the trauma of his son's death with his cancer diagnosis. Soon after, he began his own research in order to investigate a connection through his patients' experiences, discovering that all his patients had experienced an exceptionally stressful episode prior to their diagnosis. This information led the doctor on a mission to discover that *every* disease has a link to a specific area in the brain. He titled the research as *The Five Biological Laws of the New Medicine.* Despite his evidence, Dr. Hamer received a lot of criticism and condemnation despite more than thirty scientific verifications by independent physicians and associations; in 1986, he was stripped of his medical license due to malpractice, because he refused to submit to the principles of standard medicine.[1] Despite this setback, his work continued, and by the next year he was able to demonstrate his discoveries to almost every known disease known to medicine. These principles extend into the work we are doing. The trauma affects an area of the brain and inflammation is the result. The inflammation suspends the immune system, and then disease begins to form. The solution is to go back to the root cause, the traumatic event, and clear up the glitch in the memory and consistent recall of the event.

In cases of people with severe mental health disorders, the model of dopamine or serotonin dysfunction is diagnosed by most doctors. However, my ideas on what is happening seem to fall in line with newer research. There is a move to a multi-faceted neurotoxicity and neuroprogression model of impairment that is affecting inflammation and immune suppression. What seems to be missing is the solution to the inflammation, something we believe our program does assist with. You see, when we are under stress, it will cause inflammation. I believe the inflammation is a pause to allow the trauma to begin healing. The problem is, we store the memory of the trauma in high-res and every time we recall the memory we reignite the inflammation. This

---

1 Hamer titled his medical doctrine as "Germanic" because he believed his concepts were an alternative to the "Jewish" conspiracy theories regarding Western treatments of cancer, including chemotherapy and medication, which also leads to dangerous ties to former Nazi medicinal practices. As a professional, while I do not advocate for Dr. Hamer's philosophy and morality, I am certain his contributions to understanding the role of emotions in cancer should still be taken into consideration as part of the value of the Inspired Performance Program.

inflammation suppresses or compromises the immune system, and system **dysfunction occurs.**

The current solution to this dysfunction is medication, but there are more natural ways to address this. For example, natural products that are suggested by the holistic community are just as effective and do not have side effects or addictive properties. For instance, Omega-3 fatty acids, commonly found in fish oil, is recommended to help people with impaired brain functioning and also works as an anti-inflammatory. Doesn't that make sense? Reduce the inflammation, and the system goes back online. I've heard for a long time about the benefits of the anti-psychotics provided for patients suffering from various mental disorders. They work, but not for the reasons they claim: Big Pharma claims that medications affect the neurotransmitters like serotonin and dopamine. Is it possible that the patient is suffering from the dysfunction with neurotransmitters because of inflammation? The inflammation caused by trauma? The inflammation takes the neurotransmitters offline and the patient suffers various symptoms like mania **and depression.**

Here is another example, which I do not advocate by any means: The evidence is demonstrating that researchers have found that (WebMD, n.d.). LSD is effective for people suffering from mood disorders. The substance that is creating the benefit is called psilocybin, a psychedelic substance found in mushrooms (Singal, 2016). So why are people advocating for it? Because it's a quick fix that works—but that is not the answer because of its illegality and addictiveness. There are many side effects, not to mention the psychoactive and hallucinogenic properties. These effects include altering perception, brain function, difficulty thinking, and hallucinations. People use it because it makes them feel better. So then, why are they feeling better? Simply, psilocybin is an anti-inflammatory; once it is ingested, it rapidly metabolizes in the liver and converts into psilocin, which circulates in the bloodstream and reaches the brain, binding them to neurochemical receptors in the brain and soon will cause a decrease in blood flow in parts of the brain.

As you read this book, you are now beginning to understand why our program is a better solution. It is quick and natural: Clear the mind for the continuous recalling of the traumatic memory and the inflammation goes down because the threat, the trauma is eliminated. The only thing that is necessary is to remove the glitch, the error message and the inflammation goes down, and the system is **back online**.

THE VALUE OF STRESS

Notice how stress plays an important role in provoking *and* furthering symptoms of chronic stress. Even if some stress is normal and necessary, *chronic* stress is not without long-term effects. At least 40% of American adults suffer insomnia because of stress, and conditions such as cardiovascular disease, obesity, high blood pressure, irritable bowel syndrome, and diabetes are only exacerbated by stress. In reality, how do we define it, and what happens when it becomes an unwelcome, yet permanent fixture in **our lives**?

According to Salleh (2008), stress is "a process in which environmental demands strain an organism's adaptive capacity in both phsychological demands as well as biological changes that could [place a person] at risk for illness. A *stressor* includes any event or action that induces stress in the body, such as work, child-care, trauma, and unemployment (Alvord, Davidson, Kelly, McGuinness, & Tovian, n.d.). For instance, you're "stressed" about paying your bills on time, or excessively burdened about other projects at work or in the near future. In those moments, stress acts as a trigger for you to take action and solve the problem. For instance, perhaps you will schedule automatic payments during payday, or you will learn to delegate and protect your time. There's always a solution, and stress points you towards it—or at least, lets you know the answer in bright, neon colors in **your mind.**

Persistent stress is not normal; it actually becomes both instructive and destructive to the brain's pathways, which incidentally uses the same links for physical pain as it does for emotional pain (Knowledge@Wharton, 2017). Sometimes chronic stress developes through an overhwelming flood of trauma. Other times, it involves a pile-up of small stressors the person doesn't or simply refuses to handle properly (Alvord, Davidson, Kelly, McGuinness, & Tovian). Nevertheless, chronic stress is dangerous because people are more likely to suffer from depression, "experience symptoms of upper respiratory infection [...] allerg[ies] or auto-immune conditions]" and coronary heart disease, among other dangers (Miller, Chen, & Zhou, 2007).

Even worse, chronic stress brings poor lifestyle

choices that only promote more stress (Conneticut Department of Mental Health & Addiction Services, 2009). If you are stressed, what's the point in making a salad when you can smoke or eat a hamburger? Or what's the point of walking to the store when you are in too much of a hurry to drive to six other places in an hour? A fast-paced and stressful life furthers a stressful environment, which alters the neural reward pathways in your brain and entrenches unhealthy choices that only attract **more stress.**

On the other hand, *manageable* stress is a good thing. It increases your performance by "encouraging the growth of stem cells" conducive to alertness and brain growth (Jaret, 2015). Manageable stress fosters "resilien[ce] and belief" in your own skills (Jaret, 2015). You begin to seek "social support" that acts as a "buffer" against illness (Ozbay, et al., 2007). By taking (calculated) risks, stress improves your "mental toughness" as you realize that worry is only mental chatter brought to your attention by things that may very well be out of your control (Whyte, 2014; Telegraph Staff, 2015). That's why the Inspired Performance Program teaches you how to handle stress to your advantage without leading you to suffer any more chronic illnesses. With the right tools and the right attitude, you can get yourself *Out of Your Mind* and thrive over *any* **chronic disease!**

CHAPTER EIGHT

CLEARING YOUR WAY TO SUCCESS

Have you ever thought about the way you normally breathe? Do you notice how your breathing patterns change when you are excited, afraid, or angry? What about the way you breathe at night while resting? Breathing is one of the most important bodily functions we always take for granted, for mechanics are simple and under-appreciated: "When you breathe, you transport oxygen to the body's cells to keep them working and clear your system of the carbon dioxide that this work generates" (Bryce, 2014).

Despite its importance in our lives, however, many people have learned distorted breathing patterns that serve to limit the diaphragm's motion and the lungs' reception of air into the body, causing a lack of balance between the rate of carbon dioxide and oxygen in the body and shortness of breath (Williams A. , 2012; Harvard Medical School, 2016). Breath is essential, and not giving breath the importance it deserves to our well-being can cause many **problems ahead.**

As Williams (2012) discussed, "Many people breathe with a disturbed pattern that can disturb the delicate balance of carbon dioxide and oxygen in the blood." As such, learning proper breathing techniques helps you become aware of any improper breathing arrangements within the body. Things like holding your breath for too short or too long, taking shallow breaths, or breathing quickly or deeply can distort the breathing patterns and damage your body's delicate balance of nutrients. In more strenuous events like exercising, not breathing correctly can cause dizziness, headaches, fatigue, improper muscle posture, and coordination, among other ailments (**Figure 17**).

THE VALUE OF BREATHWORK

For this reason, Youst (2012) considered breathwork a therapeutic technique focused on healing the mind, body, and spirit through the breath, empowering clients to naturally develop their healing. A client's story is indelibly ingrained in their bodies, but with the energetic activation of the breath in the body, suppressions begin to soften and emerge, initiating a healing process that unfolds into conscious awareness, energetic movement, and body-mind integration." Research has concluded that deep breathing helps the body reduce its levels of carbon dioxide, allowing the blood to retain more oxygen than normal (Magner, 2017). Additionally, Alpha, Theta, and Delta brainwave patterns—most commonly found during advanced state of medication and sleep, can also occur because of "connected breathing" (Youst, 2012).

Breathwork displays two important principles: First, a person's breathing patterns aren't distorted by birth, but rather come from distressing or exciting events over which we may not have had control. This means that our conscious breathing can be changed with proper techniques that are geared towards healing. Second, returning your breathing to an optimal level improves our body's self-healing abilities (Addiction.com). By understanding these principles, you have a greater opportunity to develop better breathing mechanisms that encourage greater exchanges of oxygen within your body and improve relaxation (Harvard Medical School, 2016). For this reason, controlled breathing is a great method to combat anxiety, panic attacks, depression, and peace after meditating (Boddy, 2017).

In fact, a 2017 study led by Dr. Kevin Yackle revealed that removing an overactive pathway on 175 neurons they call the "breathing pacemaker" or the "pranayama pathway" in a group of mice caused them to lose any sense of negative arousal and alertness in the brain. This allowed the mice to breathe slowly and calmly, even when subject to potentially exciting or arousing tasks. This research led to the belief that even if breathing is considered "an autonomic behavior," people may still exercise some influence on "higher-order brain function" (Boddy, 2017; Yackle, et al., 2017; **Figure 17**). In other terms, you have much more control of your breathing than you believe, and the Inspired Performance Program will help you take advantage of **this potential.**

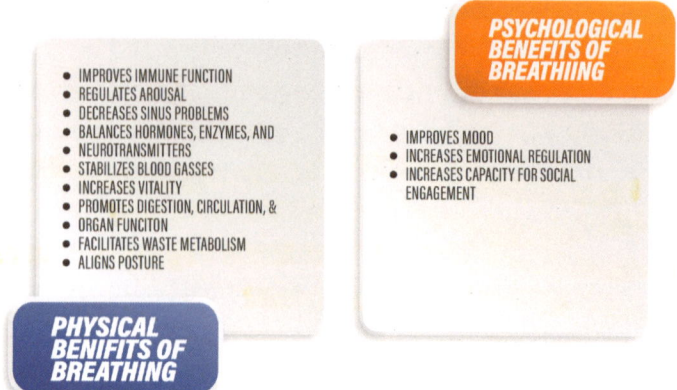

- IMPROVES IMMUNE FUNCTION
- REGULATES AROUSAL
- DECREASES SINUS PROBLEMS
- BALANCES HORMONES, ENZYMES, AND
- NEUROTRANSMITTERS
- STABILIZES BLOOD GASSES
- INCREASES VITALITY
- PROMOTES DIGESTION, CIRCULATION, &
- ORGAN FUNCITON
- FACILITATES WASTE METABOLISM
- ALIGNS POSTURE

PSYCHOLOGICAL BENEFITS OF BREATHIING

- IMPROVES MOOD
- INCREASES EMOTIONAL REGULATION
- INCREASES CAPACITY FOR SOCIAL ENGAGEMENT

PHYSICAL BENIFITS OF BREATHING

Figure 17: Graphic displaying the physical and psychological benefits of breathing.

BREATHING MODELS

Victoria and Caldwell (2013) have developed four types of breathing models that address the different aspects of breathing:

- **Relational Model: This model** considers breathing a social, communal, and individual process that fosters important relationships between people. From birth, humans can adapt their breathing patterns to a group, allowing them to mimic their interactions through breathing. As a result, proper breathing techniques can halt conflict-prone individuals, create empathetic relationships, and improve **societal harmony.**

- **Energy Model:** This model focuses on the fact that breathing increases the necessary energy to treat depression, and is associated with "feeling and expressing emotions, particularly those that allow one to experience them more intensely." Food and rest aren't the only things that fuel the body with energy. Rather, proper breathing serves as another tool for energy by eliminating muscular tension and allowing someone to experience various lengths of **emotional intensity.**

- **Regulation Model:** This model considers that breathing is not only an important physiological need, but also that it provides emotional and psychological outlets to maintain bodily homeostasis. With proper breathing, physical and emotional tolerance will improve, triggering successful changes if the breather can identify personal points **of distress.**

- **Consciousness Model:** This model reasons that conscious breathing elicits mindfulness, expands personal awareness, and improves one's spiritual connection: "A common denominator for a clean mind and body so that higher states of consciousness may emerge." Done safely, a conscious breather can improve access to other meditative states **of consciousness.**

No one breathing model offers a completely accurate description of the value of breathing in the body. Instead, these eclectic perspectives help clients "explore new perspectives of personal growth" through proper breathing, including self-esteem, self-acceptance, and the "assessment of reality" (Youst, 2012).

THE VALUE OF IDENTITY AND SELF-DISCOVERY

How do you define *identity*? How can you understand the role of your personality and enhance it for
success? Dombeck (2006) described *identity* as a concept that is not fixed or permanent, but rather shifts
according to the holder's perceptions over time. Also
known as *self-concept*, identity is something to consider
in the Inspired Performance Program because it is never
static or unchangeable. Instead, you have the capacity
to constantly develop your own self-concept and change
the one imposed by others' expectations with relative
ease—as the owner of your identity, you have the power
to develop a positive self-concept on your own.

We refer to *self* as a "warm sense or a warm feeling that something is 'about me' or 'about us'," which
considers both the thinker and the thoughts that are in
conscious awareness (Leary & Tangney, 2013). Thus, the
self-concept is structured to observe "content, attitudes,
or evaluative judgment[s]" in such a fashion as allows
us to understand the world within our perspectives. By
making sense of the world, we are free to explore the
concepts that address or enhance our identity and our
role in society.

Understanding ourselves promotes an honest discussion of our goals. People with a strong self-concept or
identity are secure and unwavering in their person; they
know their strengths and address their limitations; they
understand in what capacity they can serve and improve
in society; and they aren't dependent upon fame, attention, or reputation in order to become fulfilled (Mayer,
2014/2016; Feldman, 2011).

Your Many Identities

Are you a liberal, a conservative, a libertarian, or a moderate?

Are you spiritual, religious, both, or neither?

Do you like sports, music, television, or the Internet (who doesn't love the Internet!?)––or are none of those activities your cup of tea?

Do you consider yourself straight, gay, bisexual, or transsexual––or perhaps, asexual?

Are you urban **or rural?**

Better yet, how do others see you: your friends, family, and **work colleagues?**

These questions may be very invasive to you. Yet they also help address your identity. Your identity is not only how you finish an "I am" question, but is also an amalgam of your attitudes at work, business, and life; eating habits; your love for pets (or lack thereof); and hopes and dreams. You do not have just one identity. Rather, you adopt one identity at work, another one at school, another one at home, and another one in your private life. Alarid (2013) stated regarding the self, "the self is reflexive in that it can take itself as an object and can categorize, classify, or name itself in particular ways in relation to other social theories or classifications."

There are two types of identity: *personal identity*, where one's sense of personal attributes has either a public or private self; and *social identity*, where social definitions influence one's identity. Involving both "the internal and the subjective, and the external," in recognizing your identity is paramount to the Program's dedication to healing (Woodward, 2000). Your identity is public because your appearance, style, and personality—even on that "off" day—says a lot about your character, even if you do not mean it. Your identity is private because your thoughts, feelings, and fantasies are your own, and you have the power to change, manipulate, or transform them to your advantage. In addition, your identity is social since it is related to kinship, your ethnicity or nationality, and your religion or group affiliation, among other considerations. Ouellette (2014) described how cues manage our judgments and expectations of others' identities:

> We all rely on cues to make snap judgments when we meet new people, and those judgments can be accurate, at least in broad strokes. Physical attractiveness, race, gender, facial symmetry, skin texture, facial symmetry, or facial expressions and body language are all factions that contribute to how we form our impressions **of people.**

Even if you do not share certain personal or social identities you learned from friends, family, or institutions, they still have an impact on the development of your identity (Curtin, 2016). This need not discourage you. Instead, feel free to approach your many identities with curiosity and reality. There is no need to be afraid of what "labels" others or even you attributed to your own character. Remember: there's nothing wrong with your identity, your hopes, your dreams, and your **life expectations.**

Asking Questions about Your Identity

How many questions have you Googled today? You have probably searched a couple of them online. Now, with the information of the world at your fingertips, you only need to input some search terms and click to see your answer. The things you can find online are endless, and you can easily waste hours clicking one page over another, searching for the things that interest you. Be that as it may, when it comes to your identity, is it searchable on the Internet? Can you *truly* find yourself through five-minute quizzes, arbitrary questionnaires, personality tests? I'm not saying these things aren't useful, enriching, or entertaining. I simply believe *you* have the power to find those answers for yourself, and get a clearer picture of *your* identity through awareness. This awareness is what leads to long-lasting change.

After completing your breathing exercises and audios, you'll begin working on certain self-discovery questions that allow you to discover your inner thoughts, beliefs, and emotions. This will help you change your negative habits and trade them for positive ones, organically understand what circumstances have led you to "stick" with those beliefs, and––most importantly–– learn more about yourself: "Find out what works for YOU, not what anyone else says or wants for you. You are the expert in your own life. It's all about figuring out what you value most. With this knowledge, you can create the life you want" (Peeters, 2015). Through these self-discovery questions, you become your own coach, therapist, and **best friend.**

CLEARING IS THE NEXT STEP

By now, you have read several times about the Inspired Performance Institutes's mission to help individuals clear disturbing events from their minds. What does that really mean? If you recall, the mind has viewed old memories stored in a high-resolution format, creating an error message because the mind saw the intensity of the images and mistakenly believed they were happening in the present. If the memory of the event were happening, the subconscious mind would start a process to protect you, like fight or flight. There would be a physiological response mixed in with an emotional response, designed to prepare you for an incoming threat. It only makes sense if *something* is happening, *not* if you are only *thinking* about it.

In clearing, we fix the error messages by having the mind reprocess old data into a low-resolution format. This is accomplished by a series of different processes that allows the mind to update, reboot, reframe, and adjust. The key is to keep the individual present, aware that they are no longer in the situation. As clients learn they are safe and the memory is no longer threatening, the emotional distress will disappear, and the glitch becomes only a blip on the person's radar screen. Essentially, the goal is not to clear the *memory* of the event, but rather to clear the *intensity* of the emotions stored along with the memory, allowing the mind to recall the memory with less emotion, as just, data. Once we help clients clear at least three or four events, we then request the mind to scan and search for any similar disturbing events to be cleared automatically. The mind is brilliant on its own and makes immediate adjustments to its **stored memory.**

When I first explained this process to a client of mine, she looked puzzled and skeptical. During our session, we worked to clear the intensity of her troubling history of child abuse. Nonetheless, she still remained unsure that her memories would be cleared. More so, she wondered how the mind could adjust to clear even undisclosed events. How would she *know* her trauma was cleared? As we worked through certain events, I informed her that her mind now understood the process and would clear other traumatic events on its own. She admitted feeling surprised, yet optimistic that any other trauma would also clear soon, expressing I had been right so far, so why **challenge it?**

Three weeks later, I stumbled upon her at a supermarket and said she had great news: She went to an amusement park with her family and when she was on the escalator, she started to look over at the people below. At the top of the escalator, she looked over the railing and watched the people walking below her. When her daughter pointed out the immensity of her mother's actions, she calmly said, "I know." Mind you, she never mentioned her fear of heights during our session., She said, "I never told you about my fear of heights, and now it's gone." She finally understood how sweeping cleared and updated other distressing events in her life––and

then some!

YOUR MIND AS AN ANCHOR

Anytime you experience an intense state, a specific stimulus is applied, linking the two neurologically. This is known as an *anchor*, and it can help you access past states instantly. These can be li nked to the present to offer you resources and create change whenever you want it. *You* have the power to change your state and access resources within your mind.

The ability to access change through the use of an anchor is a theory more than 100 years old, developed by Edwin Twitmyer. In 1902, Twitmyer discovered that if he took a hammer and banged a person on the knee, the knee would jerk. He also noticed that if he told the person that he would hit the person's knee, the knee reflex would happen anyway. As a result, he presented a paper to the AMA on this study, but they weren't interested. Even so, Twitmyer's work is the basis for Ivan Pavlov's more famous study of classical conditioning (Beck H. , 2001).

You may look at learning as the topics you learn in school like Geometry, Algebra, U.S. History, or English, and you are right––to a point. However, learning in psychology is referred to as the "long-term change in behavior that is based on experience" (Andover, 2013). This is due to the work of Russian psychologist Ivan Pavlov, who read Twitmyer's paper and experimented in learning with dogs. He would show a steak to the dogs to stimulate salivation then ring a bell. After several efforts of conditioning the salivation response, he would then just have to ring the bell and the dogs would salivate. In 1936, Pavlov wrote a paper titled "Conditioned Reflexes" and presented it to the Soviet medical community regarding the conditioned response. Because of this, we now know that anchoring is only an outgrowth that perfects the body's own stimulus response.

Also known as *banking*, anchoring activates your senses—your exposure to images, colors, sounds, and experiences—in order to ease your mind. Three things help promote a clear mind necessary for relaxation: a visual symbol, a personal audio statement, and a kinesthetic touch (Racine, n.d.). I've explained how establishing a personal symbol helps you visualize peacefully and without any hassle. Repeatedly visualizing this symbol helps center your mind and calms your breath. Now, what about visualizing **your successes?**

HOW TO BE SUCCESSFUL

When was the last time you felt successful? What was your very first accomplishment? Or your most recent one? Why do you remember it so fondly? What motivated you to succeed? Did you use brains, brawn, beauty, or cunning? These questions help *you* define by yourself the role of success. Within you, there is the growing power to succeed and become a leader. This is so even when past trauma, negative memories, and even the dull and unpleasant moments of life invade your mind. For instance, Foss (n.d.) has suggested the following thought regarding the loss of a job: "Sometimes, in our panic and despair, we forget how awesome and powerful we were in overcoming an earlier curveball, mess, **or conundrum."**

That's why reflecting on your successes is a powerful mechanism to let the brain know that *you* are the
"common denominator" for your success. Regarding the
relationship between memories and success, Halvorson
(2010) suggested there are two types of memories: *general*
memories, which group "similar behaviors" together; and
specific memories, focusing on a single event for which
you are responsible. In one case, a string of general
memories could be having a string of A's, which led you
to graduate with high honors. For specific memories, it
could be winning a medal in your favorite sport, building
your favorite toy, or even finishing a grueling video game
in record time. Nobody can take away that exhilarating
feeling of victory, and nobody can ever take away the
best memories of your life—*these* are the bright memories that the Program aims to anchor in **your mind.**

THE STORY OF DARCY AND THE HOME INVASION

A therapist training in the Inspired Performance
Program referred a lady to me in her sixties named
Darcy, who suffered from the trauma of a home invasion, during which she was pistol-whipped and injured.
Two robbers ransacked her home at the dead of night,
pretending they were Drug Enforcement Agency (DEA)
agents. They did not expect Darcy to wake up—but then
she did during their robbery. As she walked in the dark
kitchen, one of the robbers told her to freeze and pre-
tended to run a drug search. Groggy and confused, Darcy
did not recognize they were fake until it was too late,

and then they forced her to *not* turn around. As soon as she realized they weren't federal agents, the robbers took the gun and bashed her over the head.

When the robbers went into another room, Darcy ran into the backyard in order to find somebody to help her. She was bleeding and screaming for her neighbors, but nobody came to her aid, so she had to run to the front yard, where she was forced to face the robbers once again. Then they chased her out on the street and began to attack her again, when a neighbor suddenly came to her aid. They could have killed her––but took off instead. Since then, Darcy suffered from severe agoraphobia. When she first came to see me, she needed to use a walker because the trauma of the home invasion had crippled her. She was crying as soon as she walked in and told me the horrors of the home invasion and how it had destroyed **her life.**

Darcy suffered from somatization, a psychological condition where "the body bears the burden of emotional experience which has not been adequately discharged, processed, or integrated" (Rodríguez Vega, Fernández Lira, & Bayón Pérez, 2005). In Darcy's case, even if she was *physically* well, the walker served as a safety-seeking mechanism that "prevent[s] phobic people from experiencing an unambiguous disconfirmation of their unrealistic beliefs about feared catastrophes" (Wells, et al., 1995). Every noise, every police siren, and every ambulance would trigger a panic attack.

To take care of this challenging case, we had to close all the drapes and silence every sudden noise. In three hours, we were able to scramble the data in her mind.

We engaged with her chosen symbol, and in the end, we had her off the walker and laughing on her way home. She was on top of the world, wondered and amazed as to how our Program had helped her so quickly. Darcy witnessed for herself how the Program healed the pain she felt over the last eight months.

Two days later, as she walked into her therapist's office, Darcy said: "I have good news and **bad news.**"

Puzzled, the therapist responded, "Well, the good news is, you are not walking with **a walker!**"

She replied, "Yeah; I'm feeling OK. I'm not walking with **a walker.**"

"Well, what's the **bad news?**"

Darcy said, "You're fired. I don't need to come back. I knew I was feeling okay after leaving Don's session, but the next day I knew I was absolutely, 100% okay when I was driving in my car and an ambulance went past me, and I just watched it go by. I felt no emotion. And that's when I said, 'I'm fine." Before the program, any memory of the home invasion, and even walking without her walker would throw her into a panic state. Now, Darcy is out of her mind and is free to **enjoy life.**

That's the freedom we aim for our clients to feel when they leave the Inspired Performance Institute. The value of getting yourself out of your mind is priceless. Beyond feeling better, you'll be empowered to carve your own path of success in the world. Why not take a jump and enjoy the power of being *Out of Your Mind*—today?

CONCLUSION

Trauma causes a glitch in the way your mind continues to replay the event in real time. This continued stress takes a toll on both the mind and body. Physical or emotional trauma creates inflammation and this inflammation is the response to trauma as it takes our natural healing system offline. It is a temporary pause to allow the healing process to engage. When you take drugs, for example, you use them to fight off disease or any bodily imbalance inflaming your body. When you exercise, you're activating the muscle that is your heart to ward off the inflammation in your arteries and your belly. When you put a warm or cold compress on your aching back, you're using it to stop inflammation on its tracks, which is simply from letting your body know it's hurt through aches and tremors. Inflammation is all round you––and it is usually a warning sign that something is, most of the time, inflammation.

Sometimes, inflammation is necessary in order to build bodily resilience and energy. This does not mean that children should not be vaccinated or play on dangerous grounds needlessly; instead, the goal is to fight inflammation, yet grow stronger by it the next time it rears its ugly head. In fact, certain studies are verifying that if antidepressants like Paxil or Lexapro are actually successful in warding off depression alone, it is only by reducing the brain's inflammation system instead of *actually* warding off depression, as normally thought. If this is true, then the question bears repeating: can you train your brain to fight inflammation without the help of **unnecessary medications?**

Of course **you can!**

Your brain is a natural, self-healing organ with an impressive amount of neuroplasticity and flexibility. It does things that are beyond our imagination in protecting every part of our bodies, giving us movement, indicating dinner, or even sleeping, with minimal effort. However, trauma and illness can disrupt the connections between your brain and your body, thus inducing inflammation to fight off an illness that never was. It disrupts your healing and many opportunities for the future. Luckily, we're here **to help!**

When I first told people the title of the book, the typical response was, "What a great title!" Of course, it is a great title because it helps you pause and reflect upon your relationship with your mind. "Do I need to be out of my mind?" Yes, because now you are fully aware how your mind was operating before. You now know what potential events and experiences have caused your mind to operate at below its peak performance levels. The solution is not as complicated as you may have believed: it revolves around fixing the problematic way your mind has been working.

Forget Big Pharma: it's time to take back control of the healthcare industry, and any change to the billion-dollar industry will be met with some heavy opposition. Not everything Big Pharma does is bad. Big Pharma has provided some life-saving solutions. There are times when the use of medications makes sense, especially during life-threatening situations. However, I take issue with drug overuse and providing drugs to a public that may not be fully aware of the side effects of their consumption. Managing the problem is in the best interest of the multi-billion-dollar healthcare industry. The Inspired Performance Institute wants to **eliminate it.**

The life-changing stories of people who have succeeded through the Inspired Performance Program served as sources of inspiration for the creation of this book. In order to make the necessary updates in your mind, one of the first keys to success is education about how your mind works. By understanding the science behind the solution, you can better improve your chances of removing any glitches in your mind, the traumatic memory that keeps the mind in fight-or-flight mode, spreads inflammation, and disables the healing process if you are not careful.

The fight-or-flight response is an emergency management system, *not* an operating system. The memory glitch keeps the error message repeating, keeping the mind in constant flight-or-fight mode. When the inflammation persists and healing is disabled, disease will be the result. We believe that emotional trauma can be linked to a large number of diseases. It may be impossible to know for sure, but the question remains: What percentage of our illnesses are created by our atmospheric conditions as opposed to our **genetic predisposition?**

The key to peace and happiness is staying present and in the moment. As you have read, most books and self-help experts *tell* you to stay present but don't tell you *how.* Now we have shown you the clue: when your mind is in Alpha state, your mind operates with complete focus and relaxation. By constantly achieving Alpha state through flow, you can learn how to relax and beat the glitches at their **own game!**

Ailments like panic, anxiety, and phobias are currently the number one reason for (unnecessary) emergency room visits. Once again, the current solution usually involves managing the problem only through costly and oftentimes addictive medications that do more harm than good for patients. Our TIPP process has been successful in eliminating the problem. What is the better answer? It should be inspiring to anyone reading this book and dealing with anxiety or panic attacks when you hear about the individuals we **have helped.**

Our entire focus is on performance, not therapy. You see, there's nothing wrong with your mind—your problems may only be a series of error messages built up over your lifetime. All we need to do is reboot your mind, update the way it processes and it will default back to the way it was meant to operate, centered and present. There you have it—the secrets that let you to know *You Must Be Out of Your Mind!*

REFERENCES

Abel, G., Lee, S., & Weeks, J. (2007). Direct-to-consumer advertising in oncology: A content analysis of print media. *Journal of Clinical Oncology, 25*(10), 1267-1271. doi: 10.1200/JCO.2006.09.5968 .

Abramowitz, J., Taylor, S., & McKay, D. (2008). Obsessive-compulsive disorder. *The Lancet, 374*(9688), 491-499.

Adams, A. (2009). *Seeing is believing: The power of visualization.* Retrieved May 9, 2017, from Psychology Today: https://www.psychologytoday.com/blog/flourish/200912/seeing-is-believing-the-power-visualization

Addiction.com. (n.d.). *Breathwork.* Retrieved May 15, 2017, from Addiction.com: https://www.addiction.com/a-z/breathwork/

Akin, U. (2014). Examining the predictive role of self-compassion on self-doubt. *Education Sciences & Psychology, 30*(4), 12-19.

Alarid, Michael. (2013). *Identity theory & social identity theory: Basics [Video file].* Retrieved June 27, 2017, from YouTube: https://www.youtube.com/watch?v=YcRNQtvOCbc

Alford, P., Martin, D., & Martin, M. (1985). A profile of the physical abusers of children. *The School Counselor, 33*(2), 143-150.

Algoe, S., & Heidt, J. (2009). Witnessing excellence in action: The "other-praising" emotions of elevation, gratitude, and admiration. *The Journal of Positive Psychology, 4*(2), 105-127. doi: 10.1080/17439760802650519.

Allard, L. T., & Hunter, A. (2010). *Understanding temperament in infants and toddlers [PDF document]*. Center on the Social and Emotional Foundations for Early Learning, Vanderbilt Kennedy Center for Research and Human Development. Nashville: Vanderbilt University.

Almashat, S., Wolfe, S. M., & Carome, M. (2016). *Twenty-five years of pharmaceutical industry criminal and civil penalties: 1991 through 2015*. Public Citizen, Public Citizen Inc. and Public Citizen Foundation. Washington: Public Citizen.

Alvarado, N. (2011). *Chapter 4: Wilhelm Wundt and the founding of psychology [PowerPoint presentation; Lecture]*. Retrieved June 30, 2017, from PSY 410: History and Systems.

Alvord, M., Davidson, K., Kelly, J., McGuinness, .., & Tovian, S. (n.d.). *Understanding chronic stress*. Retrieved July 9, 2017, from American Psychological Association: http://www.apa.org/helpcenter/understanding-chronic-stress.aspx

American Medical Association. (2015). *AMA calls for ban on DTC ads of prescription drugs and medical devices [press release]* Retrieved April 20, 2017, from American Medical Association: https://www.ama-assn.org/content/ama-calls-ban-direct-consumer-advertising-prescription-drugs-and-medical-devices

American Psychological Association. (2000). *Diagnostic and statistical manual of mental disorders (4th ed. text revision).* Washington DC: American Psychological Association.

American Psychological Association. (2013). Post-traumatic stress disorder (PTSD). In *Diagnostic and statistical manual of mental disorders, fifth edition (DSM-5)* (5th edition ed., pp. 271-280). Washington, DC: American Psychological Association.

American Psychological Association. (2014, June). How many psychologists are licensed in the United States? [Online publication]. *Monitor on Psychology, 45*(6), p. 13.

Ammons, J. (2015). *Hacking the flow state.* Retrieved June 10, 2017, from Brigade Engineering: https://brigade.engineering/hacking-the-flow-state-b2451d0bf7ba

Andover, P. [TED-ed]. (2013). *The difference between classical and operant conditioning - Peggy Andover [Video file].* Retrieved July 9, 2017, from YouTube: https://www.youtube.com/watch?v=H6LEcMoEoio&feature=youtu.be

Ankrom, S. (2017). *Anxiety vs. panic attacks: What's the difference?* Retrieved May 1, 2017, from Verywell: https://www.verywell.com/anxiety-attacks-ver-sus-panic-attacks-2584396

Anxiety and Depression Association of America. (2016). *Facts & statistics [Press release].* Retrieved May 1, 2017, from Anxiety and Depression Association of America: https://www.adaa.org/about-adaa/press-room/facts-statistics

Anxiety and Depression Association of America. (n.d.). *Panic disorder [PDF Brochure].* Retrieved June 5, 2017, from Anxiety and Depression Association of America: https://www.adaa.org/sites/default/files/panic-brochure.pdf

AnxietyBC. (2009). *Specific phobia [Video file].* Retrieved June 6, 2017, from YouTube: https://www.youtube.com/watch?v=o6HPwKCkoZo

Associated Press. (2015). *New celebrity drug ads have subtle twist.* Retrieved June 30, 2017, from NBC News: http://www.nbcnews.com/id/8563655/ns/health-health_care/t/new-celebrity-drug-ads-have-subtle-twist/#.WVb4zorkVmA

Austin, B. (n.d.). *5 ways to get in "the zone" (proven by science).* Retrieved July 6, 2017, from Stop. Start. Do.: http://www.stopstartdo.com/blog/2015/4/26/5-ways-the-zone-science-brady

Başar, E. (2013). Brain oscillations in neuropsychiatric disease. *Dialogues in Clinical Neuroscience, 15(3),*

291-300.

Baron, J. (2006). *Lightner Wilmer and the beginning of clinical psychology*. Retrieved June 30, 2017, from Department of Psychology at the University of Pennsylvania: http://www.psych.upenn.edu/history/witmertext.htm

Baron, J. (2008). *History of psychology at Penn*. Retrieved June 30, 2017, from Department of Psychology at the University of Pennsylvania: http://www.psych.upenn.edu/history/history.htm

Barras, C. (2013). *Mind maths: The sum of consciousness*. Retrieved April 28, 2017, from New Scientist: https://www.newscientist.com/article/mg21729032.400-mind-maths-the-sum-of-consciousness/

Baumeister, R., Stillwell, A., & Heatherton, T. (1994). Guilt: An interpersonal approach. *Psychological Bulletin, 15*(2), 243-267.

Beck, C. (2010). *Understanding the pain of abandonment*. Retrieved May 8, 2017, from Psychology Today: https://www.psychologytoday.com/blog/the-many-faces-addiction/201006/understanding-the-pain-abandonment

Beck, H. (2001). *The lonesome case of Edwin B. Twitmyer*. Retrieved June 30, 2017, from General Psychology: http://www1.appstate.edu/~beckhp/twitmyer.htm

Beidacki, B. (2015). *Outcome blind approach.* Retrieved July 6, 2017, from All In: http://www.allinmag.com/poker/inside-poker/the-business/april-2015-beidacki-blog-outcome-blind-approach

Bergland, C. (2014). *Chronic stress can damage brain structure and connectivity.* Retrieved July 9, 2017, from Psychology Today: https://www.psychologytoday.com/blog/the-athletes-way/201402/chronic-stress-can-damage-brain-structure-and-connectivity

Bergland, C. (2015). *Alpha brain waves boost creativity and reduce depression.* Retrieved April 28, 2017, from Psychology Today: https://www.psychologytoday.com/blog/the-athletes-way/201504/alpha-brain-waves-boost-creativity-and-reduce-depression

Berman, R. (2015). *If we're going to talk about brainwaves, we should know what they are.* Retrieved June 10, 2017, from Big Think: http://bigthink.com/robby-berman/if-were-going-to-talk-about-brainwaves-we-should-know-what-they-are

Bilgore, D. (2016). *Why you should stop asking "why?".* (The Crucible Project) Retrieved May 5, 2017, from The Crucible Project: https://thecrucibleproject.org/stop-why/

Blue Knot Foundation. (2017). *Childhood responses to threat/coping strategies.* Retrieved April 2017, 2013, from Blue Knot Foundation: http://www.blueknot.org.au/Workers-Practitioners/For-Health-Professionals/Resourc-es-for-Health-Professionals/Child-Cop-ing-Strategies

Bobelian, M. (2013). *J & J's $2.5 billion settlement won't stop Big Pharma's addiction to off-label sales*. Retrieved April 20, 2017, from Forbes: https://www.forbes.com/sites/michaelbobelian/2013/11/12/jjs-2-2-billion-settlement-wont-stop-big-pharmas-addiction-to-off-label-sales/#4a3f4850515b

Boddy, J. (2017). *A tiny spot in mouse brains may explain how breathing calms the mind*. Retrieved June 6, 2017, from National Public Radio: http://www.npr.org/sections/health-shots/2017/03/30/522033368/a-tiny-spot-in-mouse-brains-may-explain-how-breathing-calms-the-mind

Borkovec, T., & Inz, J. (1990). The nature of worry in generalized anxiety disorder: A predominance of thought activity. *Behaviour Research and Therapy, 28*(2), 153-158.

Borrelli, L. (2015). *A bad dream is more than just a dream: The science of nightmares*. Retrieved May 9, 2017, from Medical Daily: http://www.medicaldaily.com/bad-dream-more-just-dream-science-nightmares-327586

Bouton, M., Mineka, S., & Barlow, D. (2001). A modern learning theory perspective on the etiology of panic disorder. *Psychological Review, 108*(1), 4-32.

Boyce, P., & Harris, A. (2011). Childhood adversity, trauma and abuse: Context and consequences. *Australian and New Zealand Journal of Psychiatry, 45,* 608-610. doi: 10.3109/00048674.2011.602209 .

Brainworks NeuroFeedback. (n.d.). *What are brainwaves?* Retrieved April 28, 2017, from Brainworks NeuroFeedback: http://www.brainworksneurotherapy.com/what-are-brainwaves

Brill, S. (2016). *America's most admired lawbreaker.* Retrieved April 2017, 2017, from Highline: http://highline.huffingtonpost.com/miracleindustry/americas-most-admired-lawbreaker/

Bryce, E. [TED-ed]. (2014, November 14). *What do the lungs do? - Emma Bryce [Video file].* Retrieved July 13, 2017, from YouTube: https://www.youtube.com/watch?v=8NUxvJS-_ok

Busch, F. (2009). Anger and depression. *Advances in Psychological Treatment, 26,* 271–278. doi: 10.1192/apt.bp.107.004937 .

Buss, D. (2009). The great struggles of life: Darwin and the emergence of evolutionary psychology. *American Psychologist, 64*(2), 140-148. doi: 0.1037/a0013207 .

Cambridge Dictionary. (n.d.). *Optimism [def. 1].* (Cambridge University Press) Retrieved June 14, 2017, from Cambridge Dictionary: http://dictionary.cambridge.org/us/dictionary/english/optimism

Campbell, S. (2011). *Potential effects of a ban on di-rect-to-consumer advertising of new prescription drugs.* United States Congress, Congressional Budget Office. Washington: Congressional Budget Office.

Carroll, J., Gruenewald, T., Taylor, S. J.-D., Matthews, K., & Seeman, T. (2013). Childhood abuse, parental warmth, and adult multisystem biological risk in the Coronary Artery Risk Development in Young Adults study. *Proceedings of the National Academy of Sciences, 1110*(42), 17149–17153. doi: 10.1073/pnas.1315458110 .

Carter, J., Joyce, P., Mulder, R., & Luty, S. (2001). The contribution of temperament, childhood neglect, and abuse to the development of personality dysfunction: A comparison of three models. *Journal of Personality Disorders, 15*(2), 123-135. doi: 10.1521/pedi.15.2.123.19216.

Carver, C., Scheier, M., & Segenstrom, S. (2010). Optimism. *Clinical Psychology Review, 30*(7), 879-889. doi: https://doi.org/10.1016/j.cpr.2010.01.006.

Cassels, C. (2010). *Child abuse linked to increased risk for type 2 diabetes in adults.* (WebMD, LLC) Retrieved April 26, 2017, from Medscape Medical News: http://www.medscape.com/viewarticle/732279

Cecchetti, H. (. (2016). *A 10-year-old male Holland Lop rabbit.* Retrieved June 2, 2017, from Wikimedia Commons: https://commons.wikimedia.org/wiki/File:Holland_lop_rabbit.jpg

Ceccoli, V. C. (2012). *Play it again Sam: On the compulsion to repeat.* Retrieved April 27, 2017, from Velleda C. Ceccoli, Ph.D.: http://drceccoli.com/2012/03/play-it-again-sam-on-the-compulsion-to-repeat/

Cellvideoabstracts. (2012). *Brain oscillations: A video quick guide [Video file].* Retrieved July 6, 2017, from YouTube: https://www.youtube.com/watch?v=_ vQk9isSSSc&feature=youtu.be cellvideoabstracts

Center for Sex Offender Management. (n.d.). *Adult survivors of childhood sexual abuse coping mechanisms [PDF document].* Retrieved April 23, 2017, from Center for Sex Offender Management: http://www.csom.org/train/victim/2/material/Sect%20 2%20Handout%20-%20Coping%20Mechanisms.pdf

Centre for Clinical Interventions. (n.d.). *The vicious cycle of anxiety [PDF document].* (Government of Western Australia, Department of Health) Retrieved June 1, 2017, from Centre for Clinical Interventions: http://www.cci.health.wa.gov.au/resources/docs/Info-Vicious%20Cycle%20of%20 Anxiety.pdf

Cherry, K. (2016a). *What are emotions and the types of emotional responses?* Retrieved April 26, 2017, from VeryWell: https://www.verywell.com/what-are-emotions-2795178

Cherry, K. (2016). *What are the 6 major theories of emotion?* Retrieved April 26, 2017, from Verywell: https://www.verywell.com/theories-of-emotion-2795717

Child Welfare Information Gateway. (2004). *Risk and protective factors for child abuse and neglect [PDF document].* United States Department of Health and Human Services, Child Welfare Information Gateway. Washington: Child Welfare Information Gateway.

Child Welfare Information Gateway. (2013). *Long-term consequences of child abuse and neglect [PDF document].* United States Department of Health and Human Services, Child Welfare Information Gateway. Washington: Child Welfare Information Gateway. Retrieved 2017, from Child Welfare Information Gateway: https://www.childwelfare.gov/pubPDFs/long_term_consequences.pdf

Chui, H., Zilcha-Mano, S., Dinger, U., Barret, M., & Barber, J. (2016). Dependency and self-criticism in treatments for depression. *Journal for Counseling Psychology, 63*(4), 452-459. doi: 10.1037/cou0000142.

Coalition for Healthcare Communication. (2017). *About us.* Retrieved April 21, 2017, from Coalition for Healthcare Communication: http://www.co-healthcom.org/about-us/

Collins, D. (2004). *Merck yanks Vioxx from shelves.* Retrieved April 21, 2017, from CBS News: http://www.cbsnews.com/news/merck-yanks-vioxx-from-shelves/

Collins, N. (2012). *Smells can trigger emotional memories, study finds.* Retrieved July 5, 2017, from The Telegraph: http://www.telegraph.co.uk/news/science/science-news/9042019/Smells-can-trigger-emotional-memories-study-finds.html

Common behavior and coping mechanisms of childhood sexual assault survivors [PDF document]. (2014). Retrieved April 23, 2017, from Seuxal Assault and Support Centre of Waterloo Region: http://www.sascwr.org/files/www/Common_Behavior_and_Coping_Mechanisms_of_Childhood_Sexual_Assault_Survivors.pdf

Conneticut Department of Mental Health & Addiction Services. (2009). *The science of stress, bad habits, and risk of chronic disease [PDF document].* Retrieved July 9, 2017, from Yale Stress Center: http://www.ct.gov/dmhas/lib/dmhas/info-briefs/031909.pdf

Control Mind. (n.d.). *The difference between brain and mind.* Retrieved April 25, 2017, from Control Mind: http://controlmind.info/human-brain/the-difference-between-brain-and-mind

Corayer, Michael [PsychExamReview]. (2017). *Long-term memory (Intro Psych Tutorial #73) [Video file]*. Retrieved May 21, 2017, from YouTube: https://www.youtube.com/watch?v=WK4TeETxwdM

Covin, R. (2012). *Is mind reading making you depressed and anxious?* Retrieved July 8, 2017, from Huffington Post Canada: http://www.huffingtonpost.ca/roger-covin/mind-reading-depression_b_1339977.html

Cram, P., Fendrick, A., Inadomi, J., Cowen, M., Carpender, D., & Vijan, S. (2003). The impact of a celebrity promotional campaign on the use of colon cancer screening: The Katie Couric effect. *Archives of Internal Medicine, 163*(13), 1601-1605. doi: 10.1001/archinte.163.13.1601.

Craske, M. G., & Barlow, D. H. (2008). Chapter 1: Panic disorder and agoraphobia. In D. H. Barlow (Ed.), *Clinical handbook of psychological disorders, fourth edition: A step-by-step treatment manual* (pp. 1-64). New York, London: The Guildford Press.

Csikszentmihalyi, M. (1990). *Flow: The psychology of optimal experience.* New York, New York, United States: Harper & Row.

Csikszentmihalyi, M. (1997). *Finding flow.* (Sussex Publishers, LLC) Retrieved April 29, 2017, from Psychology Today: https://www.psychologytoday.com/articles/199707/finding-flow

Csikszentmihalyi, M. (2004). *Mihaly Csikszentmihalyi:*

Flow, the secret to happiness [Video file]. Retrieved April 29, 2017, from TED Conferences: https:// www.ted.com/talks/mihaly_csikszentmihalyi_ on_flow

Curtin, I. (2016). *Why should I care about my social identity?* Retrieved June 27, 2017, from The Inner Activist: http://www.inneractivist.com/social_identity

Cushman, P. (1900). When the self is empty: Toward a historically situated psychology. *American Psychologist, 45*(5), 599-611.

Cvijetic, S. (2017). *What are beta brainwaves? Improve focus and motivation with beta brainwave entrainment.* Retrieved June 10, 2017, from Owlcation: https://owlcation.com/stem/What-are-Beta-Brain-Waves-Focus-and-Motivation-with-Beta-brainwave-entrainment

Daniel, T. (2012). Losing faith vs gaining perspective: How trauma and loss can create a more spacious form of spiritual awareness. *Journal of Spirituality & Paranormal Studies, 35*(1), 16-22.

Darragh, M., Yow, B., Kiesser, A., Booth, R., Kydd, R., & Consedine, N. (2016). A take-home placebo treatment can reduce stress, anxiety and symptoms of depression a non-patient population. *Australian & New Zealand Journal of Psychiatry, 50*(9), 858-65. doi: 10.1177/0004867415621390.

DataBase Center for Life Science (DBCLS). (2015). *Thyroid gland.* Retrieved June 26, 2017, from Wikime-

dia Commons: https://commons.wikimedia.org/
wiki/File:201405_thyroid_gland.png

Davis, C. (2017). *I deserve to live: Rebuilding families one
soul at a time [Electronic book]*. BookBaby.

Dean, J. (2013). *The illusion of control: Are there benefits
to being self-deluded?* Retrieved June 14, 2017, from
Psyblog: http://www.spring.org.uk/2013/02/the-
illusion-of-control-are-there-benefits-to-being-
self-deluded.php

DeAngelis, T. (2008). The two faces of oxytocin. *American Psychological Association, 39*(2), p. 30.

DeJong, C., Aguilar, T., Tseng, C., Lin, G., Boscardin,
W., & Dudley, R. (2016). Pharmaceutical indus-
try-sponsored meeals and physical prescribing
patterns for Medicare beneficiaries. *JAMA Internal Medicine, 176*(8), 1110-1114. doi: 10.1001/jamain-
ternmed.2016.2765 .

Dennis, B. (2015). *Nearly 60 percent of Americans—
the highest ever—are taking prescription drugs.*
Retrieved July 1, 2017, from Washington Post:
https://www.washingtonpost.com/news/to-your-
health/wp/2015/11/03/more-americans-than-
ever-are-taking-prescription-drugs/?utm_ter-
m=.251acc561298

Department of Health. (n.d.). *Anxiety—reversing the vicious cycle.* Retrieved June 1, 2017, from Department of Health: http://healthywa.wa.gov.au/Arti-
cles/A_E/Anxiety-reversing-the-vicious-cycle

Diamond, S. A. (2008). *Essential secrets of psychotherapy: Repetitive relationship patterns.* Retrieved April 27, 2017, from Psychology Today: https://www. psychologytoday.com/blog/evil-deeds/200806/ essential-secrets-psychotherapy-repetitive-rela-tionship-patterns

Dickerson, I. P. (2003). *The discovery of... Schuman resonance.* Retrieved June 2, 2017, from Biblioteca Pleyades: https://www.bibliotecapleyades.net/ esp_ondas_shumman_10.htm

Division of Criminal Justice Services. (2014). *Myths and facts.* Retrieved July 2, 2017, from New York State: http://www.criminaljustice.ny.gov/nsor/ som_mythsandfacts.htm

Dombeck, M. (2006). *Self-identity problems [Online book].* Retrieved May 15, 2017, from Psychological Self-Help Tools-Online Self-Help Book: https:// www.mentalhelp.net/articles/self-identity-prob-lems/

Edelman, D. (2017). *Why is breathing important to organisms?* Retrieved June 26, 2017, from Sciencing: http://sciencing.com/breathing-important-or-ganisms-5124952.html

Eisenberg, L. (1977, April). Disease and illness: Distinctions between professional and popular ideas of sickness. *Culture, Medicine and Psychiatry, 1*(1), 9-23.

Elliott, C. (2011). *Useless studies, real harm.* Retrieved April 21, 2017, from The New York Times: http://www.nytimes.com/2011/07/29/opinion/useless-pharmaceutical-studies-real-harm.html

Elyot, A. (2008). *Character analysis: The four temperaments.* Retrieved May 22, 2017, from Blogger: http://historyhoydens.blogspot.com/2008/01/character-analysis-four-temperaments.html

Emmons, R., & McCollough, M. (2004). *The psychology of gratitude.* Oxford: Oxford University Press.

Engfer, A. (1992). Difficult temperament and child abuse: noted on the validity of the child-effect model. *Análise Psicológica, 10*(1), 51-61.

Ericson, J. (2014). *What happens in your brain when you have a panic attack? How the brain's fear and threat centers backfire.* Retrieved June 1, 2017, from Medical Daily: www.medicaldaily.com/what-happens-your-brain-when-you-have-panic-attack-how-brains-fear-and-threat-centers-backfire

Errera, P., McKee, B., Smith, C., & Gruber, R. (1967). Length of psychotherapy studies done in a university community psychiatric clinic. *Archives of General Psychiatry, 17*(4), 454-458.

Everyday Psychology. (2008). *The bobo doll experiment [Video file].* Retrieved May 26, 2017, from YouTube: https://www.youtube.com/watch?v=dmBqwWlJg8U

Fábrega, M. (n.d.). *How to enter the flow state.* Retrieved June 2, 2017, from Daring to Live Fully: https://daringtolivefully.com/how-to-enter-the-flow-state

Farkas, T. (2014). *Depression and anger go hand in hand.* Retrieved May 22, 2017, from Huffington Post Canada: http://www.huffingtonpost.ca/tere-zia-farkas/anger-and-depression_b_5381640.html

Fearnow, B. (2013). *Study: 70 percent of Americans on prescription drugs.* Retrieved July 1, 2017, from CBS Atlanta: http://atlanta.cbslocal.com/2013/06/19/study-70-percent-of-americans-on-prescription-drugs-one-fifth-take-5-or-more/

Feldman, R. S. (2011). *Understanding psychology, tenth edition.* New York, NY: McGraw Hill.

Felitti, V. [Big Think]. (2015, October 11). *How childhood trauma can make you a sick adult [Video file].* Retrieved July 2, 2017, from YouTube: https://www.youtube.com/watch?v=y3cCAcGeG8E&feature=youtu.be\

Fenstermaker, Scott [people trigger]. (2013). *Plato's psychology.* Retrieved June 30, 2017, from People-triggers: https://peopletriggers.wordpress.com/2013/06/17/platos-psychology/

Ferenciak, D. (2015). *"Am I okay?": Reassurance seeking. What is it and why is it so hard to stop?* Retrieved May 29, 2017, from Chicago Counseling Center:

http://chicagocounselingcenter.com/blog/reas-suranceseeking/

Field, P. (2014). *Are you crazy?* Retrieved April 28, 2017, from Psych Central: https://psychcentral.com/blog/archives/2014/04/25/are-you-crazy/

Fintor, L. (2002). Direct-to-consumer advertising: how has it failed? *Journal of the National Cancer Institute, 94*(5), 329-331. doi: https://doi.org/10.1093/jnci/94.5.329. Retrieved from https://doi.org/10.1093/jnci/94.5.329

Food and Drug Administration. (2009). *Prescription drug advertising: Questions and answers.* Retrieved April 20, 2017, from U.S. Food and Drug Administration: https://www.fda.gov/Drugs/Resources-ForYou/Consumers/PrescriptionDrugAdvertising/ucm076768.htm

Food and Drug Administration. (2015). *FDA drug safety communication: FDA cautions about using testosterone products for low testosterone due to aging; requires labeling change to inform of possible increased risk of heart attack and stroke with use [Press release].* Retrieved May 16, 2017, from US Food and Drug Administration: https://www.fda.gov/Drugs/DrugSafety/ucm436259.htm

Foss, J. (n.d.). *5 ways to stay positive when job searching makes you want to cry and give up.* (Daily Muse, Inc.) Retrieved June 29, 2017, from The Muse: https://www.themuse.com/advice/5-ways-to-stay-positive-when-job-searching-makes-you-want-to-cry-and-give-up

Fournier, G. (2016). *Cognitive appraisal theory.* Retrieved June 3, 2017, from Psych Central: https://psych-central.com/encyclopedia/cognitive-apprais-al-theory/

Frölich, J. (2016). *Brain waves and Beta buzz: The wild story of neural oscillations.* Retrieved June 10, 2017, from Knowing Neurons: http://knowingneu-rons.com/2016/05/18/brain-waves/

Freeman, D., & Freeman, J. (2015). *Is life's happiness curve really U-shaped?* Retrieved June 15, 2017, from The Guardian: https://www.theguardian.com/science/head-quarters/2015/jun/24/life-happiness-curve-u-shaped-ageing

Freyd, J. J. (2008). Betrayal trauma. In G. Reyes, J. El-hai, & J. Ford (Eds.), *Encyclopedia of Psychological Trauma* (p. 76). New York, New York: John Wiley and Sons.

Friedman, M. (2015). *Kim Kardashian's morning-sickness pill ad was actually a massive success.* Retrieved June 30, 2017, from Harber's Bazaar: http://www.harpersbazaar.com/celebrity/latest/news/a11866/kim-kardashian-morning-sickness-diclegis-success/

Fristcher, L. (2017). *What is anticipatory anxiety?* Retrieved July 7, 2017, from Verywell: https://www.verywell.com/anticipatory-anxiety-2671554

Frosch, D., Krueger, P. M., Hornik, R., Cronholm, P., & Barg, F. (2007). Creating demand for prescription drugs: A content analysis of television direct-to-consumer advertising. *Annals of Famiy Medicine, 5*(1), 6-13. doi: 10.1370/afm.611 .

Furberg, C., Furberg, B., & Sasich, L. (2010). Chapter 55 - What are the rules for promoting medications to consumers in the U.S.? [PDF Document] Knowing Your Medications. In *Knowing Your Medications* (pp. 184-188). Potata, Inc.

Furnham, A. (2016). *What are emotions for?* Retrieved April 26, 2017, from Psychology Today: https://www.psychologytoday.com/blog/sideways-view/201606/what-are-emotions

Gaines-Lewis, J. (2015). *Smells ring bells: How smell triggers memories and emotions.* (Sussex Publishers, LLC) Retrieved July 5, 2017, from Psychology Today: https://www.psychologytoday.com/blog/brain-babble/201501/smells-ring-bells-how-smell-triggers-memories-and-emotions

Gamboa, H. (2005a). *Eeg_alpha.svg [Image].* Retrieved June 2, 2017, from Wikimedia Commons: https://commons.wikimedia.org/wiki/File:Eeg_alpha.svg

Gamboa, H. (2005b). *Eeg_beta.svg [Image].* Retrieved June 2, 2017, from Wikimedia Commons: https://commons.wikimedia.org/wiki/File:Eeg_beta.svg

Gamboa, H. (2005c). *Eeg_delta.svg [Image].* Retrieved

June 2, 2017, from Wikimedia Commons: https://commons.wikimedia.org/wiki/File:Eeg_delta.svg

Gamboa, H. (2005d). *Eeg_gamma.svg [Image]*. Retrieved June 2, 2017, from Wikimedia Commons: https://commons.wikimedia.org/wiki/File:Eeg_gamma.svg

Gamboa, H. (2005e). *Eeg_theta.svg [Image]*. Retrieved June 2, 2017, from Wikimedia Commons: https://commons.wikimedia.org/wiki/File:Eeg_theta.svg

Gamma brainwaves: Facts & benefits. (n.d.). Retrieved April 28, 2017, from Visual Meditation: https://visualmeditation.co/gamma-brainwaves-facts-and-benefits/

Gardner, J. (2015). *The alpha state of mind.* Retrieved June 10, 2017, from Mind Body Vortex: http://www.mindbodyvortex.com/the-alpha-state-of-mind/

Gatti, C. (2016). *Preventing child abuse and neglect: Helping parents and providers understand temperament [Webinar]*. Retrieved May 22, 2017, from Pennsylvania Parents as Teachers: http://www.pa-pat.org/preventing-child-abuse-and-neglect-helping-parents-and-providers-understand-temperament/

GLOOM. (n.d.). *Delta brain waves: 0 Hz to 4 Hz.* Retrieved June 10, 2017, from Mental Health Daily:

http://mentalhealthdaily.com/2014/04/14/delta-brain-waves-0-hz-to-4-hz/

Goldberg, J. (2016). *What are anxiety disorders?* Retrieved June 5, 2017, from WebMD: http://www.webmd.com/anxiety-panic/guide/mental-health-anxiety-disorders#1

Goldhill, O. (2016a). *A "time slice" theory of consciousness suggest we're not continually aware of our surroundings.* Retrieved April 27, 2017, from Quartz: https://qz.com/663729/new-research-suggests-that-consciousness-is-developed-in-two-stages/

Goldhill, O. (2016b). *Scientists say your "mind" isn't confined to your brain, or even your body.* Retrieved April 27, 2017, from Quartz: https://qz.com/866352/scientists-say-your-mind-isnt-confined-to-your-brain-or-even-your-body/

Gonzalez, R. (2012). *The 4 biggest myths about the human brain.* (Gizmodo) Retrieved July 5, 2017, from i09: http://io9.gizmodo.com/5890414/the-4-biggest-myths-about-the-human-brain

GoodTherapy.org. (2015a). *Explicit memory.* Retrieved April 26, 2017, from Good Therapy: http://www.goodtherapy.org/blog/psychpedia/explicit-memory

GoodTherapy.org. (2015b). *Implicit memory.* Retrieved April 26, 2017, from GoodTherapy: http://www.goodtherapy.org/blog/psychpedia/implicit-memory

GoodTherapy.org. (2015c). *Parasympathetic nervous system*. Retrieved April 29, 2017, from Good Therapy: http://www.goodtherapy.org/blog/psychpedia/parasympathetic-nervous-system

Goodwin, R., Faravelli, C., Cosci, S., Trugia, E., de Graaf, R., & Wittchen, H. (2005). The epidemiology of panic disorder and agoraphobia in Europe. *European Neuropsychopharmacology, 15*, 435 – 443. doi:10.1016/j.euroneuro.2005.04.006 .

Gorbea, D. (2016). *What are brain (Theta, Delta, Alpha, Beta brain) waves?* Retrieved July 7, 2017, from Stellar Waves Cristal Light Beam: https://stellar-waves.net/what-are-brain-theta-delta-alpha-beta-brain-waves/

Gotzler, M. (2014). *Hacking flow: Achieving ultimate human potential [Presentation]*. Retrieved June 10, 2017, from SlideShare: https://www.slideshare.net/biotrakr/hacking-flow-achieving-ultimate-human-potential

Grant Halvorson, H. (2010). *Yesterday influences your performance today in surprising ways*. Retrieved June 29, 2017, from Psychology Today: https://www.psychologytoday.com/blog/the-science-success/201009/yesterday-influences-your-performance-today-in-surprising-ways

Green, H. [Crash Course]. (2015). *The nervous system, Part 3–Synapses!: Crash Course A&P #10 [Video file]*. Retrieved June 8, 2017, from YouTube: https://www.youtube.com/watch?v=VitFvNv-

RIIY&list=PL8dPuuaLjXtOAKed_MxxWBNaP-no5h3Zs8&index=10

Green, J. [vlogbrothers]. (2016). *On pain [Video file].* Retrieved June 13, 2017, from YouTube: https://www.youtube.com/watch?v=Gxz-IBgeDHc

Greene, J., & Kesselheim, A. (2015). *An age-old battle: The FDA versus the shill.* Retrieved June 30, 2017, from The Atlantic: https://www.theatlantic.com/health/archive/2015/09/fda-drug-promotion-social-media/404563/

Gregoire, C. (2016). *Consciousness works differently than you think, according to this new theory.* Retrieved April 28, 2017, from Huffington Post: http://www.huffingtonpost.com/entry/perception-brain-time-slices_us_570fedb8e4b0561c-9f043a79

Grezlik, A. (2005). *G. Stanley Hall.* Retrieved June 30, 2017, from History of Psychology Archives: http://muskingum.edu/~psych/psycweb/history/hall.htm

Griffin, D., & Tversky, A. (1992). The weighing of evidence and the determinants of confidence. *Cognitive Psychology, 24*(3), 411-435. doi: https://doi.org/10.1016/0010-0285(92)90013-R.

Gumbrecht, J. (2011). *In Sweden, a generation of kids who've never been spanked.* Retrieved April 22, 2017, from CNN: http://www.cnn.com/2011/11/09/world/sweden-punishment-ban/

Hampton, D. (2014a). *What doesn't kill you makes you stronger.* Retrieved July 1, 2017, from Your Best Brain Possible: https://www.thebestbrainpossible.com/what-doesnt-kill-you-makes-you-stronger/

Hampton, D. (2014b). *What's the difference between the mind and the brain?* Retrieved May 30, 2017, from Your Best Brain Possible: https://www.thebestbrainpossible.com/the-mind-and-the-brain-what-is-the-difference/

Hampton, D. (2014c). *Your fortune-telling brain.* Retrieved May 7, 2017, from The Best Brain Possible: https://www.thebestbrainpossible.com/your-fortune-telling-brain/

Hampton, D. (2015). *When thinking positive is a negative [YouTube video].* Retrieved July 1, 2017, from YouTube: https://www.youtube.com/watch?v=wBngYXSGLBI

Handel, S. (2012). *The purpose of thinking.* Retrieved July 6, 2017, from The emotion machine: http://www.theemotionmachine.com/the-purpose-of-thinking/

Hanes, S. (2014). *To spank or not to spank: Corporal punishment in the US.* Retrieved May 22, 2017, from The Christian Science Monitor: http://www.csmonitor.com/USA/Society/2014/1019/To-spank-or-not-to-spank-Corporal-punishment-in-the-US

Hanh, T. N. (2006). *The four layers of consciousness.* (Lion's Roar Foundation) Retrieved April 28, 2017, from Lion's Roar: https://www.lionsroar.com/the-four-layers-of-consciousness/

Hara, N. N., Yokoyama, C., Inoue, K., Nishida, A., Tanii, H., Okada, M., . . . Okazaki, Y. (2011). The development of agoraphobia is associated with the symptoms and location of a patient's first panic attack. *BioPsychoSocial Medicine, 2017*(May), 701-710. doi: 10.3346/jkms.2011.26.6.701.

Harbeck, J. (2016). *10 commonly abused psychology words—and what they really mean.* Retrieved April 27, 2017, from The Week: http://theweek.com/articles/603303/10-commonly-abused-psychology-words--what-really-mean

Hartfield, K. (2011). *Early history of psychology–Plato.* Retrieved June 30, 2017, from Go Fish Ministeries, Inc.: https://gofishministries.wordpress.com/2011/04/20/early-history-of-psychology-%E2%80%93-plato/amp/

Harvard Medical School. (2016). *Relaxation techniques: Breath control helps errant stress response.* Retrieved May 15, 2017, from Harvard Medical School: http://www.health.harvard.edu/mind-and-mood/relaxation-techniques-breath-control-helps-quell-errant-stress-response

Hawkins, J. (2015). *If you see a therapist, how many sessions are you likely to need?* Retrieved May 22, 2017, from Good Medicine: http://www.goodmedicine.

org.uk/stressedtozest/2015/04/if-you-see-thera-
pist-how-many-sessions-are-you-likely-need

Healy, M. (2003). *"Katie Couric Effect" boosts colonos-
copy rates.* Retrieved April 21, 2017, from USA
Today: http://usatoday30.usatoday.com/news/
health/2003-07-14-katie-usat_x.htm

Heflick, N. A. (2011). *Children learn aggresssion from parents.* Retrieved May 26, 2017, from Psychology
Today: https://www.psychologytoday.com/blog/
the-big-questions/201111/children-learn-aggres-
sion-parents

Heine, C. (2011). *FDA rebukes Kim Kardashian for morning-sickness drug ad on Instagram.* Retrieved July
10, 2017, from Adweek: http://www.adweek.com/
digital/fda-rebukes-kim-kardashian-morning-
sickness-drug-ad-instagram-166348/

Henig, R. M. (2009). *Understanding the anxious mind.*
Retrieved April 23, 2017, from The New York
Times: http://www.nytimes.com/2009/10/04/
magazine/04anxiety-t.html?_r=1&ref=magazine

Henriques, G. (2011). *What is the mind?* Retrieved
April 26, 2017, from Psychology Today: https://
www.psychologytoday.com/blog/theory-knowl-
edge/201112/what-is-the-mind

Hermann, N. (1997). *What is the function of the various
brainwaves?* Retrieved April 28, 2017, from Scientific American: https://www.scientificamerican.
com/article/what-is-the-function-of-t-1997-12-22/

Heyrman, H. (2010). *Brainwaves.* Retrieved June 10, 2017, from Dr. Hugo Heyrman: http://www.doctorhugo.org/brainwaves/brainwaves.html

Hill, K., Ross, J., Egilman, D., & Krumholz, H. (2009). *The ADVANTAGE seeding trial: A review of internal documents.* (American College of Physicians) Retrieved April 21, 2017, from Annals of Internal Medicine: http://annals.org/aim/article/742239/advantage-seeding-trial-review-internal-documents

Hochhauser, M. (2009). Is this a seeding trial? *Journal of Clinical Research Best Practices, 5*(6), 1-6.

Hockenbury, D., & Hockenbury, S. (n.d.). *Discovering psychology, 4th edition.* Worth Publishers.

Hoffer, C. L. (n.d.). *Chapter 7: Section 3: Emotion [ebook].* Retrieved April 26, 2017, from AllPsych: https://allpsych.com/psychology101/emotion/

Hoffman, S. (2016). *The Schumann resonance: Feeling the Earth's hidden vibrations.* Retrieved July 7, 2017, from Healing Lifestyles: https://healinglifestyles.com/schumann-resonance-earths-healing-vibrations/

Holmes, L. (2014). Reaching the repetition compulsion. *Modern Psychoanalysis, 39*(1), 26-37.

Horvath, A. T., Misra, K., & Cooper, G. (2013, August 26). Social learning theory of addiction and recovery implications.

Howard. (2017). *The repetition compulsion.* Retrieved July 11, 2017, from SystemsThinker.com: http://www.systemsthinker.com/interests/mind/repetitioncompulsion.shtml

Howes, R. (2014). *8 more reasons to go to therapy.* Retrieved May 22, 2017, from Psychology Today: https://www.psychologytoday.com/blog/in-therapy/201403/8-more-reasons-go-therapy

Huffman, J., Pollack, M., & Stern, M. (2002). Panic disorder and chest pain: Mechanisms, morbidity, and management. *Primary Care Companion to the Journal of Clinical Psychiatry, 4*(2), 54-62.

Illinois Public Health and Disability Program. (2012). *What is chronic disease? Important things to know about chronic diseases for Persons With Disabilities .* Retrieved June 13, 2017, from Illinois Department of Public Health Disability: http://www.idph.state.il.us/idhp/idhp_ChronicDisease.htm

J.C. (2016). *Gamma waves and inspiration: How is your brain working?* Retrieved April 28, 2017, from The Epoch Times: http://www.theepochtimes.com/n3/1975608-gamma-waves-and-inspiration-how-is-your-brain-vibrating/

Jabr, F. (2013). *How does meditation change the brain?— Instant egghead #54 [Video file].* Retrieved June 10, 2017, from YouTube: https://www.youtube.com/watch?v=q0DMYs4b2Yw&feature=youtu.be

Jackson, S., & Marsh, H. (1996). Development and validation of a scale to measure optimal experience: The flow state scale. *Journal of Sport & Exercise Psychology, 18,* 17-35.

Jacobson, S., & Blundell, A. (2016). *The use of symbols in psychology.* Retrieved May 9, 2017, from Harley Therapy: http://www.harleytherapy.co.uk/counselling/symbols-in-psychology.htm

Jaffee, S., Caspi, A., Moffitt, T., Polo-Tomas, M., Price, T., & Taylor, A. (2004). The limits of child effects: Evidence for genetically mediate child effects on copoal punishment but not on physical maltretament. *Developmental Psychology, 40*(6), 1047-1058. doi: http://dx.doi.org/10.1037/0012-1649.40.6.1047.

James, C. (2015). *How high expectations can lead to dissapointment, depression, and anxiety.* (Tiny Buddha, LLC) Retrieved June 14, 2017, from Tiny Buddha: https://tinybuddha.com/blog/high-expectations-can-lead-disappointment-depression-anxiety/

James, M. (2013). *Conscious of the unconscious.* Retrieved April 26, 2017, from Psychology Today: https://www.psychologytoday.com/blog/focus-forgiveness/201307/conscious-the-unconscious

Jamie. (2010). *Understanding the stages of chronic illness.* (WordPress) Retrieved June 13, 2017, from In the Shadows of Fibromyalgia: https://shadowsoffibromyalgia.wordpress.com/2010/07/14/understanding-the-stages-of-chronic-illness/

Jaret, P. (2015). *The surprising benefits of stress*. (The Greater Good Science Center at the University of California, Berkeley) Retrieved July 9, 2017, from Greater Good Magazine: https://greatergood.berkeley.edu/article/item/the_surprising_benefits_of_stress

Jarrett, C. (2014). *Great myths of the brain (Great myths of psychology)*. Wiley-Blackwell.

Jenner, B., Hamill, D., & Klippel, J. (2009). What's the best Way to combat arthritis? [Interview transcript]. *Larry King Live*. CNN. Atlanta.

Joseph, S., & Butler, L. (2010). Positive changes folllowing adversity. *PTSD Research Quaterly, 21*(3), 1-8.

Judd, L., Schettler, P., Coryell, W., Akiskal, H., & Fiedorowicz, J. (2013). Overt irritability/anger in unipolar major depressive episodes past and current characteristics and implications for long-term course. *AMA Psychiatry, 70*(11), 1171-1180. doi:10.1001/jamapsychiatry.2013.1957.

Kübler-Ross, E. &. (n.d.). *The five stages of grief [PDF Handout]*. Retrieved June 13, 2017, from McComb & Wagner Family Funeral Home & Crematorium: http://www.mccombwagner.com/download/24712/TheFiveStagesofG.pdf

Kadlec, G. (2015). *3 reasons children keep abuse "a secret"*. (Kadlec x2, LLC) Retrieved 1 2017, July, from Be A Kids Hero: http://www.beakidshero.com/posts/3-reasons-children-keep-abuse-a-secret/

Kahn, L. (2006). The understanding and treamtent of betrayal trauma as a traumatic experience of love. *Journal of Trauma Practice, 5*(3), 57-72. doi:10.1300/J189v05n03_04. Retrieved from Journal of.

Karakaş, S., & Başar, E. (1998). Early gamma response is sensory in origin: a conclusion based on cross-comparison of results from multiple experimental paradigms. *International Journal of Psychophysiology, 31*(1), 13-31. PMID: 9934618 .

Kelley, T. (2013). *The big bucks in keeping kids focused.* Retrieved July 1, 2017, from Bloomberg: https://www.bloomberg.com/news/articles/2013-10-10/shires-adhd-drugs-face-resistance-in-a-skeptical-europe

Kendall, J. (2002). How child abuse and neglect damage the brain. *The Boston Globe.*

Kennon, J. A. (2010). *Mental model: The illusion of choice.* Retrieved May 5, 2017, from Joshua A. Kennon: http://www.joshuakennon.com/mental-model-the-illusion-of-choice

Kessler, D., Rose, J., Temple, R., Schapiro, R., & Griffin, J. (1994). Therapeutic-class wars—Drug promotion in a competitive marketplace. *New England Journal of Medicine, 331*, 1350-1353.

Kessler, R., & Greenberg, P. (2002). Chapter 67: The economic burden of anxiety and stress disorders. In K. Davis, D. Charney, J. Coyle, & C. Nemeroff (Eds.), *Neurpsychopharmacology: The fifth generation of progress.* (pp. 981-992). Philadelphia: Lippincott, Williams, & Wilkins.

Kessler, R., Berglund, P., Dernier, O., Jin, R., Merikangas, K., & Walter, E. (2005). Lifetime prevalence and age-of-onset distributions of DSM-IV disorders in the National Comorbidity Survey Replication. *Archives of General Psychiatry, 62*(6), 593-602. doi:10.1001/archpsyc.62.6.593 .

Kilpatrick, D., Edmunds, C., & and Seymour, A. (1992). *Rape in America: A report to the nation.* Crime Victims' Research and Treatment Center, National Victim Center. Charleston: Crime Victims' Research and Treatment Center.

Kitron, D. (2003, April). Repetition compulsion and self-psychology: towards a reconciliation. *The International Journal of Psychoanalysis, 84*(2), 427–441. doi: 10.1516/PHT8-9K7N-ELYY-G90F.

Knowledge@Wharton. (2017). *Emotions as "power": How to handle chronic stress.* (Wharton School at the University of Pennsylvania) Retrieved July 9, 2017, from Knowledge@Wharton: http://knowledge.wharton.upenn.edu/article/emotional-wellness-can-help-handle-chronic-stress/

Koch, C. (2016). *Does size matter—for brains?* (Nature America, Inc.) Retrieved July 5, 2017, from Scientific American: https://www.scientificamerican.com/article/does-size-matter-for-brains/

Koss, M. (1979). Length of psychotherapy for clients seen in private practice. *Journal of Consulting and Clinical Psychology, 47*(1), 210-212. doi: 10.1037/0022-006X.47.1.210.

Kotler, S. (2014). *Flow states and creativity.* Retrieved April 29, 2017, from Psychology Today: https://www.psychologytoday.com/blog/the-playing-field/201402/flow-states-and-creativity

Kotler, S. (2014). *The science of peak human performance.* (Time, Inc.) Retrieved July 7, 2017, from Time: http://time.com/56809/the-science-of-peak-human-performance/

Kotler, Steven [Big Think]. (2015, October 15). *Hack your flow: Understanding flow cycles, with Steven Kotler.* Retrieved June 10, 2017, from YouTube: https://www.youtube.com/watch?v=JWy_cBcawKQ&-feature=youtu.be

Koul, S. (2012). *Culture and corporal punishment.* (Penguin Random House) Retrieved May 22, 2017, from Hazlitt Magazine: http://hazlitt.net/feature/culture-and-corporal-punishment

Krane, E. (2011). *Elliot Krane: The mystery of chronic pain [Lecture].* (Spalding Foundation) Retrieved June 15, 2017, from TED Conferences: https://www.ted.com/talks/elliot_krane_the_mystery_of_chronic_pain?language=en

Krentzman, A. R. (2015). *Ying and yang of positive psychology and addiction [PDF document].* Retrieved

April 29, 2017, from University of Minnesota: http://www.cehd.umn.edu/ssw/Documents/ KrentzmanTANNewsletter.pdf

Krueger, J. A. (2015). *Aggression beyond frustration.* Retrieved May 5, 2017, from Psychology Today: https://www.psychologytoday.com/blog/one-among-many/201507/aggression-beyond-frustration

LaBier, D. (2013). *Why the impact of child abuse extends well into adulthood.* Retrieved July 1, 2017, from Psychology Today: https://www.psychologyto-day.com/blog/the-new-resilience/201310/why-the-impact-child-abuse-extends-well-adult-hood

LaMattina, J. (2015). *Kim Kardashian, Dr. Oz, and TV drug ads.* Retrieved July 10, 2017, from Forbes: https://www.forbes.com/sites/johnlamatti-na/2015/08/13/kim-kardashian-dr-oz-and-tv-drug-ads/#5a1887c2628c

Lambert, M. J. (2013). *Bergin and Garfield's handbook of psychotherapy and behavior change, sixth edition.* John Wiley & Sons.

Lancer, D. (2015). *Breaking the cycle of abandonment.* Retrieved May 9, 2017, from Darlene Lancer, JD, MFT: https://www.whatiscodependency.com/ emotional-abandonment/

Lane, S. (2016). *The hidden side of clinical trials-Sile Lane-TEDxMadrid [YouTube video].* Retrieved

June 30, 2017, from YouTube: https://www.you-tube.com/watch?v=-RXrGLolgEc&feature=you-tu.be

LaPierre, J. (2013). *Sexual abuse is a "gateway experience" that often leads to drug addiction later in life.* Retrieved April 24, 2017, from Bangor Daily News: http://bangordailynews.com/2013/07/22/maine-focus/childhood-sex-abuse-victims-often-live-misunderstood-in-a-world-of-isolation/

LaPierre, J. (2015). *Understanding "powerlessness" and why acceptance liberates you.* Retrieved July 2, 2017, from Choose Help: http://m.choosehelp.com/topics/recovery/accepting-powerlessness-is-liberating

Law, B. M. (2004). Family circumstances, not children's misbehavior, spur abuse. *Monitor on Psychology, 35*(11), p. 15. Retrieved from American Psychological Association: http://www.apa.org/monitor/dec04/abuse.aspx

Layton, J. (2008). *How does the body make electricity—and how does it use it?* Retrieved June 2, 2017, from How Stuff Works: http://health.howstuffworks.com/human-body/systems/nervous-system/human-body-make-electricity.htm

Leary, M., & Tangney, J. (2013). Chapter 4: Self, self-concept, and identity. In M. Leary, & J. Tangney, *Handbook of Self and Identity, Second Edition* (pp. 69-104). New York, NY, United States: Guildford Press.

Lefkowitz, R. (2017). *The profits and perils of off-label use*. Retrieved October 17, 2017, from Periscope Group: http://www.periscopegroup.com/risperdal/off-label-drug-use-ris-art

Llamas, M. (2016). *Selling side effects: Big Pharma's marketing machine*. Retrieved April 20, 2017, from Drugwatch: https://www.drugwatch.com/featured/big-pharma-marketing/

Loren, F. (n.d.). *Why confidence isn't vital for athletes to win*. Retrieved May 8, 2017, from Expert Sports Peerformance with Loren Fogelman: http://expertsportsperformance.com/confidence-vital-athletes-win/

Lubin-Katz, C. (2014). *4 things you should learn about the art of losing gracefully*. Retrieved June 15, 2017, from Thought Catalog: http://thoughtcatalog.com/corinda-katz/2014/05/4-things-you-should-learn-about-the-art-of-losing-gracefully/

MacKinnon, M. (2016). *Illusion of choice: The myth of free will*. Retrieved May 5, 2017, from Psychology Today: https://psychologytoday.com/blog/neurptitde/201608/illusion-choice-the-myth-free-will

Mager, D. (2014). *Defining recovery*. Retrieved May 22, 2017, from Psychology Today: https://www.psychologytoday.com/blog/some-assembly-required/201406/defining-recovery

Magner, E. (2017). *I tried this trippy healing modality for mental clarity—and still can't believe how it made me feel.* Retrieved May 15, 2017, from Well and Good: https://www.wellandgood.com/good-advice/does-breathwork-healing-work/

Mansell, B. (2008). *Remembering your successes can boost self-confidence.* (MindPerk) Retrieved June 29, 2017, from MindPerk: http://www.mindperk.com/one-minute-motivators/remembering-your-successes-can-boost-self-confidence/

Martino, J. (2013). *Experiment proves why staying in tune with the earth's pulse Is key to our well being.* Retrieved April 28, 2017, from Collective Evolution: http://www.collective-evolution.com/2013/12/19/experiment-proves-why-staying-in-tune-with-the-earths-pulse-is-key-to-our-well-being/

Mathews, A. (2013). *Projection and identity.* Retrieved May 12, 2017, from Psychology Today: https://www.psychologytoday.com/blog/traversing-the-inner-terrain/201304/projection-and-identity

Mattejat, F., & Remschmidt, H. (2008). The children of mentally ill parents. *Deutsches Ärtzeblatt International, 105*(23), 413–418. doi: 10.3238/arztebl.2008.0413.

Matthews, K. (2015). *Hacking enlightenment with flow states.* Retrieved June 10, 2017, from Elephant Journal: https://www.elephantjournal.com/2015/05/hacking-enlightenment-with-flow-states/

Maunder, R., & Hunter, J. (2017). *How childhood trauma can lead to chronic ollness.* Retrieved June 13, 2017, from The Walrus: https://thewalrus.ca/how-childhood-trauma-can-lead-to-chronic-illness/

Mauri, M., Cipresso, P., Balgera, A., Villamira, M., & Riva, G. (2011). Why is using Facebook so successful? Psychophysiological measures describe a core flow state while using Facebook. *Cyberpsychology, Behavior, and Social Networking, 0*(0), 1-9. doi: 10.1089/cyber.2010.0377 .

Maus, J. (2010). *Transaxial slice of the brain of a 56 year old patient (male) taken with positron emission tornography (PET) [PETimage]*. Retrieved June 2, 2017, from Wikimedia Commons: https://commons.wikimedia.org/wiki/File:PET-image.jpg

Mayer, J. D. (2014/2016). *Know thyself*. Retrieved May 15, 2017, from Psychology Today: https://www.psychologytoday.com/articles/201403/know-thyself

Mayo Clinic. (2017). *Agoraphobia*. Retrieved May 1, 2017, from Mayo Clinic: http://www.mayoclinic.org/diseases-conditions/agoraphobia/home/ovc-20311918

Mayo Clinic Staff. (2016). *Chronic stress puts your health at risk*. Retrieved July 9, 2017, from Mayo Clinic: http://www.mayoclinic.org/healthy-lifestyle/stress-management/in-depth/stress/art-20046037

McLeod, S. (2013). *Sigmund Freud*. Retrieved June 30, 2017, from Simply Psychology: https://www.simplypsychology.org/Sigmund-Freud.html

McLeod, S. (2014). *Classical conditioning*. Retrieved July 1, 2017, from Simply Psychology: https://www.simplypsychology.org/classical-conditioning.html

McManamy, J. (2016). *Anger*. Retrieved July 2, 2017, from McMan's Depression and Bipolar Web: http://www.mcmanweb.com/anger.html

Mcurrie. (2010). *Child trauma and the hippocampus*. Retrieved April 26, 2017, from Serendipity Studio: Child Trauma and the Hippocampus

Merriam-Webster. (n.d.). *Mesmerize [def. 1]*. Retrieved April 20, 2017, from Merriam-Webster: https://www.merriam-webster.com/dictionary/mesmerize

Merriam-Webster. (n.d.). *Trauma [def. 1b]*. Retrieved April 22, 2017, from Merriam-Webster : https://www.merriam-webster.com/dictionary/trauma

Meuret, A., Rosenfield, D., Wilhelm, F., Zhou, E., Conrad, A., Ritz, T., & Roth, W. (2011). Do unexpected panic attacks occur spontaneously? *Biological Psychiatry, 70*(10), 985-991. doi: 10.1016/j.biopsych.2011.05.027.

Meyer, J. (n.d.). *Alpha brain waves—The science behind peak performances and creativity*. (PRYMD Labs LLC.) Retrieved April 28, 2017, from PRYMD: http://www.prymd.com/blog/science-behind-peak-performance/

Micallef-Trigona, B. (2014). *Comparing the 5 theories of emotion.* Retrieved April 26, 2017, from Brain Blogger: http://brainblogger.com/2014/10/22/comparing-the-5-theories-of-emotion/

Miller, E. (2016). *Testosterone multidistrict litigation bellwether trials.* Retrieved from Drugwatch. com: https://www.drugwatch.com/testosterone/multi-district-litigation/

Miller, G., Chen, E., & Zhou, E. (2007). If it goes up, must it come down? Chronic stress and the hypothalamic-pituitary-adrenocortical axis in humans. *Psychological Bulletin, 133*(1), 24-45. doi: 0.1037/0033-2909.133.1.25.

Miller, I. (2013). Schumann resonance, psychophysical regulation & psi (Part I). *Journal of Consciousness Exploration & Research, 4*(6), 599-612.

Miller, R. A., & Miller, I. (2003). *Schumman's resonances and human psychology.* Retrieved April 29, 2017, from Organization for the Advancement of Knowledge: www.nwbotanicals.org/oak/newphysics/schumann/schumann.htm

Mindvalley Academy. (n.--d.). *How to generate more alpha brain waves.* (Mindvalley Academy) Retrieved June 2, 2017, from Mindvalley Academy: http://blog.mindvalleyacademy.com/meditation/how-to-generate-more-alpha-brain-waves?__hst-c=122874388.94f90c52a1c049f44ac170228a5b26.1485387960856.1485387960856.14853879608 56.1&__hssc=122874388.1.1485387960857&__

hsfp=3478827707 Mindvalley Acadto help individuals achieve their peak performance by clearing the traumatic blocks ingrained throughout their lives.

emy

Mitsutake, G., Otsuka, K., Hayakawa, M., Sekiguchi, M., Comélissen, G., & Halberg, F. (2005). Does Schumann resonance affect our blood presure? *Biomedicine Pharmacotherapy, 59*(S1), S10-S14.

Morris, T. (2015). *The importance of optimism.* (Tom Morris) Retrieved June 14, 2017, from Tom V. Morris: http://www.tomvmorris.com/blog/2015/7/27/the-importance-of-optimism

Morton, K. (2013). *Chronic illness and mental health-Kati Morton [Video file].* Retrieved June 7, 2017, from YouTube: https://www.youtube.com/watch?v=RDH9cITtkFk

Morton, K. (2014). *What is social anxiety disorder? Mental health help with Kati Morton treatment scared school [Video file].* (YouTube) Retrieved June 5, 2017, from YouTube: https://www.youtube.com/watch?v=BcRobzrfc98

Muhaiyaddeen, M. B. (2007). *God's psychology: A Sufi explanation.* Philadelphia, PA: Fellowship Press.

Mukerjee, M. (2005). Hidden scars: Sexual and other abuse may alter a brain region. *Scientific Amer-*

ican.

Muris, P., Schmidt, H., & Merckelbach, H. (1999). The structure of specific phobia symptoms among children and adolescents. *Behaviour Research, 37,* 863-886.

Myers, D. G. (2011). *Psychology, ninth edition.* New York, NY: Worth Publishers.

Na, H., Kang, E., Lee, J., & Yu, B. (2011). The genetic basis of panic disorder. *Journal of Korean Medical Science, 26*(6), 201-210. doi: 10.3346/jkms.2011.26.6.701.

Nader, R. (2015). *Generalized anxiety disorder—Understanding the nature of worry and anxiety [Presentation].* Retrieved June 5, 2017, from YouTube: https://www.youtube.com/watch?v=fr3iYr_zZak

Naik. (2011). *The benefits of getting more alpha waves!* Retrieved April 29, 2017, from World Institute for Self-Healing: http://yang-sheng.com/?p=5123

Najavits, L., Gastfriend, D., Barber, J., Reif, S., Muenz, L., Blaine, J.,...Weiss, R. (1998). Cocaine dependence with and without PTSD among subjects in the National Institue on Drug Abuse Collaborative coccaine Treatment Study. *American Journal of Psychiatry, 155*(2), 214-219. doi: 10.1176/ajp.155.2.214.

National Health Council. (2014). *About chronic disease [PDF document].* Retrieved June 13, 2017, from

National Health Council: http://www.nation-
alhealthcouncil.org/sites/default/files/NHC_
Files/Pdf_Files/AboutChronicDisease.pdf

National Institute of Mental Health. (2016). *Generalized
anxiety disorder: When worry gets out of control
[PDF document]*. Retrieved June 5, 2017, from
National Institute of Mental Health: https://
www.nimh.nih.gov/health/publications/gener-
alized-anxiety-disorder-gad/generalized-anxi-
ety-disorder_124169.pdf

National Institute of Mental Health. (2016). *Obsessive-compulsive disorder: When unwanted thoughts
or irresistible actions take over National Institute
of Mental Health [PDF Brochure]*. Retrieved
June 5, 2017, from National Institue of Mental Health: https://www.nimh.nih.gov/health/
publications/obsessive-compulsive-disorder-
when-unwanted-thoughts-take-over/508-ocd-
qf-16-4676-12142016_150041.pdf

National Institute of Mental Health. (2016). *Social
anxiety disorder: More than just shyness*. Retrieved June 5N, 2017, from National Institute
of Mental Health: https://www.nimh.nih.gov/
health/publications/social-anxiety-disor-
der-more-than-just-shyness/508-social-anxi-
ety-disorder_153750.pdf

Nauert, R. (2015). *Subtle signs warn of panic attacks in ad-
vance*. Retrieved June 7, 2017, from Psych Central:
https://psychcentral.com/news/2011/07/29/sub-
tle-signs-of-unexpected-panic-attacks/28168.

html

Navajits, L., Weiss, R., & Shaw, S. (1997). The link between substance abuse and posttraumatic
stress disorder in women: A research review.
American Journal on Addictions, 6(4), 273-283.

Neumann, F. (2013). *A cure for panic disorder and agoraphobia.* (Sussex Publishers, Inc.) Retrieved June 15,
2017, from Psychology Today: https://www.psy-
chologytoday.com/blog/fighting-fear/201305/
the-treatment-health-anxiety

Orac. (2016). *All drugs are poisons, and that's OK.* Retrieved April 20, 2017, from ScienceBlogs: http://
scienceblogs.com/insolence/2016/04/07/all-
drugs-are-poisons-and-thats-ok/

Orenstein, C., Jones, R. G., & Tigas, M. (2016). *Now there's
proof: Docs who get company cash tend to prescribe
more brand-name meds.* Retrieved April 21, 2017,
from ProPublica: https://www.propublica.org/
article/doctors-who-take-company-cash-tend-
to-prescribe-more-brand-name-drugs

Osborne, D., & Williams, C. (2013). Excessive reassurance-seeking [PDF document]. *Advances in
Psychiatric treatment, 19,* 420-421. doi: 10.1192/
apt.bp.111.009761. Retrieved from Advancesd in
Psychiatric Treatment.

Osmosis. (2016). *Obsessive compulsive disorder (OCD)
- causes, symptoms & pathology [Video file].* Retrieved June 5, 2017, from YouTube: https://

www.youtube.com/watch?v=I8Jofzx_8p4

Osmosis. (2016). *Posttraumatic stress disorder (PTSD)—causes, symptoms, treatment & pathology [Video file].* Retrieved July 2, 2017, from YouTube: https://www.youtube.com/watch?v=hzSx-4rMyVjI&feature=youtu.be

Oswald, A., & Blanchflower, D. (2008). Is well-being U-shaped over the life cycle? . *Social Science & Medicine, 66,* 1733-1749. doi:10.1016/j.socscimed.2008.01.030.

O'Toole, M. (2014). The dangerous injustice collector: Behaviors of someone who never forgets, never forgives, never lets Go, and strikes back! *Violence and Gender, 1*(3), 97-99. doi: 10.1089/vio.2014.1509.

Ouellette, J. (2014). *Personal identity is (mostly) performance.* (Atlantic Media) Retrieved June 27, 2017, from The Atlantic: https://www.theatlantic.com/health/archive/2014/01/personal-identity-is-mostly-performance/283043/

Oxford Living Dictionaries. (n.d.). *Trauma [def.1].* (Oxford University Press) Retrieved April 22, 2017, from Oxford Living Dictionaries: https://en.oxforddictionaries.com/definition/trauma

Ozbay, F., Johnson, D., Dimoulas, E., Morgan, C. I., Charney, D., & Southwick, S. (2007). Social support and resilience to stress: from neurobiology to clinical practice. *Psychiatry (Edgemont), 4*(5), 35-40.

Pasti-Dickerson, I. (n.d.). *A tuning fork for life.* (Terrapin Therapy) Retrieved June 3, 2017, from Terrapin Therapy's Quantum Holographic Healing: http://quantumholographichealing.com/Tuning_Fork.html

Paul, M. P. (2015). *Are you addicted to judging yourself?* Retrieved May 7, 2017, from Huffington Post: http://www.huffingtonpost.com/margaret-paul-phd/are-you-addicted-to-judgi_b_7434968.html

Paul, S. (2016). *Risk aversion and anxiety.* Retrieved June 8, 2017, from Huffington Post: http://www.huffingtonpost.com/sheryl-paul/risk-aversion-and-anxiety_b_12354200.html

Pedersden, T. (2016). *Delta brainwaves.* Retrieved July 6, 2017, from Psych Central: https://psychcentral.com/encyclopedia/delta-brain-waves/

Peeters, J. (2015, January 14). *Self-coaching: Ask yourself these questions to find your true identity.* Retrieved June 27, 2017, from Powerpressive: http://powerpressive.com/self-coaching-ask-questions-find-true-identity/

Perkins, C. (2017). *The effects of child abuse and Its role in alcoholism and addiction.* Retrieved April 21, 2017, from Cynhia Perkins, M.Ed.: http://www.alternatives-for-alcoholism.com/effects-of-child-abuse.html

Peterson, T. J. (2015). *Mind-reading and projecting in social anxiety.* Retrieved July 8, 2017, from Healthy

Place: https://www.healthyplace.com/blogs/
anxiety-schmanxiety/2015/12/social-anxi-
etys-minions-mind-reading-and-projecting/

Pew Charitable Trusts. (2013). *Persuading the prescribers: Pharmaceutical industry marketing and its
influence on physicians and patients [Factsheet].*
Retrieved April 21, 2017, from Pew Charitable Trusts: http://www.pewtrusts.org/en/re-
search-and-analysis/fact-sheets/2013/11/11/
persuading-the-prescribers-pharmaceu-
tical-industry-marketing-and-its-influ-
ence-on-physicians-and-patients

Pillar, P. R. (2006). *Intelligence, policy, and the war in Iraq.*
Retrieved June 1, 2017, from Foreign Affairs: https://
www.foreignaffairs.com/articles/iraq/2006-03-
01/intelligence-policy-and-war-iraq

Plenke, M. (2016). *The mind-bending "time slice" concept will make you rethink perception.* Retrieved
April 28, 2017, from Mic: https://mic.com/arti-
cles/141185/time-slice-theory-will-make-you-re-
think-perception#.J5qeEIyaI

Popova, M. (2012). *Learned optimism: Martin Seligman on
happiness, depression, and the meaningful life.* Retrieved May 7, 2017, from Brain Pickings: https://
www.brainpickings.org/2012/06/28/learned-opti-
mism-martin-seligman/

Popova, M. (2013). *Kierkegaard on why anxiety powers
creativity rather than hindering it.* Retrieved May
1, 2017, from Bran Pickings: https://www.brain-

pickings.org/2013/06/19/kierkegaard-on-anxi-ety-and-creativity/

Positive Minds Psychotherapy. (n.d.). *Self-hypnosis to reach-alpha brain wave state.* Retrieved June 2, 2017, from Positive Minds Psychotherapy: http://www.positivemindshypnotherapy.co.uk/what-is-alpha-state/4561215311

Powers, T. (2015). *Simplifying the steps: Step one and the concept of powerlessness.* Retrieved July 2, 2017, from Sober Nation: https://sobernation.com/simplifying-the-steps-step-one-and-the-con-cept-of-powerlessness/

Preidt, R. (2013). *Depression may be worse when ac-companied by anger.* Retrieved May 22, 2017, from WebMD: http://www.webmd.com/depression/news/20130911/depres-sion-may-be-worse-when-accompanied-by-an-ger-irritability

Public Citizen. (2010). *Pharmaceutical industry is biggest defrauder of the federal government under the false claims act, new Public Citizen study finds.* Retrieved June 30, 2017, from Public Citizen: https://www.citizen.org/media/press-releases/pharmaceuti-cal-industry-biggest-defrauder-federal-govern-ment-under-false-claims

Qamish, A. (2016). *Arabian wolf in Jordan.* Retrieved June 3, 2017, from Wikimedia Commons: https://commons.wikimedia.org/wiki/File:Arabian_wolf_in_Jordan.jpg

Racine, M. (n.d.). *How to use anchoring to be calm on command.* Retrieved July 9, 2017, from Bar Exam Mind: http://www.barexammind.com/how-to-use-anchoring-to-be-calm-on-command/#ixzz-4mO3vtUz7

Rauch, J. (2017). *Anxiety attack vs. panic attack: Which one are you having?* (Talkspace) Retrieved May 1, 2017, from Talkspace: https://www.talkspace.com/blog/2017/04/anxiety-attack-vs-panic-at-tack-one/

Rehm, I., & Slikboer, I. (2015). *Pulling out your hair in frustration? What you need to know about tricho-tillomania.* Retrieved May 12, 2017, from The Conversation: http://theconversation.com/pulling-out-your-hair-in-frustration-what-you-need-to-know-about-trichotillomania-45228

Reiss, S., Peterson, R., Gursky, D., & McNally, R. (1986). Anxiety sensistivity, anxiety frequency and the prediction of fear. *Behaviour Research and Ther-apy, 24*(1), 1-6.

Rennie, D. (2008). *Seeding trials: Just say no.* Retrieved April 21, 2017, from Annals of Internal Medi-cine: http://annals.org/aim/article/742309/seed-ing-trials-just-say

Reuder, M. E. (2004). Mind/body problem. In W. E. Craighead, & C. B. Nemeroff (Eds.), *The Concise Corsini Encylcopedia of Psychology and Behavioral Science, Third Edition* (pp. 570, 571). Hoboken, NJ, United States: John Wiley & Sons, Inc.

Richardson, E., Kesselheim, A., Spatz, I., Lott, R., & Gnadinger, T. (2016). *Off-label drug promotion in adults.* Retrieved June 30, 2017, from Project HOPE: The People-to-People Health Foundation, Inc.: http://www.healthaffairs.org/health-policybriefs/brief.php?brief_id=159

Robbins, R. (2016). *Drug makes now spend $5 billion a year on advertising. Here's what that buys.* Retrieved June 30, 2017, from Stat: https://www.statnews.com/2016/03/09/drug-industry-advertising/

Rodríguez Vega, B., Fernández Lira, A., & Bayón Pérez, C. (2005). Trauma, dissociation and somatization. *Anuario de Psicología Clínica y de la Salud [Annuary of Clinical and Health Psychology], 1,* 27-38.

Rothbart, M. K. (2012). *Temperament.* Retrieved May 24, 2017, from Encyclopedia on Early Childhood Development: http://www.child-encyclopedia.com/temperament/synthesis

Routledge, C. (2010). *The power of symbolism: Why burning the Quran is distrubing.* Retrieved June 10, 2017, from Psychology Today: https://www.psychologytoday.com/blog/more-mortal/201009/the-power-symbolism-why-burning-the-quran-is-disturbing

Russel, W. (2001). An examination of flow state occurence in college athletes. *Journal of Sport and Behavior, 24*(1).

Sahu, A., Gupta, P., & Chatterjee, B. (2014). Depression is more than just sadness: A case of excessive anger and its management in depression. *Indian Journal of Psychological medicine, 36*(1), 77–79. doi: 10.4103/0253-7176.127259 .

Salleh, M. (2008). Life event, stress, and illness. *Malaysian Journal of Medial Sciences, 14*(4), 9-18.

Sanger, S. (2011). *The illusion of control.* Retrieved June 15, 2017, from Sandra Eng, Ph.D.: http://www.sandrasanger.com/2011/09/22/the-illusion-of-control/

Satel, S. (2013). *Distinguishing brain from mind.* Retrieved April 25, 2017, from The Atlantic: https://www.theatlantic.com/health/archive/2013/05/distinguishing-brain-from-mind/276380/

Scheve, T. (2012). *What is the link between depression and anger?* Retrieved July 2, 2017, from HowStuffWorks.com: http://health.howstuffworks.com/mental-health/depression/questions/link-between-depression-and-anger.htm

Schiavon, C., Marchetti, E., Gurgel, L., Busnello, F., & Reppold, C. (2014). Optimism and hope in chronic disease: A systematic review. *Frontiers in Psychology, 7*(2022), doi: 10.3389/fpsyg.2016.02022. Retrieved from Frontiers in Psychology.

Schilling, D. (2013). *You need to get into flow: Concentration at its best.* Retrieved July 7, 2017, from

Forbes: https://www.forbes.com/sites/womens-media/2013/06/05/you-need-to-get-into-flow-concentration-at-its-best/#360acc8d18c4

Schirp, M. (2011). *The dark side of self improvement*. Retrieved May 12, 2017, from HighExistence: http://highexistence.com/the-dark-side-of-self-improvement/

Schumann, W. (1952). Über die strahlungslosen eigen-schwingungen einer leitenden kugel die von einer luftschicht und einer Ionosphärenhülle umgeben ist [On the radiated natural vibra-tions of a conducting sphere surrounded by an air layer and an ionosphere shell]. *Zeitschrift fur Naturforschung A [Journal of National Science]*, 7(2), 149–154.

Schumann, W., & König, H. (1954). Über die beo-bachtung von "atmospherics" bei geringsten frequenzen [On the observation of the atmo-sphere at its lowest frequencies]. *Die Naturwis-senschaften [Natural Sciences]*, 41(8), 183-184.

Seif, M. (n.d.). *How to tame your anticpatory anxiety [Worksheet; PDF document]*. Retrieved July 7, 2017, from Dr. Martin N. Seif: http://www.drm-artinseif.com/pdfs/AnticipatoryAnxiety.pdf

Seifter, B. (2010). *Trauma and illness*. Retrieved June 13, 2017, from Psychology Today: https://www.psychologytoday.com/blog/after-the-diagno-sis/201012/trauma-and-illness

Seitbert, P. (2016). Short-term memory. In *Salem Press encyclopedia of health*. Salem Press.

Shackman, A. (2015). *Understanding the early-life origins of extreme anxiety—role of the amygdala*. Retrieved July 7, 2017, from Emotions News: http://emotionnews.org/amgydala/

Sharot, T. (2012). *Viewpoint: How happiness changes with age*. Retrieved June 15, 2017, from Magazine-BBC News: http://www.bbc.com/news/magazine-20591893

Shim, R. (n.d.). *Co-management of chronic physical and behavioral health conditions [PowerPoint presentation]*. Retrieved June 8, 2017, from Substance abuse and Mental Heatlh Sercies Administration.

Shue, K. (n.d.). *The basics of brain waves*. Retrieved June 10, 2017, from Dr. Karen Shue: http://www.brainandhealth.com/brain-waves/

Shuttleworth, M. (2013). *Aristotle's psychology*. Retrieved June 30, 2017, from Explorable.com: https://explorable.com/aristotles-psychology

Silva, J. (2013). *Find your creative flow state [Video file]*. Retrieved October 10, 2017, from YouTube: https://www.youtube.com/watch?v=AXwLsba2TOY&feature=youtu.be

Silva, J.(2014). *Hacking your flow state [Video file]*. Retrieved June 10, 2017, from YouTube: https://

www.youtube.com/watch?v=YUOJFB6ZGQ-
Q&feature=youtu.be

Silver, V. (2017). *The depression and anger connection.* Retrieved May 22, 2017, from Val Silver's Holistic
Mindbody Healing: http://www.holistic-mind-
body-healing.com/depression-and-anger.html

Silverman, E. (2016). *Lawmaker seeks to end tax breaks
for consumer drug ads.* Retrieved May 16, 2017,
from Stat: https://www.statnews.com/pharma-
lot/2016/03/04/drug-ads-taxes-al-franken/

Singal, J. (2016). *Psilocybin, the active ingredient in
'shrooms, is looking more and more like a potential
wonder drug.* Retrieved October 17, 2017, from
Science of Us: http://nymag.com/scienceo-
fus/2016/12/psilocybin-research-looks-very-ex-
citing.html

SMU News. (2011). *Out-of-the-blue panic attacks aren't
without warning; data show subtle changes before patients' aware of attack.* Retrieved June 8,
2017, from SMU News: http://blog.smu.edu/
research/2011/07/26/out-of-the-blue-panic-at-
tacks-arent-without-warning/

Society for Personality and Social Psychology. (2012).
*Skills that make us a good partner make us a
good parent.* Retrieved June 29, 2017, from ScienceDaily: www.sciencedaily.com/releas-
es/2012/12/121207101706.htm

Society for Research in Child Development. (2016).

Corporal punishment is still legal (and used) in US public schools in 19 states: Used dispropor-tionately on black children, boys, and children with disabilities. Retrieved April 22, 2017, from ScienceDaily: www.sciencedaily.com/releas-es/2016/10/161005090700.htm

Soucheray, S. (2012). *A Yale clinician ponders the ethics of a seeding trial masquerading as research.*Retrieved June 30, 2017, from Yale School of Medicine: http://ymm.yale.edu/winter2012/news/chroni-cle/114439/

Sparks, A. (2016). *Depression vs anger: Discovering the lesser of two evils.* Retrieved July 2, 2017, from Psych Central: https://psychcentral.com/lib/depression-vs-anger-discovering-the-lesser-of-two-evils/

Stark, V. (2014). *To get free of the past, you need to stop asking "why?".* Retrieved May 27, 2017, from Psychology Today: https://www.psychologytoday.com/blog/schlepping-through-heartbreak/201411/get-free-the-past-you-need-stop-asking-why

Staroversky, I. (2013). *Three minds: Consciousness, subconscious, and unconscious.* Retrieved June 8, 2017, from StarOverSky Conseling & Psychotherapy: https://staroversky.com/blog/three-minds-con-scious-subcosncious-unconscious

Stein, M., & Stein, D. (2008). Social anxiety disorder. *The Lancet, 371*(9618), 1115–1125.

Stevens, Michael. (2012). *What is consciousness? [You-Tube video]*. Retrieved June 8, 2017, from You-Tube: https://www.youtube.com/watch?v=qj-faoe847qQ

Stiner, M. L. (2004). *Surfing in Hawaii [Digital image]*. Retrieved June 2, 2017, from Wikimedia Commons: https://commons.wikimedia.org/wiki/File:Surfing_in_Hawaii.jpg

Storm, M. (2013). *Breathe to heal-Max Strom-TEDx-CapeMay [Video file]*. Retrieved June 26, 2017, from YouTube: https://www.youtube.com/watch?v=4Lb5L-VEm34

Strand, V. C., Sarmiento, T. L., & Pasquale, L. E. (2005). Assessment and screening tools for trauma in children and adolescents: A review. *Trauma, Violence, & Abuse, 6*(1), 55-78.

Strauss, N. (2016). *Why we're living in an age of fear*. Retrieved May 1, 2017, from Rolling Stone: http://www.rollingstone.com/politics/features/why-were-living-in-the-age-of-fear-w443554

STW. (2008). *Graphic display of the Schumann resonance [Image]*. Retrieved June 2, 2017, from Wikimedia Commons: https://commons.wikimedia.org/wiki/File:Schumann_resonance_01_en.png

Sukhodolsky, D., Kassinove, H., & Gorman, B. (2004). Cognitive-behavioral therapy for anger in children and adolescents: A meta-analysis. *Agression and Violent Behavior, 9*, 247-269. doi:

doi:10.1016/j.avb.2003.08.005.

Swann, N. (1998). Innovative treatment helps traumatized drug-abusing women. *Child Abuse
and Drug Abuse, 13*(12). Retrieved from Child:
https://archives.drugabuse.gov/NIDA_Notes/
NNVol13N2/trauma.html

Swardfager, W., Hermann, N., McIntyre, R., Mazer-
eeuw, G., Goldberger, K., Kha, D.,... Lanctôt, K.
(2013). Potential roles of zinc in the patophys-
iology and treatment of mejor depressive disorder. *Neuroscience and Behavioral Reviews, 37*(5),
911-929. doi: 10.1016/j.neubiorev.2013.03.018.

Sweis, B. M. (2012). *Basic hypothalamic-pituitary-adrenal
axis summary [Digital image]*. Retrieved June 1,
2017, from Wikimedia Commons: https://com-
mons.wikimedia.org/wiki/File:HPA_Axis_Dia-
gram_(Brian_M_Sweis_2012).png

Szalavitz, M. (2012). *How childhood trauma may make the
brain vulnerable to addiction, depression*. Retrieved
April 24, 2017, from Time: http://healthland.
time.com/2012/08/01/how-childhood-trauma-
may-make-the-brain-vulnerable-to-addiction-
depression/

Tanner, J. (2008). *Darwin's role in psychology*. Retrieved
June 30, 2017, from Brainy Behavior: http://
www.brainybehavior.com/blog/2008/02/dar-
wins-role-in-psychology/

Taratovsky, M. (2011). *Psychology's history of being mes-*

merized. Retrieved April 20, 2017, from Psych Central: https://psychcentral.com/blog/archives/2011/05/09/psychologys-history-of-being-mesmerized/

Teicher, M. H. (2002). Scars that won't heal: The neurobiology of child abuse. *Scientific American,* *286*(3), pp. 68-75. Retrieved 2007, from Scientific American: https://www.scientificamerican. com/article/scars-that-wont-heal-the/

Telegraph Staff. (2015). *Five surprising health benefits of being stressed.* Retrieved July 9, 2017, from The Telegraph: http://www.barexammind.com/ how-to-use-anchoring-to-be-calm-on-command/#ixzz4mO3vtUz7

Tenner, I., & Tenner, D. (2011). *Learn to lose as you learn to win.* Retrieved June 14, 2017, from Wisdom, sleeping: http://wisdom.tenner.org/blog/learn-how-to-lose-as-you-learn-how-to-win

Terzian, M., Hamilton, K., & Ericson, S. (2011). *What works to prevent or reduce internalizing problems or socio-emotional difficulties in adolescents: Lessons from experimental evaluations of social interventions.* Child Trends. Washington: Child Trends.

The Canyon. (n.d.). *Sexual abuse and addiction.* Retrieved April 24, 2017, from The Canyon: http:// thecanyonmalibu.com/sexual-abuse-and-addiction/

The Norwegian University of Science and Technology (NTNU). (2010). *Brain waves and meditation.* Retrieved July 6, 2017, from ScienceDaily: www.sciencedaily.com/releases/2010/03/100319210631.htm

The Ranch. (2013). *Ending the nightmare of post-traumatic stress disorder.* Retrieved April 22, 2017, from The Ranch: https://www.recoveryranch.com/articles/dual-diagnosis/ending-the-nightmare-of-post-traumatic-stress-disorder/

The United States Attorney's Office, District of Massachusetts. (2016). *Former Acclarent, Inc. executives convicted of crimes related to the sale of medical devices [Press release]* Retrieved May 16, 2017, from The United States Attorney's Office, District of Massachusetts: https://www.justice.gov/usao-ma/pr/former-acclarent-inc-executives-convicted-crimes-related-sale-medical-devices

Therabada Buddha Sasana Organization Mahasi. (2015). *About process of mind - Part 1 [YouTube video].* Retrieved May 31, 2017, from YouTube: https://www.youtube.com/watch?v=bfxY-DAS0-Mw

Thomas, C. (2014). *Is it a heart attack—or a panic attack?* Retrieved August 11, 2017, from Heart Sisters: https://myheartsisters.org/2011/08/13/heart-attack-vs-panic-attack/

Thomas, K., & Schmidt, M. (2012). *Glaxo agrees to pay $3 billion in fraud settlement.* Retrieved June 30,

2017, from The New York Times: http://www. nytimes.com/2012/07/03/business/glaxosmith-kline-agrees-to-pay-3-billion-in-fraud-settle-ment.html

Thomaselli, R. (2007). *New study lays into DTC ad-vertising.* Retrieved May 16, 2017, from Adver-tisement Age: http://adage.com/article/news/ study-lays-dtc-advertising/114654/

Toffolo, M., Smeets, M., & van den Hout, M. (2012). Proust revisited: Odours as triggers of aversive memories. *Cognition and Emotion, 26*(1), 83-92. doi:10.1080/02699931.2011.555475 .

Topol, E. (2014). Failing the public health—Rofecox-ib, Merck, and the FDA. *New England Journal of Medicine, 351,* 1707-1709. doi: 10.1056/NE-JMp048286. Retrieved from New England .

Torres, A. (2014). *Confidence is important, but it's not ab-solutely everything.* Retrieved April 29, 2017, from Thought Catalog: http://thoughtcatalog. com/art-torres/2014/04/confidence-is-import-ant-but-its-not-absolutely-everything/

Tracy, B. (n.d.). *Understanding your subconscious mind.* Retrieved April 26, 2016, from Brian Tracy Inter-national: http://www.briantracy.com/blog/gen-eral/understanding-your-subconscious-mind/

Turk, C., Heimberg, R., & Magee, L. (2016). Chapter 3: Social anxiety disorder. In D. Barlow (Ed.), *Clin-ical handbook of psychological disorders, fourth edition* (pp. 123-163). The Guildford Press.

Turner, J., & Kelly, B. (2000). Emotional dimensions of chronic disease. *The Western Journal of Medicine, 172*(2), 124-128.

Twenge, J. M. (2009). *Why confidence isn't all that's cracked up to be.* Retrieved April 29, 2017, from Psychology Today: https://www.psychologytoday.com/blog/the-narcissism-epidemic/200906/why-confidence-isnt-all-its-cracked-be

U.S. Department of Veteran Affairs. (2015). *Common reactions after trauma.* Retrieved April 24, 2017, from U.S. Department of Veteran Affairs: https://www.ptsd.va.gov/public/problems/common-reactions-after-trauma.asp

University of California––Los Angeles Health Service. (2013). *Abuse, lack of parental warmth in childhood linked to multiple health risks in adulthood.* Retrieved July 1, 2017, from ScienceDaily: https://www.sciencedaily.com/releases/2013/09/130926205005.htm

University of Chicago News Office. (2016). *Low levels of neutrotransmitter serotonin may perpetuate child abuse accross generations [Press release].* University of Chicago, News Department, Chicago.

UWaterlooPsych. (2013). *The first psychological clinic [YouTube video].* Retrieved June 30, 2017, from YouTube: https://www.youtube.com/watch?v=hIu8kkYcCBk&feature=youtu.be

Vahdat, S., Hamzehgardeshi, L., Hessam, S., & Hamze-hgardeshi, Z. (2014). Patient invovlement in health care decision making: A review. *Iran Red Crescent Medical Journal, 16*(1), Online publication. doi: 10.5812/ircmj.12454.

Vahn, M. (2014). *Is anxiety hereditary?* Retrieved June 4, 2017, from Everyday Fear: http://www.everyday-health.com/news/is-anxiety-hereditary/

van der Kolk, B. A. (1989). The compulsion to repeat the trauma. Re-enactment, revictimization, and masochism. *Psychiatric Clinics of North America, 12*(2), 389-411. PMID 2664732.

Vangelisti, A. (1994). Family secrets: Forms, functions, and correlates. *Journal of Social and Personal Relationships, 11,* 113-135.

Ventola, C. (2009). Off-label drug information: Regulation, distribution, evaluation, and related controversies. *Pharmacy and Therapeutics, 34*(8), 428-440.

Victoria, H., & Caldwell, C. (2013). Breathwork in body psychotherapy: Clinical applications. *Body Movement and Dance in Psychotherapy, 8*(4), 216-228. doi: 10.1080/17432979.2013.828657.

Volland, H. (1995). *Handbook of atmospheric electrodynamics, vol. I* (Vol. 1). Boca Raton, Florida: CRC Press.

Voorthuis, A., Bhandari, R., Out, D., van der Veen, R.,

Bakermans-Kranenburg, M., & Van IJzendoorn, M. (2014). Childhood maltreatment experiences and child abuse potential: Temperamental sensitivity as moderator? *Journal of Family Violence, 29*(7), 749. doi:10.1007/s10896-014-9624-3.

Wadsworth, R., Spampneto, A., & Halbrook, B. (1995). The role of sexual trauma in the treatment of chemically dependent women: Addressing the relapse issue. (R. Balkin, Ed.) *Journal of Counseling and Development, 73*(4), 401-406. doi: 10.1002/j.1556-6676.1995.tb01772.x.

Wagner, D., & Erber, R. (1992). The hyperaccessibility of suppressed thoughts. *Journal of Personality and Social Psychology, 63*(6), 903-912.

Wall Street Journal. (2015, November 23). *The risks of off-label uses of medication [Video file].* Retrieved June 30, 2017, from YouTube: https://www.youtube.com/watch?v=j2NlnYbAbOk&feature=youtu.be

Walton, C. (2014). *The benefits of gamma brain waves [Video file].* Retrieved June 10, 2017, from YouTube: https://www.youtube.com/watch?v=997KAkspLDk&feature=youtu.be

Warrell, M. (2012). *Too judgmental for your own good?* Retrieved May 6, 2017, from Forbes: https://www.forbes.com/sites/margiewarrell/2012/07/24/too-judgemental/#4d79fed04c6b

Waszcruk, M., Zavos, H., & Eley, T. (2013). Genetic and

environmental influences on relationship between anxiety sensitivity and anxiety subscales
in children. *Journal of Anxiety Disorders, 27*(5),
475–484. doi: 10.1016/j.janxdis.2013.05.008.

Watson, B. (2012). *Obsessive compulsive disorder [Im-
age]*. Retrieved June 5, 2017, from Wikimedia
Commons: https://commons.wikimedia.org/
wiki/File:Obsessive_Compulsive_Disorder_
(8970250666).jpg

Wazana, A. (2000). Physicians and the pharmaceutical industry: Is a gift ever just a gift? *Journal of
the American Medical Association, 283*(3), 373-380.
doi: 10.1001/jama.283.3.373 .

WebMD. (n.d.). *The facts on omega-3 fatty acids*. (Web-
MD, LLC) Retrieved October 17, 2017, from
WebMD: https://www.webmd.com/healthy-ag-
ing/omega-3-fatty-acids-fact-sheet

Wells, A., Clark, D., Salkovskis, P., Ludgate, J., Hack-
mann, A., & Gelder, M. (1995). Social phobia:
The role of in-situation safety behaviors in
maintaining anxiety and negative beliefs. *Behavior Therapy, 26*, 153-161.

Wentz, I. (2015). *Hashimoto's and our emotions*. Retrieved June 26, 2017, from Dr. Izabella Wentz,
PharmD.: https://thyroidpharmacist.com/arti-
cles/hashimotos-and-our-emotions/

Wheal, J. (n.d.). *Hacking the flow state [Webinar]*. Retrieved June 10, 2017, from Flow Genome Proj-

ect: http://www.flowgenomeproject.com/hack-ingflow/

Wheeler, S. (2014). *Bandura's 4 principles of social learning theory.* Retrieved May 26, 2017, from Teachtought: http://www.teachthought.com/learning/principles-of-social-learning-theory/

White, W., & Miller, W. (2007). The use of confrontation in addiction treatment: History, science and time for change [PDF document]. *Counselor, 8*(4), 12-30.

Whiteman, H. (2015). *Panic disorder linked to increased risk of heart attack, heart disease.* (Healthline Media UK Ltd) Retrieved August 11, 2017, from Medical News Today: http://www.medicalnewstoday.com/articles/295664.php

Whyte, J. (2014). *How stress can be a very good thing.* (Oath Inc.) Retrieved July 9, 2017, from Huffington Post: http://www.huffingtonpost.com/john-whyte-md-mph/stress-good_b_5582961.html

Williams, A. (2012). The beauty of breathwork [PDF document]. *Massage & Bodywork, 27*(4), 100-103.

Williams, F. (2016). *This is your brain on nature.* Retrieved July 6, 2017, from National Geographic: http://www.nationalgeographic.com/magazine/2016/01/call-to-wild/

Wilson Meloncelli, C. (2015a). *The neurosocience of flow state: Effects on sports athletes.* Retrieved

June 10, 2017, from C Wilson Meloncelli: https://www.cwilsonmeloncelli.com/neuroscience-flow-state-effects-sports-athletes/

Wilson Meloncelli, C. (2015b). *The 5 brain waves and its connection with flow state.* Retrieved June 2, 2017, from C Wilson Meloncelli: https://www.cwilsonmeloncelli.com/the-5-brain-waves-and-its-connection-with-flow-state/

Winson, A., Hardwick, E., & Jaberi, N. (2005). Neuropsychiatric effects of caffeine. *Advances in Psychiatric Treatment, 11*(6), 432-439. doi: 10.1192/apt.11.6.432 .

Wired Staff. (2015). *ADHD drugs make big money, but we still don't know the risks.* Retrieved May 16, 2017, from Wired: https://www.wired.com/2015/12/adhd-drugs-are-big-business/

Wonderly, K. (2011). *What happens to the blood oxygen level when a human exercises?* Retrieved June 1, 2017, from Livestrong: http://www.livestrong.com/article/548502-what-happens-to-the-blood-oxygen-level-when-a-human-exercises/

Wood, D. (2016). Linking trauma to addiction will provide the treatment solution. *Unpublished Master's Thesis.*

Woodward, K. (2000, 2004). *Questioning identity: Gender, class, nation.* London, New York: Open University.

World Health Organization. (n.d.). *Noncommunicable diseases*. Retrieved June 13, 2017, from World Health Organization: http://www.who.int/topics/noncommunicable_diseases/en/

Yackle, K., Schwarz, L., Kam, K., Sorokin, J., Huguenard, J., Feldman, J., ... Krasnow, M. (2017). Breathing control center neurons that promote arousal in mice. *Science, 355*(6632), 1411-1415. doi: 10.1126/science.aal7984. Retrieved from Breathing control center neurons that promote arousal in mice

Yamada-Hosley, H. (2015). *Remember your past successes to stay motivated thorugh a hard time.* Retrieved June 29, 2017, from Lifehacker: http://lifehacker.com/remember-your-past-successes-to-stay-motivated-through-1679915168

Yang, R. (n.d.). *Yingyang.* Retrieved April 29, 2017, from Internet Encyclopedia of Psychology: http://www.iep.utm.edu/yinyang/

You & Your Hormones. (2017). *Adrenocorticotropic hormone.* Retrieved April 26, 2017, from You & Your Hormones: http://www.yourhormones.info/Hormones/Adrenocorticotropic_hormone.aspx

Young, S. H. (2009). *Humility is more important than confidence.* Retrieved May 8, 2017, from Scott H. Young: https://www.scotthyoung.com/blog/2009/03/02/humility-is-more-important-than-confidence/

Youst, J. (2012). *Therapuetic breathwork.* Retrieved May 15, 2017, from Power of Breath Institute: http://powerofbreath.com/articles/therapeutic-breathwork/

Zera, L. (2016). *When meds didn't improve my depression, I tried retraining my brain waves instead.* Retrieved June 20, 2017, from Quartz: https://qz.com/720419/when-meds-didnt-cure-my-depression-i-tried-retraining-my-brain-waves-instead/

Zetlin, M. (2014). *Why you must celebrate small successes.* Retrieved June 29, 2017, from Inc.: https://www.inc.com/minda-zetlin/why-you-must-celebrate-small-successes.html

Zhu, P. (2015). *Brain vs mind.* Retrieved July 5, 2017, from Future of CIO: http://futureofcio.blogspot.com/2015/06/brain-vsmind.html

Zipp, B. (n.d.). *Planning for the future does not mean predicting the future.* Retrieved May 7, 2015, from Leadership Link: http://billzipponbusiness.com/planning-for-the-future-does-not-mean-predicting-the-future/